PHOTOGRAPHY
FRIENDS, FATE, & FUN

AMAZING TIMES AND WONDROUS STORIES OF A PHOTOJOURNALIST

BRIAN MCLEAN

CONTENTS

PREFACE

IT'S THE NIGHT BEFORE Thanksgiving, 2023 (November 22), and I'm thinking it's time to start my book. As I begin, I pull up the first three Legs Diamond albums on CD that have been released through Rock Candy Records. The CDs, *Legs Diamond*, *A Diamond Is a Hard Rock*, and *Fire Power*, arrived earlier in the day. The name Legs Diamond took me back to the fall of 1981. I had to stop and make a note. It only motivated me to get this undertaking going.

This book originally started out as my music-related memories and experiences. The seed was planted after phoning my friend to tell him that we, as in my daughter and I, just met Aerosmith's Steven Tyler. No fancy meet-and-greet—just a gamble and a hunch.

He could tell from just talking with me how hyped up I was about the experience. He strongly suggested that I write a book about the things I have experienced over time.

That encounter planted the seed for this book even though it's been over a decade.

The majority of the book will be music experiences that shaped me—events as a photographer, writer, or fan. Many are sports related. Those recollections come from being a photographer in the working media to working in public relations departments for several teams.

I hope that as you read through the book, you will reminisce about a special time in your life.

The main reason for writing this book is to document and leave all these special thoughts behind for E, my daughter; for once I am gone, so, too, are the special moments.

INTRODUCTION

THAT CONVERSATION OCCURRED ON Sunday, July 29, 2012. It was the day after Aerosmith and Cheap Trick played the American Airlines Center in Dallas.

Late in the band's set, Steven Tyler was doing a stage rap and quickly threw in, "Three o'clock, tomorrow, Hit Records. This is called 'Rats in the Cellar.'"

That stuck with me the rest of the night. The next day, I kept thinking about what he'd said.

(L-R) The Kiddo, Steven Tyler and Brian outside Hit Records after sweating out on a hunch to meet Steven Tyler.

I looked up Hit Records and saw it was on the other side of Dallas. I told my daughter what I heard at the show. I felt like taking a gamble.

I grabbed my *Draw the Line* vinyl, Tyler's autobiography, and my daughter's journal with an Aerosmith logo on the cover. As a place marker, a puffy version of the logo with wings is attached by ribbon.

An hour later, we arrived early in the afternoon and pulled into the parking lot. Painted on a brick wall next to the store was the squiggly-line Aerosmith logo. Seeing that piqued my curiosity even more.

In the parking lot was a lone yellow Volkswagen Beetle covered in Aerosmith and colorful daisy flower stickers. Upon seeing this car, I realized I'd heard my middle school hero correctly the night before.

Curious, I went up to the car. There was a girl sitting in the driver's seat, and the window was down. I apologized for just coming up to her, but I had a question to ask.

I asked her if she'd gone to the Aerosmith concert the night before, and she said, "Yes."

I then asked her if she'd heard Steven Tyler say something, and she had.

I asked her what she'd heard, and she repeated the same words: "Three o'clock, tomorrow, Hit Records. This is called 'Rats in the Cellar.'"

I stated I'd heard the same thing and then said, "Well, I guess I am not leaving now."

We introduced ourselves to each other.

Her name's Spring, and she's a huge Aerosmith fan, probably one of the biggest Aerosmith fans I have met.

After an hour or two, we went to the front door of the store. The hours of operation listed on the door showed the store was open on Sundays. For some "strange" reason the store was closed. Oddly, there were people inside.

The owner told us the store was closed, but I pointed to the store hours posted, showing the store was open on Sundays.

I then asked him point blank if Tyler was making an appearance at the store. He replied, "No."

I mentioned what Tyler said the night before.

He said nothing was happening at the store.

I then asked him, "If nothing is happening, why are people wearing Aerosmith swag?" A girl was even wearing Aerosmith pajama pants.

He again replied that nobody from Aerosmith was coming to the store.

I told him I wasn't buying it and that we were not leaving.

He didn't like that.

All three of us just started hanging out. Several hours turned into more hours.

People would drive by and ask if Steven Tyler was inside. We would say no because he wasn't, but we didn't offer any additional information.

By this time, we had invested roughly four hours of wait time. We didn't want others to stop and hang out. Now, if they were there four hours prior when we started, it would have been a different story.

Keep in mind, it was July in the mid- to late afternoon. It was getting hot, as in serious Texas summer heat, as in frying an egg on the sidewalk or baking cookies in a car hot.

The high on that afternoon was 105 F at 4:53 p.m. CST.

About six hours in, my daughter and I went across the street to the convenience store to purchase water and snacks for all three of us.

By this time, we were roughly six hours in. I was seriously

contemplating giving up.

About fifteen minutes later, we were sitting down, leaning up against the wall of the record store in the shade.

A white Chevrolet HHR vehicle pulled up with two people. I looked at the passenger who was holding a little dog and said, "That's an ugly woman."

I then took a double take and said, "That's Steven Tyler."

We watched with our jaws open as the voice of Aerosmith and the driver exited the vehicle. They went into the store. They walked right past us, not saying a word. The vocalist known for decorative scarves draped on his microphone stand was carrying a little Yorkie.

A few moments later, another car pulled up. Brad Whitford exited the vehicle and entered the store.

We all looked at each other and said, "We're not leaving now."

While the two rock stars were in the store, several people who were at the show drove by. They asked about Steven Tyler. We said we didn't know anything.

We were not going to let people know anyone was inside. We were the ones who'd spent roughly six hours in the trenches, waiting. The gamble was now eventually going to pay off.

After spending some time inside the record store, Tyler and Whitford came out and talked with us prior to leaving.

Tyler happily signed our stuff. I told him a story about a missed opportunity to meet him in 1987 at the Texxas Jam. I had blown it by not being assertive. (Story is later in the book) He replied something along the lines of, "Well here we are now."

Unfortunately, Whitford snuck by and left. We weren't able to meet him. The legendary vocalist signed everything, even the rear hood, mirrors, and front trunk cover of the yellow Beetle.

It was a cool experience, especially since Aerosmith was one of the first bands I started getting into after KISS. Never in my wildest dreams would I have thought that thirty-four years later, in 2012, I would be meeting him face-to-face.

A thought like that seems incomprehensible to a thirteen-year-old kid just stepping on the road to discovering rock bands.

What follows is my story of hopes, teenage daydreams, detours and disappointments.

FOREWORD

THE SOUND WAREHOUSE MEMORY lingers in my mind.

On a sunny Texas afternoon, we flipped through vinyl, suburban teens seeking the latest hard rock releases within the vast record store on Camp Bowie Boulevard. I searched for the latest Dokken album. Or was it Rush? Or Iron Maiden? I can't remember.

What I do remember is a short, rather enthusiastic fellow standing next to me. His nimble fingers browsed the *M* section, settling on a band I'd read about in *Kerrang!!* and *Metal Forces* magazines. The band? Motorhead.

"You're not a Lemmy lover?" I joked, detecting a kindred spirit, someone who not only knew about the British metal legend but also appreciated his inclusion among otherwise mainstream record-store inventory.

"Yes, I am," he laughed.

Enter Brian McLean.

From the moment we met, I knew this jovial, fun-loving fellow would become a lifelong friend. A brother. Someone not only in whom I could confide my passion for underground heavy metal music, but also a fellow misfit. Someone beholden neither to the preps nor freaks. No, we were too cool for cliques!

Since then, I've watched Brian blossom. Whether behind the camera lens or standing before a classroom chalkboard, Brian pours his soul into everything he touches. With an all-consuming devotion to his passions—photography, journalism, teaching, fatherhood—this man, short in physical stature but tall in character, is an inspiration.

Decades since striking up our record-store conversation, Brian and I have only grown closer. We've withstood the slings and arrows of life without surrendering to the mundane. "We grew up, but never grew old" became our mutual mantra while navigating the challenges we all face.

Imagine my excitement at learning that Brian planned to chronicle his eventful life in the book you hold in your hands. It's no typical screed penned by a heavy metal fan, nor is it an autobiography from an author with nothing to say. Brian has plenty to say.

Whether honing his photojournalism skills in college darkrooms and local nightclubs covering Pantera concerts or inspiring classrooms of public school students while struggling with maddening child-custody issues, among other challenges, Brian never gave up.

Where Brian obtains his indefatigable energy is beyond me. He packs more into a single day than almost everyone I know, with an unquenchable thirst for knowledge and experience. He's someone I can't imagine sitting down for more than a few minutes at a time.

He's a Tasmanian devil, a whirling dervish whose infectious laugh and likable demeanor belies an otherwise stone-cold serious determination to fulfill his dreams. His hopes and dreams—and achieving those dreams—are chronicled in this book.

Why should you read it? What does this Brian R. McLean fellow matter in the big picture? Turn this page and find out . . .

A. Lee Graham

April 2024

ONE

ELVIS COMEBACK SPECIAL

1968

I CAN'T SAY IF my first music memory comes from the original broadcast of the '68 *Elvis Comeback Special* on December 3, 1968, or not. The only rebroadcast dates I found occurred in 1977 after Elvis's death and an HBO special in 1985.

If my faint memory comes from the original broadcast, that would put me at just a little over three years of age. I do recall a time but unknown age when I saw an image of Elvis in his black leathers. Whether he's on the stage with the other musicians or alone, I do not remember. This faint visualization is how my journey begins.

Two

Elvis and Aloha from Hawaii

1973

THE ELAPSED TIME FOR this section seemed so vast back then, but actually, it was maybe twenty months, tops. It seemed like a forever that was moving slowly.

For a seven-year-old boy in early 1973, twenty months into the future seems so distant.

One year is one-seventh of a boy's life, whereas one year for an individual who is fifty-eight years old is a much smaller percentage than the child's percentage.

As time progresses, one year becomes a smaller percentage of life with each passing trip around the sun.

By this point, a lot in regard to music-related experiences happened to me, especially for a seven-year-old. I just didn't put much thought into it.

It all begins with Elvis and the *Aloha from Hawaii* broadcast. This was a major feat. Something of that magnitude had really never occurred, but with Elvis and Colonel Tom Parker, nothing was ever too big.

Aloha from Hawaii was a live performance that was aired via satellite on January 14, 1973. People think it was live worldwide, but it wasn't. The show aired live in the sense that it was happening. Only the viewers in Asia and Oceania were able to watch in real time.

The following day, the footage was aired in Europe. It wasn't until April 4, 1973, that the footage of *Aloha from Hawaii* aired in the United States on NBC. When *Aloha from Hawaii* was finally on TV, we, as a family, watched it. I sat on the dark olive-green, 1970s shag carpet, glued to the television. This I remember, and it was mesmerizing.

The recording was released as a double live album in February 1973 before the airing. My brother had the album, but there was an unwritten rule that I didn't even ask to borrow it. I don't know why. That double live album seemed so mystical and mysterious.

Now, I would look at the die-cut cover, sleeves, and gatefold artwork with the phrase "We Love Elvis" written in various languages. The phrases were pointing at the countries the phrase was written in.

I would also look at the record sleeves. I specifically remember looking at the sleeves where there was a full-body image of Elvis. He was in a white jumpsuit on tropical green grass in front of a grass hut. He was wearing the *As Recorded at Madison Square*

Garden outfit in the middle of fourteen women. All the women were wearing Hawaiian dresses with leis around their necks.

Even at that young age, the image didn't look natural to me. I knew something just wasn't right. I was mainly curious how this group of women were calm with Elvis in the middle of them. It's because the image was superimposed.

What's strange about the album copy I have is that the fine print on the bottom of the back cover shows 1972, not 1973. The year is correct, though, on the copies of the 8-track and cassette I own.

I didn't realize how big of a deal the broadcast was at the time. Things like that just fly over the head of a kid. To this day, the *Aloha from Hawaii* broadcast reigns as a legendary and impressive feat.

THREE

TEXAS

1973

I ALWAYS THOUGHT MY Elvis story was my first live music experience. It wasn't. Upon starting this book and compiling my information, I realized that the following started my journey.

———◆———

Growing up in 1973, my older brother's best friend at the time was the youngest of three siblings, all boys. The oldest of the three was a drummer/musician named Gary. The middle brother was a high school baseball standout. His name was Larry. The youngest, Terry, was a ten-year-old kid, just like my brother.

The eldest sibling was my brother's first drum teacher. One of his snares would become my brother's first snare drum. I am fairly certain he received it for Christmas in 1973 or 1974. The drum itself was hidden behind the living room/kitchen door on Christmas morning.

It was not uncommon for our family to go visit their house. They lived about a mile from us. I have vivid memories visiting the household—playing pool upstairs, the Raquel Welch pillowcase, running up and down on the stairs next to the kitchen.

They lived in a two-story house, so I always thought it was supercool to go visit them.

Located at the top of the stairs, there was a black rotary phone mounted on the wall. I specifically remember my brother and Terry calling people to wish them a Happy New Year in 1974. They were also asking the stupid juvenile question to the random person: "Is your refrigerator running?"

All these memories pretty much come from 1973, give or take.

One night when visiting, my brother, his friend Terry, and I were digging through one of the closets of the downstairs bedroom. I remember seeing a black bass drumhead with "BANG" in pinkish letters with a burst that illustrated a "bang" behind it.

Bang was an American rock band out of Philadelphia. Gary and his friend, vocalist Mace, were part of the lineup for a bit in 1972. The two are pictured on the cover of the *Mother/Bow to the King* album. The band is sitting at a table, and Gary is on the left. Mace is on the right. From my understanding, the two did not play on the album.

The band recently released new material. I made a comment on social media about finding the Bang bass drum head. One of the members replied, "I was wondering where it went."

This brings me to 1973.

After their stint in Bang, Gary and Mace reformed one of their previous bands, called Texas. The band released one album in September of 1973, *Texas*, with Bell Records. "L.A. Lights" and "Rock and Roll Eyes" were the two 45 RPM singles.

One weekend afternoon, my family went to a floral distribution convention for florists and flower shops. I remember running around and being able to eat free hot dogs.

Nothing there was foreign to me. I was always around a flower shop as a kid. I recognized a lot of the floral-related items on display.

As we were leaving, we passed two older guys. Each had a healthy stack of records under one arm. I saw the albums and I said, "Look, Mom, it's Texas."

The guys stopped and handed a copy to me and one to my brother. My mother made us give one copy back. I am fairly certain that the two didn't expect an eight-year-old kid to recognize the albums.

As I look back on this encounter, it reminds me of the very early workings of a promotional "street team" promoting a band's release.

The cover consisted of Texas sitting on the front porch of the Wild West Saloon at Six Flags Over Texas in the Texas section of the park.

There was an ad that ran for the album in *Rolling Stone* with Three Dog Night tour dates. It was the November 8, 1973, issue on page

33. The ad only ran once. The tour ran from October 21 through November 16, 1973, with the first night in Dallas.

Under the band's logo, the ad read in capital letters, "HOW CAN YOU GO WRONG WITH A NAME **THIS BIG!**"

Why do I know this fact? I ran across the ad on eBay in the spring of 2007. I knew that there was no way I was going to miss winning that auction. Actually, I think I may have been the only bidder. To me, that didn't matter. What did matter was I had a rare piece of Texas album memorabilia.

I have since seen this ad listed on eBay as a "promotional poster," which is incorrect, for $70. I just laughed. I only paid around $13.

It's hard to believe that the Texas album is fifty years old—half a century. Still, the music impacts me.

———◦———

There was an evening our family was visiting, and my brother was going to do a sleepover at Terry's. I recall the typical kid stuff—running around and acting like an eight-year-old boy with ADHD coursing through my veins.

There's an impactful memory I have from this night, and it's not begging to be part of the sleepover or even related to it.

I was coming down the stairs, and I recall Gary sitting on the sofa, sewing sequins on his white 1970s jumpsuit, his stage outfit.

I am not sure if this was for the upcoming tour with Three Dog Night or if it was for the night Texas played at the Tarrant County

Convention Center. The show at TCCC was a Toys for Tots gig on December 16, 1973, with the headliner Lee Pickens. Texas, Michael Murphy, and Pecos Star were also on the bill. There may have been tickets, but admission was a new, unwrapped toy.

I don't have a lot of memories of the show, but I do remember being at the front of the stage. I was dancing away with a hippie girl. She was probably in her twenties, wearing a brown suede jacket with long fringe on the arms. As I was grooving away, she would pat me on my head.

Being at the front of the stage, I remember waving to Gary and he waved back.

At that point of the show, Gary was at the front of the stage hyping up the crowd, but he wasn't doing any vocals.

I even remember the car ride to the show. A concert commercial came on the radio. The station was KDFW 102.1 FM, and "Rock and Roll Eyes" was played in the commercial. I made the comment along the lines of, "Duh, that's where we are going"—typical stupid eight-year-old stuff. As weird as it is, I remember being at the stop light near the house, about to turn onto the highway.

———◦———

I like to say I have a good memory and always have, especially related to music. More on that later, during my high school years. Details of the Toys for Tots show came from a good friend of mine, Lance.

We were having lunch at a pizzeria, and for some reason, the topic of Texas came up. He mentioned the Toys for Tots show, date, and lineup. His cousin Charlie Bassham played in Lee Pickens's band.

Lee Pickens was in the Fort Worth band Bloodrock that had a hit with the song "D.O.A."

Actually, I saw Lance earlier today at a record store. I asked him a few questions about the Toys for Tots show. The information he shared inspired me to write this section.

⎯⎯◇⎯⎯

During the lockdown on April 20, I was browsing eBay. It's just something I do. Something I search on a regular basis is "Texas" and "Bell Records." Normally, the hits I get are for the debut Texas album and the singles. Only one time have I had a unique item come up. That was for the album advertisement I purchased in 2007.

On that April night, I was scrolling through looking at all the listings when I ran across an 8-track tape of the Texas album. I was blown away and literally had to look closely. I couldn't believe what I was seeing. Actually, I wasn't even aware that the Texas album was released in 8-track format. This was a "holy grail" find for me that relates to music. I immediately became very nervous. I had to make this purchase ASAP. The tape was listed for $12.99. The most amazing part—the tape was still factory sealed. I was speechless.

The shipping took longer than expected. I was extremely nervous and on pins and needles. I waited and waited for the tape to arrive. Every day I would wait for the mail carrier. It took a little over a week for the tape to be delivered. I was so relieved when I actually had this vintage Texas factory-sealed 8-track in my hand.

It's hard to believe the tape is now fifty-one years old.

I didn't tell my brother about the tape. I just had it with me one day when I had to stop by his house. When he put on his glasses and saw the tape, he asked me where in the world I found it. I explained to him that I found it on eBay. He immediately took a photo with his phone and texted it to his friend Terry. Even Terry, the youngest of the brothers, was amazed at seeing it.

Needless to say, the tape is one of my most prized possessions in my entire music collection. I am very proud to own it.

Four

The Angry Punch

1974

I GREW UP IN an airline family. My father was a career airline employee and eventually retired at the age of fifty-five with early retirement. His office was located on the first floor of what was then the Sheraton Hotel in downtown Fort Worth. He ran the city ticket office (CTO). His office faced east, looking at Houston Street. All major airlines had ticket offices on this floor. There was American, Braniff, Continental, Delta, Eastern, Pan Am, TWA, and United.

It was normal for my mother to go pick up my father from work. We would sit in the family car, a black Pontiac, and wait for him to get off work.

I remember sitting in the car, outside his office, facing north. I was gazing at the time-and-temperature clock. One afternoon, the Watergate hearings were on the radio. I knew Watergate was something bad, but I just didn't understand what was going on.

Inside the hotel, there was another ticket office, the central ticket office. It was a box office that sold event tickets. This was several years before Ticketron and Ticketmaster.

The hotel building itself has been under several names over the years: the Texas Hotel, Sheraton Hotel, Hyatt Regency, and more recently, the Hilton Fort Worth. The hotel sits directly north at walking distance from what is now the Fort Worth Convention Center. The convention center used to be called the Tarrant County Convention Center (TCCC).

The hotel building itself is very historic. It's the place where President John F. Kennedy gave his last address in the Crystal Ballroom on the second floor.

On a daily basis, my father dealt with what I consider now "high rollers" and other distinguished clientele. One afternoon, my father took me to a restaurant in the hotel called the 6666 or Four Sixes. He introduced me to a waitress whose name was Corky. I remember this, as we had a Collie named Corky.

I also met a really nice gentleman. He was the bartender and maybe a waiter at the restaurant. He gave me a basket of popcorn. Of course, I didn't turn down the free popcorn. Actually, no kid would.

My father had one regular customer who was a professional gambler. He would always bring my father something, whether it was a deck of cards that was used in Las Vegas or fancy turquoise jewelry for my mother. It could be a ring, bracelet, necklace, or something else. He would open a handkerchief and tell my father, "Pick something for your wife."

Mr. Underwood was always a very nice man. Simply, he was a legendary gambler. As a nine-year-old kid, I thought he was a pretty cool gambling man who was born in 1890.

One day, a regular customer of my father's gave him four front-row tickets to see Elvis. The tickets were for the 3:00 matinee show on Sunday, June 16, 1974, at the convention center.

Elvis would play four shows that weekend, two on Saturday and two on Sunday. All were sold out.

That afternoon before the show, we had lunch at the Elks Club on White Settlement Road. The banquet hall sits across from Greenwood Memorial Park. In fact, Mr. Underwood is buried there.

After lunch, we drove east, making our way into downtown Fort Worth and eventually to TCCC.

Our seats were on the front row but to the right side edge of the stage. To give perspective, J. D. Sumner and the Stamps Quartet, Elvis's male backup singers, were just a bit to our right.

I don't recall a support act such as a comedian or anything like that. My first memory, once inside the area, is a pair of blue boots behind a curtain. I pointed them out to my brother, but he said it wasn't Elvis.

I don't remember Elvis taking the stage. Maybe it was just information and sensory overload. I do vividly recall my mother snagging a baby blue scarf out of the air. She wasted no time stuffing the scarf into her purse. My father took a photo with the Instamatic camera, and there's a slide with my mother's hand grabbing the scarf.

Throughout the night, I had my hands on four or five scarves tossed to me by Elvis. Notice, I said "had" because what followed was several encounters with crazed female Elvis fans. These women would run up from the back of the floor and engage me in a tug-of-war match. Obviously, I lost every effing time.

By the fourth or fifth time, I was fed up—really fed up and very distraught when that last scarf was yanked from my hands. I fought with all the might a nine-year-old boy could muster. Still, I lost, and I was pissed.

My opponent was a crazy woman with no regard for a kid. She was wearing a blue polyester jumpsuit. When she yanked that scarf from my hands, I felt a rage in me I'd never felt as a kid.

I was eye level right at her waist, and without a second thought, I punched with all my built-up anger below her waist. I hoped she was sore for several days. I didn't forget what she did to me, but I knew she wouldn't forget what I did in return.

My father saw how upset I was, so he talked with the officer on duty working security. My father explained to the officer what was happening. He asked the officer if he would hold the women back next time Elvis came to our side of the stage. My father would then lift me up to the stage.

There was no barricade separating the stage from the audience, but it was higher than normal.

Elvis eventually made his way back to our side of the stage. The women came running up, and the officer held them back. My father was able to lift me up to the stage.

Elvis knelt on one knee, and I was face-to-face with the King. I could see the beading sweat on his forehead. I began to pull a baby blue scarf off his neck from his left side. The scarf got caught up on the chain of his German Iron Cross. I pulled with a bit more force, and the scarf started coming off. Now I had it in my hands.

My father brought me down, and I quickly gave the scarf to my mother. Like a flash of lightning, she shoved it in her purse.

This occurred toward the end of the show. I don't know what song or how many songs were played after this. I was just high on happiness.

I do remember driving south on I-35 W toward home. My brother and I were in the back seat of the car, a Volkswagen 411. We were waving the scarves through the back window at cars behind us. Some people probably didn't understand what we were doing, but others did. One lady was excitedly pointing at us.

———◇———

The scarves stayed tucked away for years. It wasn't until I purchased my house that I finally brought the scarf I pulled to my house. In the summer of 2014, I decided to have my scarf put into a shadow box. I purchased a colorful metal Elvis sign with images of him from Las Vegas. He's sporting one of the *That's the Way It Is*–era white jumpsuits.

I obtained two replica Elvis concert tickets. The tickets are for shows that didn't happen, dated September 27 and 28, 1977.

I had the shadow box put together when I went to study abroad in Ecuador and the Galapagos Islands. The shadow box is displayed in my music/game room/man cave with several other Elvis-related items. It's in the section I call my "Elvis Wall," flanked with a neon light and autographed albums.

—◆—

There is another segment that brings this whole story full circle. Originally, I was going to include this later in the book, but I have decided to close out this section with the following:

In 1999, Follow That Dream or FTD was created by Sony Music's Official Elvis Presley Collectors label. The purpose is to serve the dedicated Elvis collectors. FTD releases material that is of high interest to serious Elvis fans and collectors like me.

I really didn't know much about these releases. I honestly didn't realize these releases were being put out until one day when I stumbled across one in 2021.

I went to the Elvis Shop and couldn't decide if I wanted to purchase an Elvis CD for $34.99 or something else along those lines. Obviously, I procrastinated, and when I finally decided to do it, the CD was sold out online. A sinking feeling hit me.

I went to eBay and found the CD for roughly $25 more out of Europe, but this time I didn't hesitate to make the purchase. The CD is the FTD's Elvis, Fort Worth, Texas 1974, and consists of two shows. The 3:00 p.m. and 8:30 p.m. shows on Sunday, June 16, 1974. That 3:00 show is the show mentioned above.

I have a live recording of the Elvis show where I pulled the scarf off his neck. It's a soundboard recording and fairly decent; if only I knew when I'd pulled the scarf off his neck, I would be musically complete.

The only difference between the two shows is that "Heartbreak Hotel" is in the afternoon set, whereas "How Great Thou Art" is in the evening set.

It's super nice knowing that I have this recording in my collection. Honestly, it means the world to me.

FIVE

THE BICENTENNIAL YEAR

1976

1976 WAS A STRANGE year for me.

I wrapped up fourth grade in May of 1975 and started my fifth grade year. By this time, I was almost ten years old, the youngest in my class as a late August kid. As the school year progressed through the fall of 1975, I wasn't settling down like my classmates. I was still bouncing off the classroom walls. My grades were suffering.

Every day, I would have to go to the principal's office and take my little yellow pill, which, in pharmaceutical terms, is Ritalin.

I was presented the option by my parents to go back to fourth grade at another school. It was explained that I would be one of the oldest in the class. There would be more kids my age. I agreed. When school returned after winter break, I was in a new school in a new year surrounded by new kids. This was January 1976.

Academically, it was the right move.

My teacher, Mr. Parker was more than a cool cat—he was an awesome teacher. I actually enjoyed having him.

A high point of fourth grade was taking our History of Texas test toward the end of the school year. The test had maybe twenty questions, but it was multiple choice with three or four answer options. I actually earned a 100 on the test. Not even the little geeky, blonde-haired, super-smart girl who always read super-fast out loud earned a 100. I think I may have been the only one, and it was a huge deal for me.

On the last day of school I was trying to make conversation with a girl in our class. I told her I was going to see Elvis several days after school ended. She didn't seem too impressed when I told her. That was about it.

Several days later, we went to go see Elvis, but this time, we were in the balcony, about halfway up on the left side, stage right. I do recall my brother being able to have the binoculars when Elvis hit the stage. He wanted to watch Ronnie Tutt, Elvis's drummer, when Elvis hit the stage.

Fans would bring teddy bears and other things to Elvis. Besides those items, one fan gave him a huge trophy. It was a two-tiered trophy, several feet tall.

As July 4, 1976, descended upon Fort Worth, I took part in the bicentennial parade that was held downtown. My participation in the parade with my father's employer consisted of handing out little white plastic jets to people in the crowd.

The float consisted of a flatbed truck with advertisements on it. The adults were on the flatbed, and the kids were handing out the toy planes. It should have been the other way around when I look at it. In other words, we were all punked into our part. Either way, it was fun to participate in the city's bicentennial parade.

Summer was now in full swing with June gone. The remaining afternoons would be spent at the Elks Club swimming pool.

There was a brother and sister I became friends with at the swimming pool. She was fifteen, and her sibling may have been sixteen or seventeen. He had a friend closer to his age. All three were super nice to this ten-year-old kid who would be turning eleven in August.

The brother's friend may have been on a high school diving team. He would teach me how to dive. Nothing fancy, just keeping the legs together and toes pointed as I entered the water. He was always very encouraging.

The trio of friends frequented the pool on a regular basis. One afternoon, in early to mid-August, I was talking with the sister. She said that she and her brother were going to the KISS show that night. I knew what she was talking about, but I really didn't think much about the statement. It was cool as a kid, meeting someone who was going to see KISS. Now, it was such a 1970s thing—a KISS concert.

I don't know how I knew at that point who KISS was, but I just did.

It must have been that night, August 11. I recall seeing the advertisement for the show in the paper. The black-and-white ad was the cover of *Destroyer*, the album KISS was touring on. *Rock and Roll Over* wasn't released until November 1976.

I actually phoned the radio station listed with the ad. I asked if they would be broadcasting the show. Obviously, the answer was no, and I was bummed. I had a brand-new blue Realistic 8-track tape ready to go for the broadcast. All I had to do was push the red Record button on my father's Sony stereo.

I don't recall speaking with my three friends again at the pool after the KISS concert. If I did, the conversation probably didn't impact me very much.

I never forgot how kind they were to a ten-year-old kid. I have wondered where life took the three. I do know they would be in their mid-sixties now, as 1976 was forty-eight years ago now.

People my age who are massive KISS fans all remember the *Paul Lynde Halloween Special* that aired Friday, October 29, 1976. It featured Margaret Hamilton, who reprised her role of the Wicked Witch of the West from the *Wizard of Oz*, Billie Hayes as Witchiepoo from *H. R. Pufnstuf*, and other big names at the time. The most memorable part of the show was the appearance of KISS. It gave many of us our first visual of the band in action.

The band played, well, more like lip-synched, to "Detroit Rock City," "King of the Night Time World," and "Beth." It was cool seeing the band, but I remember my mother's comment the most. She said, "They're probably a bunch of hoodlums that ran away from home."

I don't recall any big talk at school on Monday. I am certain the talk of the playground would have been the candy haul made the previous night on Halloween.

SIX

ENTERING SIXTH GRADE AND 1978

1977

THE SUMMER OF 1977 blew by in a blur. What I do remember is that Elvis died and we, the neighborhood kids, played outside every day.

I was told about his death by my friend Kristi. We were out playing around like we did every day, and she said Elvis had died. We were near or sitting on a stone wall when she told us.

It was a strange feeling for me. I really didn't know how to react. I didn't see any tears on the faces of people I knew. All the sadness I saw came from TV news footage.

Of course, I'd seen Elvis twice in concert, the last time just fourteen months earlier in June of 1976. At that age, 14 months seemed like such a "long time ago," but in reality it really wasn't.

Several weeks after Elvis died, I was entering sixth grade. What's strange is that just ten months prior, I saw the *Paul Lynde Halloween Special*, yet it seemed like another long time ago.

I would get bused to another school for sixth grade. During this time, I would discover KISS. I wanted to learn about them. I don't recall making any connection to them from the *Paul Lynde Halloween Special* though.

Around this time, KISS was touring on the *Love Gun* album. They actually played two shows in Fort Worth at TCCC on September 4 and 5, 1977.

Styx was the opening band. They were touring for their *Grand Illusion* album.

The younger sister of a friend of my brother started giving me KISS clippings from *16 Magazine*. One set of clippings consisted of mysterious biographical information on each member. She also gave me live photo clippings and a color photo used in TV Guide.

The biographical information, as mentioned, was "mysterious." The one "biographical fact" I recall the most was that Gene Simmons had stated he was born in 1776 on Mars. All this crazy information only made me want to learn more.

At the time, never in my wildest dreams would I have thought that Simmons and I would share the same birth month and day. It was one of those mind-blowing facts I learned later on.

Unfortunately, my passion to learn more about KISS received resistance from my parents.

When *KISS ALIVE II* was released, on October 14, 1977, my friends would have their KISS *Book of Evolution* with them. We would look at it on the school bus. I would study how their outfits changed each year. Everything about the band was fascinating to me.

———◆———

One day after school, more specifically on October 20, 1977, I was watching NBC's *Nightly News* while my mother was preparing dinner. My father wasn't home from work yet.

While watching, I saw the story of the Lynyrd Skynyrd plane crash. I didn't know who the band was. To me, the band name was a bit odd, but it stuck with me.

This was the second news story from which I learned about a rock band or artist tragedy. Obviously, the first was Elvis just three months prior. I was too young for Jimi Hendrix, Janis Joplin, and Jim Morrision.

———◆———

For Christmas I received a black General Electric cassette tape recorder that came with a blue cassette tape. I could record five minutes on each side.

During winter break, one of my friends in band class went to New York. The big thing she had upon her return was a black-and-white photo of KISS. She bought it for $5 on the street. They were in costumes that I had never seen before. I thought these costumes were the new outfits for 1978.

The *American Music Awards* aired on January 16, 1978. With my new tape recorder set in front of the TV, I was ready to push the Record button.

KISS was to make an appearance. The appearance wasn't on the awards program, it was live footage from their December 20, 1977, show in Largo. The footage was edited together for a quick version of "Shout It Out Loud" and "Rock and Roll All Night." I recorded the audio. This was my first time getting any type of KISS music in my possession. Most of all, it was jaw-dropping to see KISS on stage.

Again, I still didn't make a connection to this and the *Paul Lynde Halloween Special*. Maybe it was just my age and thoughts spinning around constantly. I just thought it was way cool to finally see KISS on stage, if only for a short bit.

I cherished that tape, but at some point, I recorded over part of it. I was devastated, as it was the only KISS music I had.

I was still envious of all my friends who had KISS's *Alive II* and all the cool things that came with it. Sometimes I felt that I didn't belong because I didn't have any KISS music. I felt I wasn't really able to add anything worthy to conversation about their music.

It wasn't until sometime in the spring of 1978 that I was able to purchase KISS music for the first time. Needless to say, I had to work hard for it.

I made the B honor roll in what may have been the fourth six weeks period. It was a big deal academically for me. In doing so, I was able to purchase KISS's *Alive II*. I don't recall if my mother bought it for me or if I used my money. All I can say is that it finally happened.

Making the honor roll only occurred once when I was in public school but never while I was earning my bachelor's. For graduate school, I cruised through with nothing below an A. By that time, I had all the KISS albums I wanted—the makeup era only.

What's odd is that as big of a deal as it was for me to get *ALIVE II*, I don't remember where I got it from. I don't remember riding in the car to the mall, record store, or wherever I picked it up. I don't even remember buying the album. I can't say, then, if it was waiting for me one afternoon after I got home from school. I don't even remember dropping the needle for the first time. I would think for something as big as this, I would have some type of memory, but I just don't.

I do remember putting the KISS logo temporary tattoo on my bony-ass chest in the spring. I had to lie down on the bathroom floor to do it. Once done, I covered it up with my shirt. That night, I went to the roller rink. As I was skating, I had my butterfly-collar silk shirt unbuttoned, showing off the KISS tattoo. It was probably a very silly, adolescent look.

<hr>

In the spring, the KISS Donruss Series 1 cards were released. The set consisted of sixty-six trading cards. The back of each card was part of a puzzle. It was always a feeling of victory turning the card over and seeing what part of the puzzle you had. The piece could be part of a member's face or a portion of a costume. Either way, it was a rush and brought you one step closer to completing the puzzle.

There was one card that seemed just so over the top, image-wise. It was card number 50, a photo of Gene after he spit blood. He had his mouth on his microphone with blood dripping. It was so intense looking for 1978. The card was highly sought after by those who were collecting the series.

Looking at the cards made the bus ride to and from school that much more fun.

Along with the cards, friends would have a copy of the latest issue of 16 Magazine. While thumbing through the latest published KISS photos, there would be new album ads and pictures of other bands and artists. There was always something on Shaun Cassidy, Andy Gibb, the Bay City Rollers or others.

There was one album ad that immediately caused me to lock my eyes on the image. It was for Angel's new album White Hot. They were on Casablanca Records, the same label as KISS.

I had never seen a band that had that type of imagery. Even though the photo of the band was an artistic illustration, the entire band looked so polished. There were no flaws. What really caught my eyes was the hair of Greg Giuffria and Punky Meadows.

The ad put Angel on my music radar. For some reason, though, I would never purchase their music. I would see their albums all the time and would look at them.

I knew about Angel. I remember when the band last came through on the Rock & Roll Marathon Tour in 1980. I just never purchased their music until years later.

I will say with the limited information I had on the band, guitarist

Punky Meadows was very mysterious. He was more of a mystery to me than Ace Frehley, whose face was hidden by makeup.

———◦———

During the fall of sixth grade, I started taking private saxophone lessons at a music store called C&S. My teacher was an elderly gentleman. The first thing he did was correct my embouchure. That's the proper positioning of your mouth and teeth in order to play the saxophone correctly.

When I first started playing, my top teeth were not on the mouthpiece. My top lip was under my top front teeth. My teacher corrected that by placing several layers of white medical tape on top of the mouthpiece. The tape created a slight cushion for my teeth. After a week or two, he removed the tape, and I was finally using the proper embouchure when I played.

He was an extremely knowledgeable teacher, so I was disappointed when he retired. I think I only took a few months of lessons from him, but during that first lesson, he made a major change that quickly improved my playing.

I am not sure why I was taking lessons; maybe it was to give me something to focus on.

I switched to another teacher around winter break at another location. The lessons were in a smaller music store for the spring of sixth grade and partway into seventh grade. I know at one point that I switched to another building.

It was at a small music store called DC Sound, but I don't know what the two letters stood for. The location wasn't far from our house at all—less than a mile. Actually, the store was walking distance from Gary, Larry, and Terry's house mentioned in an earlier section.

Besides offering private music lessons, the store always had records. It's where I was allowed to purchase a 45 RPM of "Shout It Out Loud" by KISS. I never knew why I was allowed to purchase the KISS 45 but not the album.

———◦———

One day after lessons, I was looking at the albums and saw *Street Survivors*. That was the album that Skynyrd was touring for when their plane crashed. As I looked at the cover, I felt this eerie feeling. It was from seeing Ronnie Van Zant and Steve Gaines in the flames. I knew several members of the band died, but I didn't know who.

While the album was in the racks, I would look at it each time I was there for my lesson. I would just stare at the cover while holding it.

My knowledge of the band and a sincere appreciation of their music would come several years later. I would be exposed to their music through my brother's band.

SEVEN

A YEAR OF CHANGE

1978

THE YEAR 1978 WAS a year of change that started in the spring and continued from summer into the fall of my seventh grade year.

I started my final season of Little League Baseball. It was my second year of what was called the Majors. When I was playing, there were three levels of Little League. The bottom level or division was Peewee, followed by the Minors, and finally the Majors. These days, there are more divisions.

At some point during my five seasons (1974–1978), tee ball was introduced, maybe about 1976. It was explained but difficult to understand. I just had to go watch a game for a few minutes, and then I understood.

All the teams in the Majors were named after Major League Baseball teams. My team was the Cubs, but our letter C logo was more like the C for the Cincinnati Reds. Our colors were not blue and white like the Chicago Cubs but yellow and blue. Yellow was the dominant color. We had a few new team members, but the majority of the team was in place from the previous year.

Our leader, Coach Kennedy, rocked. He was a B-52 pilot, and with his military background, he worked us hard. Prior to each practice, we would run a huge lap at the park. It started to become a competition between players to see who could finish first. I always finished second. I could never seem to get the edge on my teammate Chris. He always came in first. At the end of our session, we would repeat the lap. Again, I would finish second.

Coach Kennedy was our leader. I never questioned why he ran us so hard. It wasn't until several years later that I realized why. He was building up our physical stamina for game days. It worked.

From all that running, I learned that I had endurance for long-distance running. When we had our twelve-minute walk/run test in PE that spring, I knocked out seven laps around the track by keeping a steady pace the whole time. For a twelve-year-old, running 1.75 miles in twelve minutes was impressive. The coaches noticed, and so did other students.

Some students were saying that I didn't complete seven laps. I was accused of grabbing more than one popsicle stick on each pass. There was some serious jealousy. I shrugged it off by saying I was in baseball and we ran every day.

I was asked by one of the PE coaches if I wanted to run in the cross-country city meet and represent the school. I was very surprised but declined. I'd heard stories of athletes tripping others and making them fall to gain an advantage. I didn't want to deal with or experience that.

Our baseball team won the championship with an impressive record. Maybe only two losses for the twenty-game schedule. We went into post-season play. Now, we were practicing on the league fields.

I noticed my hitting was getting stronger. During batting practice, I hit the ball over the fence. The news traveled very fast. Players from other teams couldn't believe I actually did that. It was crazy.

We went four games deep into the first round of playoffs. The first game, I had a deep two-run double to left center field. The left fielder wasn't able to catch the ball. If I hadn't jacked the ball so high, I truly believe the ball would have cleared the fence.

I don't remember much of the second game, but in the third game, I caught the winning out in right field. The center fielder, Peter, mobbed me with excitement.

We advanced to the fourth game and faced an undefeated team out of Arlington. Their pitcher was a beast on the mound. He threw serious heat. I'd never experienced the speed of a baseball like I was seeing in this game. Many of my teammates were mowed down easily in three to five pitches.

On my last at-bat late in the game, I decided to swing early—much earlier than normal. It worked. I hit a weak blooper over the first baseman. The ball kissed the grass just inside the foul line. It wasn't a big hit, but it was a game-changer. My weak single broke the pitcher's no-hitter.

We lost 7–0, but the opposing team was very impressed by our play. Prior to playing us, the lowest number of runs they were held to in the regular season was 15.

I didn't continue to play after that last season. Everyone was getting taller and bigger, but I was still a small, skinny kid. In other words, I chickened out and didn't want to move up to Pony League. The thought of getting hit by a fastball at that level was scary.

During the summer, I had a bowling pass to the bowling alley for one free game each day. I had bowling shoes, so it didn't cost me anything to bowl that one game daily.

By this time of the summer, I had a KISS shirt. It was the *Love Gun* album cover on a blue T-shirt that I wore religiously. My aunt had sent it to me.

On July 31, 1978, my best friend Randall and I rode our ten-speed bikes down to the bowling alley. It was something we did every day. Unfortunately, this trip would end up differently.

The bowling alley was located about a quarter mile from the bottom of a steep hill. We took this hill daily. As we were heading down the hill, two cars came racing toward us. One was a blue Corvette. We both aimed for a driveway to our right. Randall made it into the driveway. I didn't. I hit the rounding of the curb at the driveway's edge and went over my handlebars. I landed next to a small tree. That tree was nearly twenty feet from my bicycle's point of impact.

All the following is information I was told after the fact:

Randall said the two cars stopped but then drove away. I really don't remember anything.

My friend ran across the street to get help from a man who was outside his house. I vaguely remember this. There's something about a yellow station wagon with wood paneling. I don't know how my bicycle and Randall made it back to my house.

I recall waking up in the family car as my mother drove frantically to the ER. I kept going in and out of consciousness. I was tired, sleepy, and extra lethargic.

I don't remember getting wheeled into the hospital. I do start to have memories of being on a stretcher or gurney in the ER, looking up at the ceiling. There was a pressing pain in my shoulder. That was a portion of my collarbone protruding from my left shoulder. My mother told me later the bone sticking out was the size of her fingernail.

To get to my injury, the ER staff had to cut off my KISS shirt. I was "promised" I would get another. Spoiler alert: it never happened.

I went into surgery, and the surgeon pinned my collarbone back together.

If memory serves me correctly, I stayed overnight. I know that friends of my brother came to see me. They brought me the first KISS album. Now, along with *ALIVE II*, I had the first album. I got to know songs like "Strutter," "Deuce," "Cold Gin," "Nothing to Lose," "Firehouse," "100,000 Years," and "Black Diamond"—all classic-era KISS songs.

However, the joy of having a new KISS album for my collection and hopes for others was short-lived. Once I began to heal, I started going to the mall and visiting the record store. I was a teenager, or right on the cusp of it. I was entering that phase of discovering rock music. The first album I purchased with my own money wasn't a KISS album, but Foghat's *LIVE*. I had heard my brother and his friends talk about it many times. It had to be good if the album was a topic of conversation.

My next purchase was Foreigner's *Double Vision*, followed by Boston's *Don't Look Back*, and Styx's *Pieces of Eight*. I am thinking Aerosmith's *Toys in the Attic* followed for number five.

After that, I don't remember. I have been unsuccessful in any attempts to jog my memory. Several weeks or months passed before I purchased another album. I can't say. What I can say is that I was in seventh grade.

Putting another KISS record into my collection around this time was a mission that had to fly under the radar. I had to be very stealthy.

One afternoon, I was in the mall record store with my mother. She said I could purchase any album I wanted. I was so excited that I went directly to KISS's *ALIVE*. Then she added, "Except a KISS album."

I felt so defeated.

———◦———

There was another KISS-related event that was the talk of my friends:

KISS Meets the Phantom of the Park was airing. For us KISS fans, this was a must-see. I am honestly surprised my parents let me watch it when the movie aired on Saturday, October 28, 1978.

The best part of the movie was the live concert scenes. This was my third time to see KISS in a live setting on TV. Like the first, it was amazing. It only fueled my fascination with the band even more.

Yes, the plot was silly, but that didn't matter. The movie was still cool to me and my friends.

Every Sunday we would get the major daily newspaper. It would be packed with full-color comics, coupons, the latest news, and the *TV Guide* for that week. The *TV Guide* for the week leading up to the KISS movie had the mad scientist and members of KISS as an animated illustration on the cover.

When I saw the TV Guide and the artwork, I told my parents that I wanted to have the *TV Guide* by the end of the week. They agreed.

I still have the TV Guide, and it's in really nice condition, considering it's forty-six years old. It's a great thing to look back at how TV was before cable. There were the three major networks, ABC, CBS and NBC. Then there was PBS and one or two UHF/VHF channels. That's it.

It's great to see and reflect on what shows were on during primetime, after-school hours, and the coveted Saturday-morning cartoons.

—◇—

Besides discovering more rock bands and artists such as Aerosmith, Ted Nugent, Alice Cooper, and Cheap Trick, I was becoming a disciplined saxophone player. I had the first chair in the seventh-grade band for the saxophones locked down. Nobody could outperform me and take it away.

With an ever-growing passion for school band and discovering rock music, I wanted to learn how to play the guitar. I was disciplined enough and would practice my tail off.

I would always ride my bike down to the music store and gaze at the black Gibson Les Paul with white piping. It was a beauty displayed high above the sales floor. The price tag was $600, and it's what Ace Frehley played. That's what I wanted to learn to play guitar on.

One afternoon, I said to my mother that I wanted to learn how to play the guitar. Her response was a quick five-word response that halted any potential.

She said, "No. You have your saxophone."

That was it—end of discussion.

For the school band, our teacher, Miss Winchester, wanted to put together the best band she could with seventh- and eighth-grade students.

When she became excited about something or wanted everyone's attention quickly, she would screech out a high-pitched, loud,

39

"Hey!" It was her trademarked phrase.

To put together her dream band for the upcoming semester, she brought in judges. Every student had to try out. These judges weren't just regular judges. These judges were the real deal judges. Band students had to audition in front of these judges to try out for City, State, or Regional Band. This was serious stuff, with the top score being 100.

The scores from tryouts would determine what band Miss Winchester would assign the students to. Obviously, the top band would be the Symphonic Band and consist of the best players, no matter what grade.

Most likely, our tryouts were held late in the fall semester so schedules could be shuffled around for the spring.

One day, Miss Winchester was looking over the judging sheets. She excitedly shouted, "Hey! Someone made a 94."

Everybody started asking, "Who? Who? Who?" but she wouldn't say. She did mention it was the highest score overall.

Imagine my surprise when I was told I scored the highest out of all the band students. I was informed that I would move to the Symphonic Band. There, I would take over the first chair for saxophones. There were a few other seventh graders, but me achieving this feat wasn't expected. It blew everyone's minds. Everybody knew me as a rock music fan, prankster, and clown.

EIGHT

KISS DYNASTY TOUR

1979

THE YEAR 1979 WAS another memorable year for me. Not only did I return to school as an eighth grader, but I also still had a firm grasp on the first chair for saxophones. I was also discovering more rock bands. Some that come to mind include Triumph, Electric Light Orchestra, Ted Nugent, Van Halen, Black Sabbath, Journey, and Bad Company. I was introduced to the greatness of Pink Floyd through *Dark Side of the Moon*. This was courtesy from the older brother of a friend down the street.

I would see RUSH's *Farewell to Kings* album quite a bit in the cutout section of record stores. The cover creeped me out every time I saw it. Not even the $3.99 price tag would entice me. It wasn't until the neighbor's garage sale that I finally gave in. I picked up *Farewell to Kings* on 8-track for a quarter. It was then that I realized what an incredible album it was. I would listen to that tape over and over. The album still ranks one of my top three Rush releases to this day.

There was a local band called Point Blank on MCA Records. I would see their album *Airplay* everywhere. It was always a promotional giveaway at radio live remotes. It's a great record that I have in cassette and 8-track formats along with the album.

—◦—

The notable story from 1979 for me was obviously related to KISS. They were going out on tour for the *Dynasty* album and playing TCCC. I really, really wanted to go, but no matter how much pleading I did, the response was a firm no.

Brian standing outside the square dance building on October 23, 2019 holding a copy of the photo that ran in the paper the day after the KISS concert and a square dance record.

That night, Tuesday, October 23, 1979, was pure torture. Not only was I missing the KISS concert, but I was constantly thinking about what was happening at that exact moment. I had to go with my parents to their square dance lessons. I was so defeated just being there, knowing that KISS was a fifteen-minute drive away.

The date, October 23, 1979, is forever ingrained into my music-loving mind. No matter how old I become, I remember that night. The thought of missing a KISS concert as an eighth grader still stings to this day. Square dance lessons vs. KISS, the battle of that memory will never fade.

Forty years later on October 23, 2019, I went back to that specific building. There's a photo of me standing out front in a KISS Army 1996 tour shirt, a print of the photo that ran in the paper, and a square dance record.

What makes matters worse is the fact that I pass by the "swing your partner round and round" building on a regular basis. I laugh but still think of what could have been.

———◇———

Three days later on October 26, 1979, one of the local album rock stations, KTXQ 102.1 FM—or simply Q 102—put on a concert with free tickets. The only catch—there was a ten-ticket limit. The headliner was Triumph with their *Just a Game* album. Supporting Triumph was Gamma, and the first band was a local hard Southern rock trio called Blackhorse.

My brother went to the Triumph show, but again, no matter how much I pleaded, I wasn't allowed. By this point, I had started to pay close attention to the rock concerts coming through town.

Pretty much the five W's—the who, what, where, when and why of these shows—were logged in my brain. Concerts were starting to become a major part of me as a person.

Ironically, on the date that I am writing this passage, December 4, I saw Triumph live on the *Allied Forces* album in 1981. It was my second show to attend. A year later, 1982, I saw The Who on the *It's Hard* tour.

The local band Blackhorse was making some serious waves. At one point I recall the band being offered a deal with CBS/Columbia Records, but I never saw anything. The talk about Blackhorse was hot, especially after the Triumph show.

Years later, I was at a venue and saw Blackhorse play. As I was leaving, I was driving toward one of the members of the band in the parking lot. I stopped my truck, said that I enjoyed their set, and asked if I could ask a question.

Whoever the member was replied, "Of course."

I told him I remembered the talk about the band being offered a deal with CBS/Columbia Records.

He said, "Yes, the band was offered a deal."

I asked, "What happened?"

His reply was actually sad. He said, "We told them we weren't ready. It was the biggest mistake we ever made."

It's a real shame the band never got their dues. That band was a serious can of Southern-fried rock whoop ass. They were never again able to grasp what was once offered to them. I didn't ask for details of the record deal; I just wanted confirmation if the stories I had heard over the years were true, especially in middle school. Indeed, the stories were true.

Several years after this encounter, I saw the band at a small hole-in-the-wall bar west of Fort Worth. I purchased the album for $5.00. The album these days fetches $49.99 on the low end, and I have seen listings as high as $99.99. The album in CD format is out there as well. It just takes a bit of searching for that reasonable price.

It's a great album, and the tunes "Fox Huntin'" and "Lucille" are bona fide killer Southern rock songs. The tracks would have been classics but never received their proper justice. Those tunes kill.

This is how important music was becoming to me as a seventh and eighth grader. I remembered all this stuff. I had such a curiosity for information regarding concerts and bands. I remember the shows and tours like Alice Cooper's Madhouse Rock Tour with The Babys and Legs Diamond, for instance. These are music details I remember to this day. A quick search of the internet only confirms what I remember.

———◄O►———

In middle school, we had what was called a *rotating schedule*. To me, a rotating schedule seemed normal. Today, I can see middle school students being confused and lost if they had to deal with a rotating schedule. The schedule was based on five class periods a day.

On Monday, students would attend class periods one through five in order. Classes on Tuesday then ran periods two, three, four, five and one. Wednesday's class schedule would run three, four, five, one, two. Thursday's would be four, five, one, two, three, and then Friday's would be five, one, two, three, four.

This schedule was normal for high school. I don't think we had a rotating schedule during my sophomore, junior, or senior year though.

If there was no school on a Monday, whatever day of the week students returned, that day's schedule would run. The schedule would then run normally through the end of the week.

For lunch, certain classes were designated with one of the three lunch periods. There was a rotating lunch schedule as well. All classes were assigned one of the three designated lunch periods. For example, all math classes would have a first-period lunch. History and English classes would have the second-period lunch, the split-class lunch. Students would attend the first half of class, and then class would dismiss for lunch. When students were supposed to return for the second half of class after lunch, some students wouldn't show.

All electives would have third period lunch. So students would have a lunch schedule and often, it was a different lunch period every day. For some reason, I have a recollection of 3, 2, 1, 3, 2 as a lunch schedule.

I used that persona of disciplined saxophone player and great band student to my advantage. I guess in Miss Winchester's eyes, I could do no wrong. I did no wrong, except for one small, tiny teenage adventure in the auditorium.

On more than one occasion, I would go to Miss Winchester and explain to her that I'd left my books behind in the auditorium and needed to get them. She then would give me the key, and I would go to the auditorium stage door and unlock it.

My girlfriend at the time would go in, I would take the keys back to Miss Winchester, and I would return to the auditorium. There, on stage right, off to the side, we would have a lunchtime make-out session. It happened more than once.

Since the middle school ran on a rotation schedule, my girlfriend and I wouldn't have the same lunch every day. We may have had the same lunch once or twice a week, so these adventures were not a daily occurrence. This might have happened three times at the most, but I am leaning more toward twice.

At some point, my girlfriend got me one of those racy cards from Spencer's Gifts in the mall. It had a set of big red juicy lips on the front. It was a tri-folded card, and she wrote me a love note calling me "Hot Lips."

I was a bit embarrassed by it, but I did sense an imaginary pat on my back and an "attaboy." I hid the card in my closet on the top shelf under my old baby blankets, thinking no one would ever find it.

One day a year or two or years later, I went looking for the card, and it wasn't there. I freaked, and the only conclusion I made was that my mother found the card under the blankets. She never said anything, and I never asked.

NINE

GOODBYE MIDDLE SCHOOL, HELLO HIGH SCHOOL

1980

As THE SCHOOL YEAR for 1980 was winding down, I was looking forward to the next few months. Of course there were some shenanigans as the school year was closing out that are worthy of mention. For me, fun in the classroom never seemed to cease. Especially if it occurred in science.

I will be the first to say I don't remember squat from eighth-grade science. Literally, I have only one memory.

It's from the end of the year, even maybe on one of the last days when we were learning about various types of rocks. This wasn't just a unit on igneous, sedimentary, or metamorphic rocks. This particular lesson involved various rock samples and hydrochloric acid.

All I remember is that students were tasked with finding out how hydrochloric acid reacts with various rock samples. One would think there would be lots of bubbles and fizzles. A few did react, but that was the extent of it.

The samples were in small brown prescription bottles with little white lids that popped off. I don't even think there were childproof lids yet, just tops that could be popped off with the thumb.

One of the samples we tested was pebble stone, and it did react with the hydrochloric acid—rather well, I might add. This reaction made us go, "Wow, that was cool."

Well, leave it to me to take it a step further. We observed a bubbly reaction in the bottle, so I suggested to my lab tablemates to test it again. This time, though, we would seal the bottle to see what would happen. That's exactly what we did. We weren't gifted and talented, just mischievous.

After we waited a couple moments, the reaction occurred. The pressure inside the bottle from the gas created shot the cap off the bottle with a loud pop. We all busted out laughing. To us, it was way too funny to do just once, so we did it again.

We put the hydrochloric acid in the bottle with the pebble stone sample and put the lid back on. As soon as we put the lid on, our teacher, Mr. Hackford came to our table. Meanwhile, our prescription bottle was loaded. We were waiting for it to blow as our teacher stood at our table. The look in our eyes said it all: "Oh sh*t."

We waited for the bottle to blow. By the grace of powers outside the classroom, the bottle didn't blow.

Mr. Hackford left our group and went to check on another table. The sense of relief amongst every mischievous boy at that lab table was immeasurable. Why the bottle didn't blow, I have no idea. Maybe the lid wasn't firmly secured, or we needed fresh pebble stone. I just know that if it would've blown, we would have been sent down to the office. There, we would've had to assume the position and receive pops with that flexible, white fiberglass paddle named Snap 'n' Pop. Yes, that was ACTUALLY the name of the assistant principal's paddle.

***

The last few weeks of eighth grade were extremely important, especially for us band students. For two weeks, we would attend the after-school marching band boot camp at the high school. There, we would learn the basics of high school marching band mechanics and, most importantly, how to properly march in the style the high school band director built the shows upon. There were other things as well, such as being able to play your instrument, reading/sight reading music, and having an understanding of basic components related to music theory.

The marching band had a solid reputation of winning. This was a big time for us middle school kids. I was aware of the band's success, as my brother was a junior in the marching band when I was attending boot camp. Of course, since I was his younger brother, I immediately had a target on my back.

The boot camp lasted two weeks. We had to try out at the end of camp. If we made the cut, then we would receive a letter in the mail welcoming us. It was a badge of honor to become a member of the Big Red Band from Rebel Land.

I received the highly anticipated letter and was stoked that I'd made the cut.

Unfortunately, not everyone received the welcome letter, not because they were unable to do what was required but because of doing what shouldn't have been done.

The following is an example of what should not be done.

One of my fellow middle school bandmates pranked the band director with several upperclassmen. Wrong move. He was removed, kicked out, or whatever is the best way to say it, from boot camp.

I know that was a big-time gut punch to him. He was one of the leading brass players in the middle school band. Being removed from boot camp was like receiving the death penalty in the high school band.

On the first Monday of August, all band students, including the incoming freshmen, reported for marching band. He was there but not in the band. He would march along on the sidelines and even dismiss with the band. It was a sad sight to watch. I think him showing up lasted a couple of days, and then I never saw him again.

Somehow, through the grapevine, I heard he attended high school in a different district. Through a friend, I met a girl six years after high school graduation that had gone to high school with him. She was in the band and was in the same brass section as he was. She may have been in eighth grade when he was a senior, but she had high praise for his playing. I am sure deep down, he wanted to be part of the Rebel band.

Competition-wise, we were untouchable.

The band won the city marching contest, walking away with the Best in Class trophy in the years 1971–1979 and 1980–81 through 1983–84, the year I graduated. I stopped following the winning streak after I left high school. The only year the band didn't win during those years was 1979–80, my eighth grade year. That meant, when I was in competition as a freshman, we won the Best in Class trophy back.

During the summer at one point, the church youth group took a trip to Red River, New Mexico. I think the trip was about five days.

In our little group of mischievous boys, there were a few intense music fans such as my friend Trent and me.

At the camp, we met what I guess would be a camp counselor. He was a few years older than us, had long hair, and was from Los Angeles. He was totally cool, and we could really relate with him. His name was Paul.

One afternoon when we had time to burn, we gathered on the front porch of his residential quarters. He proceeded to describe in detail Pink Floyd's *The Wall* concert he attended in LA. It was a wow moment for us rock music lovers, meeting someone who actually saw *The Wall* in concert.

Production for the tour was so massive, there were only two locations of tour stops in the United States—seven shows at the Los Angeles Sports Memorial Arena and five at New York's Nassau Veterans Memorial Sports Coliseum. All the dates were in February of 1980.

As rock fans who were craving anything concert related, we were captivated and enthralled by his narration of the show. Actually, his dialogue was more like a play-by-play of the concert. It's a shame we didn't have tape running. If there was a recording of Paul's Pink Floyd play-by-play, I would still listen to this day, forty-three years later.

———◦———

Throughout the summer, our youth minister had been battling leukemia. I didn't understand what exactly was happening medically. Information would be shared with us here and there.

He was hospitalized and didn't make the trip to Red River with us.

I admit that I was extremely active at times, but that was just me. I was high energy, high metabolism, full throttle more of my waking hours than I should have been. It was genetics.

Fun fact, I didn't break 120 pounds until I was thirty-five. When I saw that on the scale for the first time, I flipped out.

Our last hurrah for the youth group consisted of going to a waterslide park. The next morning I would start my freshman year. I even remember the date. It was Sunday, August 31, 1980. Why do I remember that? AC/DC was in town in support of the *Back in*

Black album at the Dallas Convention Center. That's why.

One of the girls in our youth group went to the show. I was so envious of her while I was just sitting around, hanging out at the water park. It was prehistoric when compared to the water parks of today.

Toward the end of the night, I heard one of the chaperons get paged to take a phone call. For some reason, I watched him walk to the office.

I told my brother that Mr. Davidson was asked to report to the water park office. He didn't think much of it, but I did.

Mr. Davidson finished the phone call. I watched him return to the waterslides. He had a stunned look on his face. He was expressionless.

I asked him if everything was alright, and he didn't answer me. I asked him again, and he said something, but I really didn't hear him.

I told my brother what had happened, and he paused for a moment.

I was the only one who noticed Mr. Davidson taking the phone call and then the look on his face afterward. Nobody else did, as they were having too much fun on the last night before school started the next morning.

Probably ten minutes later, the bus was loaded and on its way back to the church. I was riding with my brother in his friend's convertible. I just kept looking up toward the sky and stars. I just knew something wasn't right.

When we arrived at the church, everyone unloaded from the bus. We were instructed to go to the sanctuary, so we did.

As I walked down the hallway, I was getting a bad vibe, a sickening gut feeling.

Once we were in the sanctuary and seated on the maroon carpet at the front, Mr. Davidson told us. He said our youth minister had passed away from leukemia.

It was terrible to experience all the grief that hit like a ton of bricks, especially for my brother. It was horrible. I never want to witness reactions like that again. Tears and wailing of grief. Pure devastation.

It didn't matter who—all the kids were hit hard, but especially my brother. He and the youth minister were tight. His reaction is still chilling to this day.

I've never forgotten where I was sitting when we were told.

Whenever the youth group would come together in the sanctuary for the night, I would sit in that exact same spot. Every time we were brought in there for a group gathering in the sanctuary, I never sat anywhere else.

That was not how I'd anticipated starting my freshman year in high school.

I will say on the day of the funeral, there must have been at least eighty early dismissals from my high school. That's how much of an impact he had had on our group as our youth minister. Each year, when August 31 rolls around, I think of him as well as the AC/DC show.

As for the one member of the youth group who went to the AC/DC show, she told me she would have rather been with the group that night instead of being at the concert.

TEN

THE START OF MY FRESHMAN YEAR, BIG MUSIC NEWS, AND MORE SHENANIGANS

THAT FIRST DAY OF summer, marching band practice sucked. Since my brother was now a senior, I had to deal with a bunch of crap.

One of the first orders of business for that first day was to elect "property managers." I was nominated very quickly, along with a couple of freshmen who had older siblings who were upperclassmen.

The elections didn't go my way. I was quickly elected with several other of my fellow ninth graders.

The basic duties of the property managers were to transport and haul bulky accessories vital for marching band. That included the drum major's wooden podium, ladder, and other things to the practice field and back. We also had to load those things on the bus for football games, unload, transport, reload, and other nonsense.

I didn't like doing it, plain and simple.

———⋅◇⋅———

My freshman year was underway. Each school day started an hour earlier than normal. The marching band would report to the band hall and be ready on the practice field by 7:00 a.m. every morning. That means, I was arriving at school before seven each morning.

After we practiced on the field, we would make our way to the band hall for music rehearsals. By a certain time, band members would be dismissed. For the girls, that meant they would be getting ready for school—in other words, makeup and hair. Makeup mirrors and plugged in curling irons were scattered throughout the band room. It was strange to see.

As the fall weeks progressed, the temperatures became cooler in the mornings. That meant I needed to dress in layers. I will say, it was no fun practicing on the cold mornings.

To keep my head warm, I would wear what was called my "Elmer Fudd hat." It was more of a winter hat with black and orange checkered squares, topped off with a black puff ball. It even had flaps that folded down. The flaps allowed my hair to dry flat.

Several years later, as in 1989, I was out and about with a friend several years younger who was in the marching band. We decided to go up to the school, and we walked through the open gate to get to the marching field. As I passed between the two fence poles, a flood of memories came rushing back. It was such a surreal feeling.

I found several of the upperclassmen fascinating. They were going to concerts and always talking about bands. These guys were leaning more toward British invasion bands, new wave, some punk bands and traditional rock bands.

I recall conversations about Fleetwood Mac's *Rumours* and music by the Kinks. I would just listen even though I was leaning more toward the hard rock side of things.

By the end of the first week of school, the Labor Day weekend was upon us. Later in the week, Van Halen played a sold-out show at Reunion Arena in Dallas on the *Women and Children First* album.

Reunion Arena was a mythical place to me, as it was a big twenty thousand-seat arena for major concerts. Once it opened, the Tarrant County Convention Center saw little concert action. Unfortunately, pyrotechnics were not allowed at Reunion in the early years of the arena.. It wasn't until years later that I started seeing pyrotechnics used at Reunion Arena.

The next school day after the Van Halen show, 1980 Invasion shirts were everywhere. When I mean everywhere, no matter what hallway I was walking in or what direction I was looking, I would see Van Halen concert shirts. Then, the shirts were always in pairs, not just worn by a single person.

As a kid just craving the experience of a concert, it was truly an amazing sight to see. I was in awe. It was my first time seeing masses of people wearing their concert shirts the day after a show.

Three weeks later, the music world would be jolted to its core.

The big music news event happened in the middle of September. The first full month of my freshman year wasn't even complete. This was the shattering music event of my freshman year, maybe even the decade: the passing of Led Zeppelin's John Boham.

I didn't know much Zeppelin, as the band wasn't quite on my listening radar yet. I do recall people were camping out for Zeppelin tickets for the May 22, 1977, show at TCCC. Local news stations even covered the people at their spots. Some started lining up three days in advance.

I didn't grasp the magnitude of Boham's passing until a year or two later.

Just a few days prior to Boham's passing, the band announced a fall US Tour. I remember upperclassmen talking about how they were planning on camping out once tickets were announced for the DFW date.

It's difficult to comprehend that the passing of Boham has been over forty years. That puts the passings of Hendrix, Joplin, and Morrison at fifty-plus years.

There would be more.

The Cars' *Panorama* album was released in mid-August, and those upperclassmen were into it. The band would be rolling through Dallas on Sunday, October 12, 1980. I remember wanting to go and even asking. I don't recall having a plan about how I was going to get there. When I inquired about wanting to go, the answer was still no. It wasn't an affirmative no this time around. There was a blip of light on my concert radar.

I have often reflected back—what if I'd gone? Would I have still been a hard rocker, or would I have had more of a taste for new wave?

Several years back, I purchased an unused ticket from that show on eBay. An upper balcony ticket was only $9.50. The ticket has been sitting in a protective case on display at my desk ever since. I can't give a reason as to why I purchased the ticket. Maybe it had something to do with taking me back to a time when life was much simpler, when society was a tad nicer and music was truly appreciated and supported. The Cars were definitely one of the great American rock bands, and I never saw them.

During my freshman year, I made some new friends. One of them became my "Let's Talk Music" buddy, Mark. He introduced me to some great bands. He had two older brothers who were rockers. He went to many of the great rock concerts our freshman year with his brothers. I was very envious.

The show I remember the most was Nazareth and Krokus at Moody Coliseum on May 9, 1981. Krokus was touring on the

Hardware album. Eventually, I was fascinated with the band. They became one of my go-to bands for high school. To this day, I listen to them on a regular basis.

I know that Mark and several others were in my Introductory Algebra class. That meant we would have the same lunch one day a week. The high school ran on the rotating schedule like the middle school did.

Many times, a group of us would hang out in the band hall. We would just goof around—except for that one time.

Remember, it only takes one time.

We, being the group of us, were playing catch or football with a peanut butter and jelly sack lunch. I am fairly certain there were chips and a dessert in there as well. With those contents, it sounds like a disaster waiting to happen, but just wait.

At some point during our roughhousing and monkeying around, a pint can of white oil-based paint made its way onto the floor. It just sat in the open.

One of the guys, I don't remember who, was nailed with the sack lunch or a chalkboard eraser. It was a direct hit to the face, and he was pissed, like in severely pissed and raging. He picked up the first thing he could get his hands on. That just happened to be the can of white paint. He threw it across the room with force.

Mark was on the other side of the band hall just standing around. He was maybe thirty feet from the guy that got nailed. The paint can landed next to Mark. The impact of the can hitting the floor knocked the lid off, and Newton's first law of physics went into effect: the liquid contents continued in the direction the can was traveling. Unfortunately, Mark was in that pathway. The paint covered the entire side of his body, from bicep to shoes. This wasn't a light sprinkling or misting of paint—paint was dripping off him.

Not only was Mark covered in paint, but there was paint all over the carpet by the entrance and band director's office, storage areas, and doors for orchestra instruments. Several standup basses used in the orchestra sustained paint splatters.

I don't recall what happened next. I literally think the possibility of something staying in long-term memory was scared out of me. I vaguely remember being called to the office. After that, I don't remember a thing.

Our punishment was that we had to clean the paint up after school. No matter what cleaning solution we used, the paint would not come up. It was set and not going away. It was oil based.

I think we tried for an hour or two and just gave up.

For the next several years, the white paint stain was on the carpet. I think it was still there several years after I left.

———◇———

There were many exciting things coming in the coming months of 1981. Most importantly, ninth grade was coming to a close.

My freshman year had been unique. Obviously, some crazy things happened. Out of all this, I did learn one major life skill that I still utilize to this day.

As an incoming freshman, I was allowed to enroll in a second elective class. The first was a marching band, and the second was a speech. It was my second period of the day taught by one of the track coaches, Coach Freeman. In today's terms, the class could be known as Public Speaking. His class was highly recommended by an upperclassman from church.

By the end of the semester, a student should be able to get up in front of a group of people and give a presentation or speech. Some of the traditional speeches included introductory, entertaining, persuasive, informative and explanatory speeches.

There was a specific main reason I took the class. I wanted to get adjusted to standing up in front of people and speaking. I wanted to rid myself of any lingering "stage fright" I might have. I'd heard horror stories about reciting useless poetry or giving an oral book report in front of your classroom peers. Some people were terrified of having to do that. By the end of the semester, I wasn't. That's the reason why I took the class.

What I enjoyed about this class was that students from all grade levels were enrolled. Several of my brother's friends were in the class. It wasn't a blowoff class at all. I don't recall anyone slacking in the class actually.

I have utilized the speaking skills I gained in this class for forty-plus years, whether in a classroom, at a state conference, or in the role of a guest speaker.

I even majored in speech communications at TCU where I only

sharpened those skills. With all this said, lifelong gratitude has been extended to Coach Freeman. He has just never known.

ELEVEN

DRIVER'S ED POINT OF ENTRY INTO THE SUMMER

TWO BIG EVENTS WERE happening for me in June 1981.

The first is that rite of passage called driver's ed. As soon as school let out, class started on Monday. We would report to the school's cafeteria.

Our instructor was old school and a straight-to-the-point type of guy. He was a tad on the heavy side. It didn't matter to him what we called him. His pet peeve was someone shouting, "Hey, Teach," or "Hey, you." He was fine with anything else and even poked fun at his weight. He said we could even call him "Fat Guy" or something along those lines.

The class laughed, but we all knew out of respect we wouldn't do that.

During our three-week stint in driver's ed, we had to take a written test at the local DPS. It was walking distance from the southeast corner of the high school property. If the student passed their test, they would receive the coveted learner's permit. Without the permit, we would not be able to drive on the roads with our driving instructor. It was imperative to pass the test.

One of the DPS troopers overseeing the students taking the test had a serious Napoleon complex. I guess his uniform and shiny badge gave him an excuse to be a d*ck to those of us there for the test.

I never forgot his name, but he's not worth the effort to name. There is irony though. With a letter tweak or two in *phallic*, his name will magically appear.

I don't recall who was in my driving group, but we learned the rules of the road in a blue Chevrolet Chevette. It wasn't the fanciest thing, but it worked. One lucky group of students did their learning in a Camaro Z/28, Trans AM or something. It might have been cool to cruise around while styling and profiling in the fancy ride, but I wouldn't have liked dealing with the cramped quarters in the back.

Besides hitting the streets, another thing the students were looking forward to was the films. The films showed results of not following standard safety protocol and not practicing common sense driving. Images in these films were supposed to be disturbing, but I really don't recall anything too bad.

I remember one image. Maybe it's because of the funny caption our instructor added.

The scene had a car that went down a hill with the driver's-side door open. The driver somehow was slumped over and leaning out the door while the car traveled down the hill. The door hit a tree stump, causing it to slam shut on the driver's head. The vehicle then came to a stop.

I don't remember the moral or lesson of the photo, I just remember the instructor saying, "Take two aspirin and call me in the morning." Of course there was laughter.

Some of the fun days in the classroom had us in the driving simulators modeled after the Pontiacs of the 1970s. Of course, the guys like me who enjoyed having fun pushed our speed to the high nineties all in good fun.

The good news is that all students earned their permits and started driving with an eighteen or older adult in the front passenger seat.

A new freedom for us wasn't that far off.

———— ◆ ————

My point of entry into rock concerts finally occurred on Saturday, June 13, 1981, at Moody Coliseum at Southern Methodist University.

Judas Priest was touring in support of their February 1981 release *Point of Entry*. On tour as support were Humble Pie and Iron Maiden, which was a fairly new British band touring for their second album, *Killers*.

Finally, I was able to attend my first rock concert.

I had a ticket in hand about a month prior to the show. The days crept by slowly. A lot of people knew I was going and even wrote about it in my yearbook during those last few days of school.

The yearbook and the signings were new to me. I knew what the annuals were. My brother had a yearbook for each year in high school. This would be the only edition that would have both of us in there. It was his senior year and my freshman year.

In my record collection, I already had a copy of Judas Priest's *Unleashed in the East* album. With that, I was familiar with classic Priest tunes like "Sinner," "Victims of Changes," "Green Manalishi," "Diamond and Rust," and "Running Wild."

Besides never having attended a rock concert except for Elvis and Texas, I wanted to be familiar with songs in the Priest setlist. I wasn't familiar with any music from Humble Pie. As for Maiden, the only thing I knew was the cool album artwork. I didn't know any music at all.

I remember the wow factor when we walked up the stairs to our lower balcony seats. I saw a wide-open space with chairs on the floor, a haze of smoke lingering in the air, and a Frisbee or two flying. Then I looked at the stage and saw some netting above the PA system.

I had visual information overload. I was finally at a rock concert. Literally, it was a dream come true.

Prior to Maiden taking the stage, an announcement was made that Humble Pie would not be playing due to an illness in the band. Priest and Maiden would play extended sets.

With the research capabilities of the internet, it's very easy to see the differences in sets between the Maiden show in Dallas and the following night in Houston.

The Houston set consisted of eight songs, whereas the Dallas show had an additional five songs.

For the Dallas show, a roadie came out in an Eddie mask hyping the crowd up like a witch doctor during the "Ides of March." The band then launched into "Wrathchild" and never looked back.

Maiden added "Innocent Exile," the instrumental "Transylvania," and a Dave Murray guitar solo, followed by "Running Free" and "Drifter" as encores.

The five additional songs were a pure classic set of the Paul Di'Anno era. The front end of the set remained the same. The additions were more toward the middle and end of the set. What a gift with those additional songs.

Since I really wasn't familiar with any material from *Point of Entry*, I was a bit confused when the lights went out and "Solar Angels" started. I didn't really know what was happening. Then the first chords hit. The members elevated slowly upward on platforms that flanked both sides of Dave Holland's drum kit.

The stage setup reminded me of the *Love Gun/KISS Alive II* era stage. If there was a Priest tour that should have been filmed, *Point of Entry* was it.

I heard and recognized the classics listed from the *Unleashed in the East* album as well as top tracks from *British Steel*. The crowd was treated to "You Don't Have to Be Old to Be Wise," "Breaking the Law," and "Living After Midnight." It's a shame that "Grinder" and/or "Metal Gods" wasn't included.

In the fall of 1981, there was a radio broadcast of the *Point of Entry* tour. I made sure to record it on a Maxell 120-minute tape. It might have been the *King Biscuit Flower Hour*. I listened to that tape on a regular basis when I took many road trips to Houston later in the decade.

It was a sad day when the tape finally broke around 1989, but I still have it. I will not throw it away. Who knows? Maybe I can repair the cassette.

Seeing Judas Priest and Iron Maiden was the highlight of my summer. I would talk often of the show while hanging out at the local YMCA swimming pool with friends. Just being able to attend my first rock concert was a milestone for me. My friends had yet to attend a show though.

We would talk about music and bands we were being introduced to by an older brother of one of my friends, guitars in general, or the next album on the purchase wish list. Anything related to rock music was fair game.

The major grocery store located across the creek and behind the YMCA was Skaggs Alpha Beta. Along with the standard grocery store items, they had a decent inventory of albums. This is where I would purchase the majority of my albums, as the prices beat anything in the mall.

A standard album such as Judas Priest's *Unleashed in the East* or Skynyrd's debut, *Pronounced 'Lĕh-'nérd 'Skin-'nérd*, would be priced at $5.99 or $6.99. That was a great price for someone still on the neighborhood yard-mowing payroll.

Prices on the albums weren't the only thing that appealed to me. The price for a pound of banana pudding was less than $2.00. There were times I wouldn't come back with an album in hand but instead a pound of banana pudding.

Once back at the swimming pool, my small-framed self would devour the entire contents in one sitting, followed by a thirty-minute timeout before hitting the deep end. Of course my diving board activity involved executing a gainer and any shenanigans or stupid stuff I could pull off with the dive.

There were good things about the start of summer marching band rehearsals in August.

First, there were freshman girls coming in, but I quickly learned that they wanted nothing to do with sophomore guys. It was either juniors or seniors for those girls. Understandable.

Second, I was no longer a property manager. I was more than happy to pass the torch and title down to a few incoming freshman boys.

Did I feel that being a property manager was a load of BS? Of course I did. Now halftime marching band shows are extremely elaborate and require parental assistants or, shall I say, parental property managers. These supportive marching band parents are more than happy to volunteer their time. They have access to the field, and normally, they are sporting some type of cool-looking parent band-crew shirt. They are basically marching band roadies. My, how times have changed.

———◇———

During the fall, I was speaking on the phone with a friend of mine named Gail. I met her through one of her friends at a church gathering. Gail and I became good friends, and we would talk often.

One night, we were talking about music. I mentioned how good the guitar player was in my brother's band. I explained to her how I watched him listen to the solo in the Styx song "Renegade." He played the solo note for note with the song the second time. I was blown away just watching, as he had only been playing a year and half at that point. He had a walnut-top Les Paul with gold hardware.

I told her that he could play all the leads in songs like "2112," "Stairway to Heaven," "Crazy Train," and "Free Bird" with little to no effort. It was his playing and watching up close that was to become my first introduction to Van Halen's "Eruption."

Gail mentioned there was a kid in her class who was a great guitar player as well. She said his name was Darrell Abbott.

For some reason, that name stuck with me, and I never forgot it.

Several years later, Gail would introduce me to a friend who was a huge Sammy Hagar fan. She had blonde hair and loved the color red. Her nickname was Sammy.

TWELVE

LEGS DIAMOND

THE TURNING POINT FOR me in regard to rock concerts was the fall of 1981.

With high school football season in full swing, so was the marching band season. By this point, I was no longer a property manager, a title I was more than happy to shed.

For the marching band, there was a game-day routine that included the band arriving early at the stadium for "inspection." Inspection was simply what it was called, an inspection of each student in their marching uniform. For the inspection, we were in what was called "block formation." The squad leaders, normally two for each section, would inspect each student in their squad.

During this time, you would see the Goody Two-shoes band nerds exert their so-called power. They took things a tad on the too-serious side. Now, there were some squad leaders who were more laid back and not so uptight. It was as if the others wanted to act like drill sergeants.

It's understandable to keep things in check, but raising your voice was a bit overdoing it. It is actually comical and even more laughable all these years later. At times, it was just a pitiful look. That's why there were people like me, who liked to keep things lighthearted.

We were judged on the tidiness and cleanliness of our uniform and things related to it: the whiteness and noticeable scuffs on our marching shoes, the pickle bucket that served as the container for our hat and plume, the flip-folio that held our music, the sheets of music themselves, the lyre that held our music, and even the presentation of our instruments.

The inspection had a points system. Flaws in any of the things listed above resulted in point deductions. Those inspection points were part of the criteria for lettering in band for the year as a whole.

Near the midpoint of the second quarter of the games, the band would exit the stands and head down to the track. This is where we would file into formation. When it was showtime, the formation would allow us to align ourselves on the sidelines. All we had to do was take a few steps forward. With our call to readiness by yelling "Southwest" and snapping to attention, the crowd would go nuts.

It was a good feeling.

As I mentioned previously, the band had a winning reputation for being the Best in City year after year. I think that's one of the reasons there was so much support. Back then, times were different for being in the band.

These days, some marching bands receive little support. At some schools, the programs are basically nonexistent. It's truly sad to see, but I digress.

After the band's performance, we would march off the field to the track and make our way out. While on the track, we were still in step with chants of "left, left, left, right left." That way everybody would be in sync with each other as we marched away from the field. From the stands, it looked razor sharp.

Once we cleared the track, we would make our way to an area off to the side of the stadium to unwind. Here, we would have drinks from the concession stands.

It was during this time parents, boyfriends, girlfriends, siblings, and others would come down to talk to band members. It was one of these third quarter breaks that a light switch went off in regard to concerts.

———◆———

In high school, the homeroom rosters were alphabetical. That means the last names in my homeroom went from Mas–Mi. The rosters and names were fairly consistent from year to year, going back to sixth grade.

There was a girl who had been in my homeroom since sixth grade due to the alphabetical closeness of our last names. She would come down and say hello to her friends. I would talk with her as well.

There was one night the guy she was seeing at the time came to visit. I am sure he visited more than once, but it only took one introduction. His name was Tom. Like me, he was a huge music fan, just a few years older than me. He may have even been out of high school; I just don't remember. What I do remember, though, is that he would go to concerts. That's an automatic coolness factor in my book—but he took it a step further: he had photos from concerts.

I really don't think he had a media credential to photograph a show, but he'd somehow get his camera in. Photos I recall seeing were shot from the floor, and seeing those just blew my mind. Some were closer than others.

The two sets of photos I remember the most came from the same show. It was Alice Cooper's 1979 Madhouse Rock tour at TCCC on April 13, 1979. Legs Diamond and The Babys were the support acts.

The photo I remember the most was of the Legs Diamond guitarist, Roger Romeo. He was leaning back directly in front of the drum riser, giving the audience more of a profile view. On the front of the drum riser was a Legs Diamond banner. I don't know why I remember this image the most out of the photos he showed me, which included photos of The Babys, but I just do.

I specifically remember that show and all the cool shirts from the tour. The high school newspaper had a review that I cut out. I had it hanging on my wall for the longest time. From the spring of my seventh grade year through early college, the review was on the wall. I think the review served as inspiration in those formative years without me realizing it.

For the next year or so, I would see Tom, and he would give me a few concert photos. He gave me photos from the Scorpions' *Blackout* tour with Iron Maiden and Girlschool. There were several photos of Iron Maiden and one photo of Girlschool.

There was one shot of Maiden vocalist Bruce Dickinson that he'd enlarged to an 8×10. That photo was displayed in my locker for several years and would become part of special moments in time years later.

I am still very appreciative of Tom and his sharing of images with me. Unknowingly, he was molding my still impressionable, rock-concert-loving self.

THIRTEEN

LIFE LESSON AND THERE'S NOT A NEXT TIME

1981

MY SOPHOMORE YEAR WAS in full swing. I had my first teenage job, and I had my driver's license. For my job, I worked in a baked potato shop in the mall called Paddy's Place. My manager Danny was super cool and a hippie from the late '60s and early '70s. I didn't believe him until he showed me a photo with his hair near his waist.

Danny and I connected. I could do no wrong and never tried to pull off any mischief or unethical behavior at work. I just wouldn't. I couldn't do that to him.

Payday fell on Fridays. Once a week, I would cash my check upstairs at Montgomery Ward. They took 1 percent, and I was fine with that. I would walk away with cash in hand and head directly to the mall record store. There, I would purchase an album for my expanding collection.

By this point, I was no longer writing my name on albums as I had in middle school. Many of my albums and covers from high school are still in immaculate condition.

As for the school year, I walked away at the end of the year with a different take on life in general. I pocketed a life lesson or two while at it.

Of course, the big event was my second rock concert. This time around, it was Triumph on the *Allied Forces* tour at Reunion Arena on Friday, December 4, 1981. To this day, I am still highly disappointed with the tour roster. It could have been much better and more impressive. I think it was the most unimpressive tour package I ever attended. I felt shortchanged.

Instead of some really cool hard rock bands, the bill consisted of Harlequin, a boring band from Canada. The second was Survivor. Yes, the "Eye of the Tiger" band, but their massive hit wasn't released until May 31, 1982.

I never did like the song even after hearing it for the first time.

I really wanted to see two up-and-coming hard rock bands. I saw two bands that were not impressive. I just couldn't handle being at a rock concert and seeing some guy wearing a beret singing on stage. It collided with my vision of hard rock.

Now, I will say, years later, the beret-sporting Survivor vocalist, Mr. David Bickler, redeemed himself with the Real Men of Genius ad campaign.

I was familiar with Triumph and their music. I purchased their *Allied Forces* album shortly after it was released. I immediately thought the opening track, "Fool for Your Love" was an incredible tune. I knew, just knew that Triumph would storm the stage with that song. They didn't. Instead, they kicked off with "Tear the Roof Off" from 1980's *Progression of Power*. "Fool for Your Love" wasn't even on the setlist.

There were two songs that helped propel the album to number 23 on the Billboard Charts—"Magic Power" and "Fight the Good Fight."

That Monday morning while taking a shower, I knew the week would move at a turtle's pace, all because I was going to a concert Friday night. I was correct. The week slowly passed.

I didn't know it at the time, but I would experience and walk away with a life lesson from the concert: the use of earplugs.

This was the second time my brother had seen Triumph. He recommended that I wear earplugs, which I did. Along with my brother was his guitar player, Mike, who was a huge Triumph fan. He was the one who secured the tickets, fourth row. Not bad for my second show.

Back in 1981, earplugs were not form fitting and were very uncomfortable. There was a metal filter covered in a rubber or silicone housing. After a while, my ears would get very tender from the plugs—I mean, tender to the touch. The outer edge of the ear canal area would seriously hurt.

Eventually, I removed the ear plugs because of the tenderness I was experiencing.

Since we were on the fourth row, we started hanging out on the barricade directly in front of the PA cabinets on Mike Levine's side. By this point, the plugs were out, and my ears were getting blasted.

It wasn't until the next day at work that I realized how loud it was. I had to ask customers several times to speak up. I was having a difficult time hearing them.

<hr />

For Christmas 1981, I received a General Electric clock radio. What made this alarm clock unique compared to others was that it had a working cassette tape player. Along with the volume slider, there was one for music tone, as well as the other standard features on a clock radio. The digital numbers for the clock were in a light bluish-aqua color with a slight hint of green.

For the technology geeks, it was model number 7-4975 B and was a staple of every teenager's bedroom at the time.

The best part is that I could set it to wake up to the alarm tone or a cassette, which I did every morning.

Since I had this new cool clock radio with a tape player, I needed to purchase a cassette. My selection, Krokus's *Hardware*. At this time, the band was high on my musical radar and I would listen to them on a consistent basis.

Every morning I would wake up to side one and the song "Burning Bones." For the teenage guy humor, it's funny waking up to a song of that title, especially during the hormone-raging high school years. This would happen for the remainder of the school year.

Now, the song itself has nothing to do with raging teenage hormones or irritated morning wood, but rather the atrocities of war. Still, just the song title is funny in itself, especially when waking up to it.

I don't own the original cassette anymore. It's long past the glory days of reeling in the cassette deck at home or in my truck. I have acquired a copy of *Hardware* on cassette as well as *Metal Rendez-vous, Once Vice at a Time,* and *Headhunter* in the last several years.

These are the only four Krokus releases that matter to me. This is classic-era Krokus before label executives started to put their money-hungry mittens into the band after the *Headhunter* album in 1983.

When I joined the world of eBay in 2000, my first two CD purchases were German imports of *Hardware* and *One Vice at a Time.*

With two concerts under my belt, I had my sights set on my third show. This time it was Ozzy's tour for *Diary of a Madman* with UFO and Starfighter as support.

I was introduced to UFO about nine months earlier. I immediately liked their music. I thought the show was a great bill, Ozzy and UFO. What a great pairing, unlike my previous show of Triumph and those two other bands.

Trying to get permission to see the Ozzy tour was like pulling teeth. Even though my brother was going with his guitar player and one other person, the odds were against me. I was, however, almost there in convincing my mother to let me go to the show.

My grandmother on my mom's side was visiting us from Ohio. When I was deep in the trenches of convincing my mother to let me go the day before the show, my grandmother heard me.

She said, "Ozzy Osbourne. Isn't he the one who urinated on the Alamo?"

My best analogy for that moment is simple: "You just sank my battleship."

On the day of the show, I was told, "If you can find a ticket, you can go. You can always just see them next time"—a typical response for me and my efforts to go see a concert.

I remember being so dejected that night—if only I had been told that when my brother and his friends purchased tickets.

My brother did purchase me a UFO *Mechanix* jersey, which I thought was supercool, but it didn't soften the blow from missing the show.

Not all hope was lost, though, in my bid for a concert.

I was able to get a yes for the Molly Hatchet and Saxon show at the Dallas Convention Center on Saturday, March 20, 1982. I was pumped and excited for that day. Concert number three would be in the books.

—◦—

On Friday, March 19, 1982, I completed my typical payday routine. I cashed my check and went down to the record store. On this day, I bought Emerson, Lake & Palmer's three-record set, *Welcome Back My Friends to the Show that Never Ends*. With the record in hand, I went to say hello to Marcie, a girl in my brother's class or a year younger. She worked in the pastry-and-sweets shop next to where I worked. I never knew she was a hard rock fan until the day after Triumph.

She didn't work the day after the Triumph show, but she went by her shop and popped in to say hi to me. She was wearing an *Allied Forces* baseball jersey with red sleeves. It was signed by the band. I specifically remember the large looping letter R in Rik Emmitt's signature in blue ballpoint pen. I thought it was way cool.

Turns out, she knew someone who worked with the promoter or something along those lines. Her cool factor and stock dramatically increased in my eyes from that day on.

I showed her the ELP album, and she asked me, "Did you hear about Ozzy's band?"

I asked, "What do you mean?"

"Someone in his band died today, but I don't know who."

With a sense of urgency, I asked, "Was it the guitar player?"

She couldn't remember. I left the pastry shop and drove home.

I can't recall how I was able to confirm it was Randy Rhoads, but I did. I was so devastated, pissed, and then angry.

Once I got home, my mother was sitting in her chair in the TV room. I looked at her and said, "You always tell me I can just see them next time. Well, there won't be a next time. He's dead. He's (expletive) dead."

I told her Ozzy's guitarist was killed in a plane crash, then turned around and went to my room.

The next night was the Molly Hatchet concert. This time around, I went with several friends. I think two were in marching band and the third wasn't.

When we arrived and were walking to the venue, I noticed an ungodly number of *Diary of a Madman* shirts. They were everywhere. I did see a few *Blizzard of Ozz* 1981 tour shirts, but an overwhelmingly high percentage of shirts were from DoAM. As I looked around, I just shook my head and thought to myself that I should be wearing one of those.

Our seats were in the lower balcony located near the soundboard. One of my friends pointed out that Dave Hlubek, guitarist and a founding member of Molly Hatchet, was there. We went down to the rail behind the mixing board, and he signed our ticket stubs with an ink pen. It was my first rockstar autograph.

*The Molly Hatchet ticket stub founding
member and guitarist Dave Hlubek signed
the day after Rhandy Rhoads passed
away.*

It was a great show, and Saxon blew the doors off the Dallas Convention Center. I didn't know anything about them, but they killed it. I walked away as a new fan.

One thing I noticed during their set was that a fan tossed a Saxon banner onto the stage. The vocalist, Biff Byford, gave a thumbs-up and displayed the banner on Nigel Glockler's drums. As a kid craving rock concerts, I thought it was so cool he did that. It was a kind gesture in the way he showed appreciation to the fan's efforts.

The show was on a Saturday, and the record store was closed on Sunday. Thus, on Monday, I went and picked up Saxon's live album, *The Eagle Has Landed*. When I got back home, I listened to that album five straight times, front to back that afternoon. The album was incredible back then, and it still stands to this day.

The 1982 World's Fair was held in Knoxville, Tennessee. That was our destination for the band trip in the spring. We would depart the school early Thursday evening and then change drivers in Memphis. From there, we'd drive into Knoxville.

Before leaving, I swung by the record store and purchased the Michael Schenker Group's *MSG* cassette for some fresh music. My friend Brian brought his boombox along with loads of cassettes. The music freaks in the band had everything we needed.

As I introduced the Michael Schenker Group to my friends, my friend Jack introduced Jeff Wayne's *Musical Version of the War of the Worlds*. This tape would play an important role during our trip. Eventually its inclusion became legendary among us.

Along with my new cassette tape, I brought a large bag of Cheetos. It was during the band trip that my friends started calling me Cheeto. I can thank my dear friend Joylita Mama for the nickname. She still calls me Cheeto to this day.

I was sixteen at this time, and five months out from seventeen. At this age, I was thin and slender. Junk food such as Cheetos never had an impact on me. I can't say for certain if I was above one hundred pounds at this time or not.

Our bus was a red Trailways with seats in pairs and an open area above for luggage. There was surgical tubing that ran the length of the bus in the overhead luggage area. The tubing served as a barrier to confine the luggage or bags overhead. Passengers did not have to worry about bags falling over the edge.

The bus departed from the high school around 7:00 p.m. We would drive straight through to Memphis. That would put us in Memphis, give or take an hour for an arrival time, around five or six in the morning.

Everyone got their energy out of their systems after an hour or two on the road. That included the group of us rockers exploring and discovering new music such as the Schenker tape.

Eventually, it was time to turn in and chill for the remainder of the drive to Memphis.

Since I was a slender and skinny teen, I elected to climb up into the overhead luggage area. I was actually able to stretch out and sleep on our way to Memphis.

Once we arrived, someone had to wake me up. I was still half asleep when I started to climb down from the overhead storage area. In doing so, my foot became tangled in the elastic, and I fell out of the rack. My right side landed on one of the armrests of an aisle seat below me. That hurt for quite a while.

Inside the bus station, everyone stretched their legs, and some of the kids started playing Donkey Kong. This was the first time that I actually watched someone play the game.

Within forty-five minutes to an hour, we loaded back onto our bus and continued to Knoxville. We were looking at another six hours of drive time. Do I recall anything during that time? No, not really, but some opposing-sex band members were starting to pair up under blankets.

Once we arrived at our destination, we would be housed in two-bedroom condos. The condo building consisted of three floors. Every member in our housing group was cool, and we didn't have to worry about anyone.

Of course, being the active one, I started scaling up and down the back patios. I think our room was on the second floor, so I would climb to the unit above us instead of using the stairs.

The time came for a room check, but I wasn't ready to turn in. I still wanted to hang out with my fellow woodwind friends, the cool girls.

The chaperones actively started searching for me since I wasn't accounted for in our room check. They had a good idea where to look, and they came knocking while I was still in the girls' room.

As mentioned, these were condo units, so they had full kitchens with cabinets. Since I was, in a way, trapped, I had to think quickly about hiding. I was not about to get busted.

In the kitchen, there were the standard-size cabinets, and then there was a slender cabinet. It was maybe eighteen inches wide, tucked between a standard cabinet and the oven.

I slid into this narrow cabinet when the chaperones came looking for me. They were certain that I would be found. I could hear them searching and looking, but I was nowhere to be found. They came up empty-handed and left.

As soon as they left and the door was locked, I exited the narrow cabinet. I climbed down the third level back patio to our patio directly below on the second floor. I sure didn't want to fall because there was a nasty biology-project swimming pool, complete with green fuzzy water, outside the first level patio.

Eventually, everyone in our room went to bed around 4:00 a.m., before waking up around 7:00 a.m. or so to go to the competition. We had watched *Night Flight*, and one of the videos we saw was "Centerfold" by the J. Geils Band.

I remember one the roomies said to watch the drum when the snare fill came. There was a white liquid that splattered every time the drummer hit the fill. It was a cool effect. I have seen other bands do it since.

For that early wakeup call, I will say my eyes have never burned so much from lack of sleep than that next morning. I was falling asleep on the baritone sax case prior to competition that morning.

After the competition, we left and took a bus tour of the Smoky Mountains. I really didn't care; I was more concerned with getting some much-needed sleep. I will say it was a bit difficult with a tour guide on the bus intercom.

At some point during the tour, I was zonked out, and my friends queued up a part of the *War of the Worlds* tape. It's the part where space aliens are saying, "Oooo-La, Oooo-La."

This was how they woke me up from my afternoon slumber. I didn't know what it was, as I was in a deep sleepy fog. I had a confused look as to what would be best described as a WTF look. Everyone laughed, and the "Oooo-La" sound bite became legendary for the rest of our band trip.

The trip was a great experience, and I behaved myself for the remainder of our time away. We experienced a day at the fair, and then on another day, we spent time in Gatlinburg. My World's Fair shirt was modeled after a baseball jersey concert shirt.

In Gatlinburg, I found a round river rock with little rocks glued on top. The smaller rocks were painted in various colors and had a pair of eyes painted on each. Behind the rocks was a sign that read "Rock Concert." I thought it was the coolest and funniest thing. At this point, I was a full-blown fan of rock concerts.

I still have the rock concert to this day. It sits with my stereo in my music room. Now, on second thought, I should move it to where I am doing all this writing. It would only serve as more inspiration.

FOURTEEN

CONCERT SEASON SUMMER PASS

EVENTUALLY, MY SOPHOMORE YEAR was done, and I moved forward toward my junior year. The only thing between me and my junior year was the summer. There was nothing wrong with that, actually.

For the first time, I purchased a season pass to Six Flags over Texas, the original Six Flags, I might add. I must say it was one of the best things I did entertainment-wise for the summer. I really didn't purchase the pass to ride the rollercoasters over and over again—I went for the concerts.

Shows were held in a wide-open parking lot, and tickets were very cheap. Bands played two shows, back-to-back. For the rock-concert-craving hunger in me, that was an ideal setup.

There were some decent acts. What year those acts played has gotten a bit foggy over time. I can list two bands that played Six Flags in the summer of 1982. Blue Oyster Cult played two shows on July 16, 1982, and Joan Jett played two shows on August 28,

1982.

Tickets for the Blue Oyster Cult shows were $2 a show. My friends and I went to both shows. As soon as the first show ended, we ran out of the parking lot, circled around, and purchased tickets for the second show. Back in line for the second show we went.

The two tickets Brian used for ticket stubs when he saw Blue Oyster Cult at Six Flags over Texas.

Both shows were in the heat of the day, but that didn't matter; I was just excited to be there, experiencing a concert. The best part—I didn't have to beg and plead. Of course, I purchased a Blue Oyster Cult shirt. It was a standard black, two-sided shirt with the symbol of Kronos Saturn in blue on the back with one of the album covers on the front.

With only a few band shirts in my closet, I had to add to my concert shirt collection at every opportunity.

When school was underway, I was amazed at how many people in my class had gone to the show. My good friend Brian took his camera. One of the photos from the show ended up in the yearbook.

Tickets for Joan Jett were cheap. I had a Whoppers candy coupon that I was able to exchange for one ticket. I only went to one of Joan Jett's shows, as I really wasn't a fan. The only reason I went to the early show was to experience another concert—that's it. Her song "I Love Rock and Roll" has annoyed me from day one.

The Whoopers concert coupon for Joan Jett at Six Flags over Texas.

The Joan Jett date was the last Saturday in August. I think it was the last hurrah before school started on Monday, August 30. Prior to the show, I stopped by the merchandise booth and considered purchasing a shirt. The shirt wasn't that bad looking, but Joan Jett wasn't hard rock enough for me to do so. Several years ago, I did a search on eBay and found the type of shirt being sold that day. Looking at it provided a nice trip down memory lane.

———◇———

During the summer, besides the Six Flags concerts, I was able to catch a few arena rock shows. The most important one for me was the Scorpions' on their *Blackout* album with Iron Maiden and Girlschool.

The Scorpions were making waves with their single "No One Like You." The single took them from being a main support act on their previous tour for the *Animal Magnetism* album, to arena headliners.

Iron Maiden had a new singer, Bruce Dickinson. The Bible-thumpers were going nuts with their new album, *Number of the Beast*. The album is a landmark in Maiden's career. It was the first step in them becoming the stadium headlining superstars they are today.

To attend this show, I had to do some serious asking. I didn't want to miss it. There were two reasons for that, the first being the Scorpions were a hot metal act. The second reason was that it would be my first time seeing a band for the second time: Iron Maiden.

In the end I was able to go, and to this day, I consider that tour one of those tours that was not to be missed.

The summer of 1982 witnessed my transition to seventeen. My

mother asked me what I wanted for my birthday. I told her I wanted to go see the Doobie Brothers. I really wasn't a fan, but it was a concert that fell on my birthday. There was something about seeing a concert on my actual birthday. If memory serves me correctly, that's the only concert I have ever attended that has been on my birthday. There hasn't been one since. That's forty-two years' worth of shows and tours that have come through town.

———◆◆◆———

One of the popular movies at the time was *Fast Times at Ridgemont High*. I went and saw that movie at the local theater close to the house. One of my friends in the percussion squad met me there.

As I watched the movie, I wondered how it would relate to my upcoming junior year in high school. I was now an upperclassman. I truly was looking forward to the school year.

I was able to relate to the movie. By this time, I was working in the mall record store and meeting lots of new people. Many times, I was also securing concert tickets and selling them. Now, I wasn't scalping them like the character Mike Damone in the movie—I was just hooking up friends with tickets at face value, as I had a contact in a ticket office.

There were times I would get tickets and hang on to them till the very last minute. Why? Just in case I was magically I was able to go to the show the day of.

At the end of the movie, the first thought that came to my mind was that I hoped the school year would go by that fast.

I was ready to start my junior year the following day. I wasn't ready for the ups and downs I would experience.

As for the concert landscape, things looked very promising for the upcoming months. Cool tours would roll through town—I just didn't know it at the time.

The first metal show of the school year went down on Saturday, September 11, 1982, at Reunion Arena. The rising British metal band Judas Priest was out supporting their *Screaming for Vengeance* album. Along for the ride as main support was Krokus and the New York power trio The Rods.

For starters, my mother did not like nor appreciate the name Judas Priest. This show was a firm "no" along with a new reason. "You saw them last year," is what I heard after my pitch to see the show.

Yes, I was interested in seeing Judas Priest, but the band I truly wanted to see was Krokus. There was just something about them. They were touring on their *One Vice at a Time* album. To me, it's just a straightforward, hard rock album; and to others, it's the best album AC/DC never made.

The *One Vice at a Time* album ranks in my personal Top 5 Albums of All Time. Along with that, there's Priest's *British Steel*, Def Leppard's *High 'n' Dry* and Black Sabbath's *Heaven and Hell*. These four have been fairly consistent over the years, but the fifth album seems to change.

Then, rounding out my Top 10, there's Riot's *Fire Down Under*, Pink Floyd's *The Wall*, Queensrÿche's *Operation Mindcrime*, Rainbow's *Rising*, Metallica's *Ride the Lightning*, and Opeth's *Blackwater Park*.

As I type this, I am leaning more towards Opeth's *Blackwater Park* for number five. What an incredible album from start to finish. It's been out for over twenty years, but it's still regarded as the band's magnum opus.

This leads me back to Krokus and touring with Judas Priest. It was a very important album to me. Not being able to see them on that tour just didn't sit well with me even to this day.

I was able to experience them the following year but not really in a visual sense.

Brian standing at his locker in the Biology hall wearing his Doobie Brothers concert shirt in November 1982.

FIFTEEN

TAKEAWAYS FROM MY JUNIOR YEAR

1982

SINCE I WORKED IN the mall record store by this time, I would see the weekly issue of *Billboard Magazine*. On the front cover in the center, there was a section highlighting up-and-coming bands with a photo and brief informative news blurb for readers and retailers.

Brian at work in the mall record store.

During the summer, one of the weekly issues arrived. I immediately noticed a photo of a band I had never heard of. It wasn't a typical photo, but a full-blown, intense band promotional photo. There were four band members; three were decked out in black leather and had jet-black hair. The fourth was a bleached blond in red leather. He was pushing a sword into the throat of another member.

All members had chains, leather belts, studs, spikes, and black platform boots.

There was red light illuminating all the fog and smoke, skulls, two candelabras, and a large black pentagram flag. One member was standing in front of the flag with his arms raised, showing the horns with both hands. In his left hand, he had a device that just added to the fog. Around his neck, he had an inverted cross for shock value.

For 1982, this was a very intense image that challenged European metal bands and their imagery. Actually, this promotional photo was out prior to Venom releasing their second album, *Black Metal*.

Along with the photo, there were songs such as "Merry-Go-Round," "Public Enemy #1," and "Live Wire." The two band member names I remembered the most were Mick Mars and Nikki Sixx. The band was Mötley Crüe.

At this point, I had never really seen a band with such imagery. I think it was the platform boots that did it for me, along with the accessories and black leather. Then to have the pentagram flag in the photo. That was pushing it. I will say, the band as a whole just looked really cool for that time period.

The photo itself was used as a black-and-white insert for the

Elektra Records debut release. One just needs to see the image in color to understand how intense it was for that time.

Just the photo made me pick up the album on the day it was released, August 20, 1982, for $4.99. There were four copies at Sound Warehouse on Berry St.

I took it home, gave it a spin and then took it over to a friend's house. He liked it, and then we took it to another friend's house. He and another friend liked it.

We all hopped into my truck and drove back to the record store. My three friends then purchased the remaining three copies.

———◆———

My junior year was in full swing. Within the first few days of the year, my social studies teacher, Ms. Johnson, had subscriptions to the Fort Worth *Star-Telegram*, the major daily newspaper. Every day for the first few minutes of class, we were to read the newspaper. The purpose was to learn about news and current events.

Being the music person that I am, I was always looking at the "Entertainment" section. I was seeking out articles by Roger Kaye, the rock music critic. I always enjoyed his concert reviews, but many times there weren't any photos. If there were no reviews, then he would just have entertainment news.

I do recall one brief news article in particular.

Tommy Lee, drummer for Mötley Crüe, was jumped in Los Angeles by a group of bikers.

I don't think the group of bikers were new-wave thugs. I know that new wave was at its peak around this time, but I wonder if Lee's look at the time or a sharp tongue had something to do with the incident. I don't really recall any other information in the news blurb.

Once I finished the entertainment news, then I would go to the comics and read the *Family Circus, Nancy and Sluggo, Blondie, B.C.,* and many other classic cartoons.

Now, I read the daily news because of the availability, speed, and flow of information. I attribute this routine to Ms. Johnson. I am very grateful for her foresight to do this for her students.

———◦———

During the fall, I was enrolled in typing. My thinking was that computers were making their way into the business world. I just thought it would be wise to take the class and learn how to type.

I also thought that since I played sax, I had the coordination between my two hands and all my fingers and two thumbs. This made absolute sense to me and justified taking the typing class.

Several of us active band students added fun to the class. I do remember that two percussionists from the marching band were in the class. There may have been another one or two members from the band as well.

I can remember when we had to do exercises on the home keys, letters *A, S, D,* and *F* for the left and *J, K, L,* and *;* for the right. We would start typing away on those electric typewriters. As band people, we took it to the next level. We would get and lock in on a rhythm. It was the coolest thing I have ever heard in a class.

We were able to do this with certain assignments, and it made the learning that much more fun. Unfortunately, one day I arrived for class, and the teacher confronted me at the door. She wouldn't let me in. She looked at me in a menacing manner and said in an aggressive tone, "Where is it?"

I replied, "Where's what?""The element from that back typewriter. It's gone, and you were the only one at that typewriter yesterday."

I told her, "I didn't take it, and why would I take it?"

She didn't buy anything I said to defend myself against her false accusations.

I was escorted to the office. I had to make a phone call to get a parent up to the school for a parent conference. One of my parents showed up and went off on the teacher. Basically, what was said was, "If my son said he didn't take it, he didn't take it."

The element on an electric typewriter was the round ball with the letters and punctuation symbols on it. It would spin and hit the ribbon, thus imprinting the letter or symbol on the paper. Instead of little hammers popping the paper and imprinting the letter or symbol, the element did the same thing, just faster.

I will be the first to admit, I was one of the more "active" students in class, but I sincerely did enjoy typing. I was learning a skill I knew would be useful. I appreciated that and the opportunity.

What superseded that skill years later was what I learned from that encounter. I was able to apply this expertise to the fifteen years I spent as an educator. Here's what I keep with me: do not make false accusations against a student unless you have the documentation to sign, seal, and deliver the accusation.

I utilized those typing skills starting in college and still do in the present.

It's a small world at times. In the process of researching and digging around for this book, I learned that the lovely teacher was a neighbor. Just two houses away at one point during my teaching career. How ironic.

It's a shame I didn't know at one point during those years. I would've shared my lessons and experiences in a neighborly way of what *not* to do. It could've been an apple pie with a sweet note attached.

I saw my concert calendar filling up a bit more than it had in the past. I was fine with that. I felt that it was long overdue. Still, I missed some shows that today I would have really liked to attend.

The first show for me during my junior year occurred on the Friday night we left for Thanksgiving break. It was the mighty Van Halen for *Diver Down*. They played two shows at Reunion Arena—November 18 and 19, 1982. I went to the second show. I am not sure if the fact that it was on the Friday night that kicked off Thanksgiving break had anything to do with it. By this time though,

I think Van Halen had started their decline from their peak on the *Fair Warning* album the year before.

A week later, I was back out at Reunion Arena for 38 Special and Eddie Money. When it came to airplay, both bands were doing great. The show wasn't sold out, but it was a full house.

The show was actually a rescheduled date for 38 Special. They were originally scheduled to play the Wintergarden in Dallas during the summer, but it was postponed. Vocalist Donnie Van Zant sustained a broken leg, and the band came back in November. In hindsight, it was a good move, as the band played a much larger venue—the 20,000-seat Reunion Arena, versus the 1,500–2,000 standing-room-only Wintergarden.

A week and one day later, I was at The Who for their December 4, 1982, show at the Cotton Bowl. This was a cool show for me to attend because one year ago to the day, I was at Triumph. This was the second concert I attended on December 4.

The show was pro shot, and footage of individual songs can be watched on YouTube. Unfortunately, the entire show isn't up as a whole. I will say it's nice being able to watch, for example, "Eminence Front." It's one of my favorite Who songs. The surreal part is watching on video what I was watching at a show on a chilly Saturday night.

What's crazy is that I am older now than the members of The Who were when they played that show.

By my junior year, I was starved for new Aerosmith music. It had been nearly three years since Aerosmith released *Night in the Ruts*. That album was released in November of my eighth grade year, and I now had upperclassman status. As an older teen, that's still a significant amount of time.

That new Aerosmith came in the form of *Rock in a Hard Place*, released two days after my birthday in August 1982. I couldn't have been happier. My appetite for new Aerosmith was satisfied.

Several songs help place *Rock in a Hard Place* in my top Aerosmith album categories. Those are "Lightning Strikes," "Bitches Brew," "Rock in a Hard Place (Cheshire Cat)," and "Push Comes to Shove."

The opening track, "Jailbait," is in its own category. That first time I heard it, I could easily see Steven Tyler spinning around with the microphone stand in his signature stage move. The long gypsy scarves that adorn the mic stand would be flowing as he spun. It's nothing but total classic Aerosmith vibes.

Unfortunately, I wasn't able to attend Aerosmith the night after Christmas due to a poor grade in geometry. Missing that show still stings to this day, as the *Rock in a Hard Place* album is one of my favorite Aerosmith albums. I think the lineup without Joe Perry and Brad Whitford was solid.

Since it was the day after Christmas, could I have gone somehow without my parents knowing? Absolutely, but the factor against me was at that time, my brother was working concerts as security and ushering. It wasn't worth the risk. With my luck he would've seen me, and then that would have been it. He would've wasted no time in ratting me out. I knew better.

In all honesty, keeping me from the show didn't improve my mathematical skills; I am just not a math person. Obviously, I am more of a creative person.

Six weeks later, Sammy Hagar rolled through town on *Three Lock Box*. He was receiving heavy airplay, and Dallas has always been a special place for him.

I had a pair of tickets and asked a fellow student if she would like to go. She looked at me in disgust, as if she was offended I'd even asked. No harm, no foul.

It's just funny how people today try to associate with something that wasn't possible in high school. I never left and never turned my back on live music and albums.

A week and a half later, on February 28 and March 1, 1982, Rush played Reunion Arena for *Signals*. I am so glad I was able to catch this show, as today, *Signals* is one of my top three Rush albums. It's the album right before the Canadian trio took off, no pun intended for those who get it into the synth music phase. The other two were 1977's *Farewell to Kings* and 1980's *Permanent Waves*.

On Sunday, April 10, another Canadian trio, Triumph, played Reunion Arena, supporting their *Never Surrender* album. This was my second time seeing Triumph. I will say, *Never Surrender* didn't hit me as hard as *Allied Forces* did. The show was fantastic, especially the blinding light show they always presented. It just wasn't a mind-blowing show experience.

Two days prior to the Triumph show, tickets for Def Leppard went on sale. The last time Leppard was in town, they played with Blackfoot as support on their *High 'n' Dry* album in November 1981. Around this time, I was starting to seriously get into the *High 'n' Dry* album. I knew that was a don't-even-ask show. It was on a school night in the middle of the week. The show was at the Wintergarden, a smaller, standing-room-only venue.

Tickets for Leppard's *Pyromania* tour at Reunion Arena were on sale. It really didn't make sense. I thought to myself that it was a half-arena show like Triumph's *Allied Forces* tour, but it wasn't. Instead, it was a full-blown arena show with twenty thousand seats available.

The *Pyromania* tour was the hot concert ticket for the spring. As an added bonus, Krokus was the main support, touring on their *Headhunter* album. I liked Leppard, but Krokus was the reason I wanted to see this tour.

The *Headhunter* album was a great heavy metal follow-up to *One Vice at a Time* with the title track, "Eat the Rich," "Stand and Be Counted," and "Russian Winter." With the release of "Screaming in the Night," the song's airplay and video started to put the band in front of more people.

Unfortunately, I was unable to purchase a ticket for the show, but I could work as an usher. Maybe the show being on a Sunday night in May was the reason I couldn't go as a fan. It really made no sense that I could work as an usher and experience the band sonically but not really visually.

In hindsight, I should have elected to work in the lower balcony so

I could fully take in their show. Instead, I caught a glimpse of the band here and there from the floor.

As soon as the lights went out, the album cover on a large backdrop appeared with a lone spotlight. The crowd went nuts, and the band kicked in with "Long Stick Goes Boom." The sheer power, energy, and volume that came from the stage was something I had never experienced before. It was incredible to feel it but literally sucked to only see a glimpse or two of the band live.

After Krokus left the stage, ironically, I suddenly became thirsty. I entered the tunnel that served as the main artery to locker rooms, dressing rooms, backstage areas, and dining rooms under the concourse of Reunion Arena. My path just happened to cross with vocalist Marc Storace on my way to the water fountain. I was mesmerized seeing the voice of Krokus walk toward me.

I said, "Great show, Marc," as he passed.

His reply with a Maltese accent on the way to the dressing room was simple, "Thanks."

With that one word, I was instantly enveloped by a cloud of awestruck in the Krokus atmosphere.

At one point during the set, the Krokus executioner smashed a guitar with a large Viking battle ax or something of the sort. The guitar was given away the day after the show on one of the local radio stations.

As fate would have it, a senior from my school won that guitar after being the correct caller. I wanted that guitar so badly.

I eventually saw him in the hallway several days later and asked him if I could buy the guitar from him. He said, "No, I am going to sell it to a museum." I was totally defeated.

Obviously, what he didn't know was that a guitar was destroyed every night on stage. There really was no significant value except for it being stage used during the *Headhunter* tour.

If I had been able to get my hands on that guitar, I would still cherish it to this day. I am just curious if he still has possession of it.

In early 2000, I did come across a smashed Krokus guitar on eBay for a whopping $99, but it was from *The Blitz* tour, so I had no desire to pursue it. The reason for me was simple: the tour it was from.

Even though we didn't have cable TV at this point, I began to realize how much airplay their first single, "Photograph," was receiving. The video was in heavy rotation and played several times a day. That's when I realized the power of MTV.

When I looked at MTV as a whole, the best part for me wasn't the videos. I enjoyed the Saturday night concerts. MTV would air shows that had been recorded on video. For someone still craving the rock concert experience, this was great.

The shows I remember the most that aired were Rainbow for *Straight Between the Eyes* from San Antonio, Journey's Escape tour from the Houston Summit, and Triumph's Allied Forces tour. The Triumph show's sound was weak and couldn't even come close to the sense of being live.

The Journey show was released on CD/DVD in 2005 and captures Journey in the band's prime.

Unfortunately, that business model of music videos has been tossed out the window. Now the majority of MTV is just reality shows or whatever nonsense they are showing. There may be a video or two, but I have no desire to tune in and see for myself.

Today's music industry is totally different. I can say with certainty I did experience pieces of the golden age of concerts. I started to notice a change around 1985 or '86 when the LA Glam scene started making its way across the country.

<hr />

Because I was hitting a decent number of concerts, I always preferred to get the tickets as soon as I could. Many times, I would hit the ticket office and pick up the tickets I had put to the side. This normally occurred during my woodshop class, which also fell around lunchtime. By this time, the rotating schedule was a thing of the past.

The instructor for my woodshop class was one of the football coaches, which was totally cool. Coach Smith would let me leave to pick up concert tickets on any given day. The only thing I needed to do was to bring him back a McRib from McDonald's. No problem at all.

Ironically, the woodshop class was across the hallway from the band room. Go figure.

There was a set of double doors that led to the band room and then another set of double doors that led into the band room. The set of doors in the hallway had two pullout handles, one for each door.

One day when woodshop class was letting out, me in my infinite wisdom and another student decided to leave with a two-by-four piece of wood. At this point, the bell had already sounded to dismiss class. We quickly slipped the piece of wood under the two pullout handles and walked away. The students in the band hall were not able to exit.

If there had been cameras back then like there are today, there would have been no way I would've done that.

A day or two after this little stunt, only the right door of the exterior double doors had a pull handle. I think I know the reason.

Years later when I was teaching, I had my first general professional development at my former school in 2007. Let me say it was supercool walking the hallways between classes on the lunch break some twenty-three years later.

Yes, I went down to the band room, and the two double doors were still there. Still, the door on the right was the only door with a handle.

Some ten or so years later, a science professional development would be held at the high school in 2018. Again, only the right door had a handle. I am honored that I have had a lasting impact on my former alma mater forty-plus years and counting.

The two outer doors of the band hall with only one door handle. Photo taken in 2007 when Brian was attending professional development at the school.

The only difference is, now the former band room is more of a practice room or a smaller orchestra room.

———⋄———

When I chaperoned a band contest trip when my daughter was in band, it was at the high school. The band warmed up in the old band hall. I pointed out to her the double doors and explained the story. I don't think she expected something like that from her father, who was acting as a chaperone with the band.

Obviously, I enjoyed taking the woodshop class. I enjoyed Coach Smith's class so much that I enrolled for his class my senior year as well.

When I look back, I think what meant the most to me was not him letting me leave to get my tickets or bringing him back a McRib. It was something else. One afternoon he asked if I would go put on his new license plates for his car. I was more than happy to do it.

I did run into him at Will Rogers on a Sunday in 1990. Even though six years had passed, I was so excited to see Coach Smith. I told him how much I appreciated him as a person and as my instructor. I sincerely meant it.

On an additional note, when I made the jump from elementary to middle school as an educator, Coach Smith taught at the high school the middle school fed into. Unfortunately, he retired the year before I made the transition. I would have immediately sent him an email hoping to go see him. He meant that much to me years later.

Sixteen

The Great Computer Paper Caper

My junior year was winding down, and there would be one last adventure. This time, though, it was not a rock concert, but it was music related—the school band. I decided that this little undertaking deserved its own chapter. I consider it my magnum opus, an important piece of art since it is related to band or, in technical terms, the fine arts portion of my junior year.

I was asked if I'd like to join in on a tad bit of fun after school one day. Of course I was all in and ready to go. The squad consisted of three seniors and two juniors.

In the early 1980s, the digital world was still years away. Physical copies of paperwork, records, and other sensitive information needed to be destroyed somehow. The way companies and businesses did this was via shredding documents in an industrial shredder. The destroyed documents would then be disposed of in industrial- or commercial-sized garbage bags. The bags would eventually end up in a dumpster for proper disposal. This wasn't an uncommon practice.

One of our fearless leaders had access to the school, more specifically, the band hall. No information will be shared.

This adventure consisted of gathering these rather large bags of shredded computer paper from the dumpster of a local bank. Ironically, the bags came from a bank dumpster not far from the fearless leader's house. There were seven bags total. The contraband was transported to our locale, outside of the band room, via a truck belonging to one of the seniors.

We were all to meet one afternoon in the parking lot: our fearless leader, a fellow saxophone squad member, a clarinet squad member, a percussionist, and yours truly. We all arrived at said location to meet up with the truck transporting our bags of paper.

We were just chilling out on the tailgate an hour or so after school, ready to deliver our cargo. As we were sitting there, one of the underclass band members just happened to exit the school and see us.

After this individual left, we decided it was game on.

We made our entry into the band room with the bags of paper. From there, we gained entry into the band director's office, creating a wintery white scene in late May. It wasn't Christmas in July but close enough.

By the time we were done, the paper was waist-deep in the office. We cleaned up the area to make sure our artistic endeavor was pleasing to the eye, and departed. Prior to leaving, we made sure no school or personal property was broken or destroyed.

The following morning, the band director had a difficult time gaining entry into his office. Instead of forcing his way in, he closed the door, locked it, and left the band room. He then went straight to an administrator.

The police were called but didn't show up until late in the day. When they arrived, the band director demanded a full criminal investigation that would include pulling fingerprints off the door knob. He also demanded that a report be made.

The responding senior officer had to explain that since nothing was broken, it was just a prank. Actually, the officer had to calm him down.

The next day or the day after, our fearless leader was escorted from class to the office. As he began to sit down, he was grabbed by the shoulder by one of the administrators and was patted down. The keys in one of his front pockets were removed. The administrator then began to feverishly check each key with the lock to his office.

Our prank leader was threatened with jail time, expulsion from school, and the possibility of not graduating.

What the administrator did was illegal. There was no warrant, and rights were not read. It needs to be noted that over the years, our fearless leader was a LEO in Texas and California. He was also an Air Marshall for eighteen years.

Eventually, we all had to report to the office. One of the administrators was still trying to play tough guy with us. Individually, we all had to write statements, but that wasn't it.

Following the statements, there was a parental conference set for all five students and parents. Since one of the five of us was not represented with a parent present, the administrator dismissed the parents. His reasoning was that since one student didn't have a parent or parents present, it wasn't fair.

Admin then tried to play tough guy again and attempted to intimidate and scare us by saying they could file charges of breaking and entering. While all this nonsense was spewing from his mouth, his phone rang.

The administrator picked up the phone and briefly spoke to the person on the other end. All of a sudden his whole demeanor changed.

Following this conference, I was told one of the family attorneys contacted the school and was immediately transferred to the administrator leading the conference. The attorney basically told the administrator something along the lines that if you want to play around, we are ready.

I don't recall exactly what was said to us next, but at one point we were told by the administration that we would all be put on probation for the rest of our high school career.

For the three seniors, that only meant a couple weeks. For my friend and me, that meant the rest of our junior year and then our senior year. We were specifically told if we messed up, we would be out. That wasn't our punishment though.

The load capacity of the seven large trash bags equaled roughly twenty-three regular, black kitchen trash bags. How did I come to that conclusion? There was one student from the brass section who cleaned, cleared, and removed our artistic creation in standard black trash bags. When the cleanup was all done, an impressive stack of bags were put into the corner of the band room. The pile reached to the ceiling or very near it.

From my understanding, a photo wasn't taken, but I would certainly like to see a copy if one indeed was snapped.

This leads me to our punishment. We, as in the five of us, had to pick up trash and litter after school. How much did we have to pick up? Twenty-three bags worth of trash.

We accepted our punishment with no problems and went about our task for several days. There were times that were challenging due to very little amounts of trash and litter scattered over our large 5A high school campus. We were able to combat that with the help of the 55 gallon metal drums used as outdoor trash receptacles. We faced adversity straight on with creativity or thinking outside the box of trash bags.

After trash was collected for the day, we were instructed to take the bags to the second-in-command administrator's office. We did as instructed for the first day at least.

Overnight, the bags of trash sat on the carpet in his office. Unfortunately for him and his office carpet, the bags leaked. A not-so-pleasant smell started to linger.

The next morning, he was met with the wonderful aroma of garbage leakage.

It didn't take long for maintenance to arrive with the

industrial-strength carpet cleaner to rid the stain and smell.

At the end of the year, there was one last band function. It featured a slideshow.

Several days out from the function, the five of us got together and took a quick little photo. This was no ordinary photo of five guys just standing around. We took it a step or two further.

The truck used was brought in and parked on the walkway, facing north, with the school doors where we entered behind us. We all jumped into the bed of the truck and leaned over the cab. We put our wrists and hands together individually to give the appearance that we were wearing handcuffs. BUSTED was written in large capital letters with white shoe polish on the truck's windshield.

The photo was a final nod to our little adventure. Somehow, the photo ended up in the end-of-the-year slideshow at that band function.

Three decades later, the drum major and squad leaders were meeting to brainstorm. They wanted to pull an end-of-the-year trick on the then band director. Someone mentioned nothing would ever top the computer paper incident from the early 1980s.

The drum major in this meeting just happened to be the daughter of our fearless leader. She perked up and said, "That's my dad."

She then referenced the large band photo collage shot in 1983 that still hung high in the back of the band hall. She pointed to the drum major in the photo and said, "See, that's my dad."

Her street cred immediately went off the charts.

As the captain of our prank explained over lunch one afternoon, our little adventure with shredded computer paper is major folklore.

In the end, it didn't take a rocket scientist or an aerospace engineer to determine who'd narced on us.

SEVENTEEN

HELLO, CLASS OF 1984'S LAST SUMMER AND FALL SEMESTER

As HARD AS IT was to believe, the summer of my senior year had arrived. By this time, I was seeing somebody from a different high school in another district. In doing so, I had to endure the ideology of Southern Baptist parents.

I kept my love for music and concerts fairly suppressed, that is until a concert was the focus of date night. Those shows would be lower-key events such as Rick Springfield and Alabama. I tolerated the shows, but at least I was able to get her out to a concert or two.

I did utilize my Six Flags Seasons Pass for a few shows. If memory serves me correctly, I caught Molly Hatchet, Air Supply, and Point Blank. I truly believe the Point Blank show was in the summer of 1983, but until I find my concert list from high school, I can't confirm.

Journey was riding high on the charts with the *Frontiers* album from serious airplay of their singles "Separate Ways" and "Faithfully." I am actually surprised that "Faithfully" didn't chart higher than its peak position of #12.

Journey was the hot act of the summer with *Frontiers* reaching number two on the charts. Along with the power of the previous album *Escape* that reached number one, the band played three shows at Reunion Arena in the second week of July. When I look back, I consider myself very fortunate to have experienced the band at the top of their game. Several years later, the Journey machine would be a shadow of its former self.

Adding to the tour's appeal, Bryan Adams would be the opener. Three nights of two great acts.

Thirteen days later, the concert of the summer for me would roll into town.

———◦———

There was one show that summer I definitely didn't want to miss. It was Iron Maiden for their *Piece of Mind* album. This tour saw Iron Maiden headlining for the first time. It would be my third time seeing Maiden live. I considered this an important fact for a concert enthusiast like myself.

Saxon was the main support along with a straightforward hard rock band called Fastway.

I was already a full-blown Saxon fan from my experience in 1982. They were coming back for a great album called *Power and the Glory*. The tour would hit the Dallas Convention Center on

Saturday, July 23, 1983. It's a date I remember to this day.

I had tickets in hand the day they went on sale. I secured a great pair on the third row. This was a concert I was going all out for. I was pumped.

As a Saxon maniac by this point, I wanted to create a Saxon concert banner. I kept it simple. It was just the band logo with the eagle sitting on top. The banner itself took several hours to create and was made from the typical white sheet for a twin bed. Everything that was sketched out was in pencil. The Saxon logo was painted and outlined in red. The eagle was outlined in black with a red eye. My friend Paul and I used model paint and brushes to accomplish this.

The Saxon banner Paul and Brian made for the Iron Maiden, Saxon and Fastway show on July 23, 1983.

I considered this show a three-shirt show. I like all three bands and typically purchased shirts from all three bands. Instead, I bought two baseball jerseys, one each for Maiden and Saxon, then a tour book for each as well.

There was big news associated with Fastway. The band was formed by Fast Eddie Clarke, the former guitarist for Motorhead. Back in 1982, Motorhead was still considered an underground metal band. Seeing Clarke in the flesh was like seeing a mythical creature.

The vocalist for Fastway was a skinny redhead named Dave King. For those who aren't familiar or are just casual music fans, King now fronts a band called Flogging Molly. I have been told those shows are definitely an experience.

During Saxon's set, maybe in the first song, I wadded the banner up and threw it as hard as I could toward vocalist Biff Byford. Keep in mind, the banner had to clear three rows, the barricade, and the photo pit. The banner was unraveling and traveling at an angle, not a direct shot.

I stuck the landing with the banner at Byford's feet. He picked it up, unraveled it, showed it to the crowd, and then hung it up on the drum riser. I was flipping out. This was a huge deal for me. This took my Saxon fandom to a new level. I was on such a heavy metal, thunderous high.

Miraculously, I was able to retrieve the banner and brought it home from the show. It adorned my curtain rod for the next eight months.

It wasn't much of a huge concert, but what an atmosphere. One of the local radio stations, KZEW 98 FM, had a concert birthday celebration at Reunion Arena. The station brought in Eddie Money, The Fixx, and Mitch Ryder and the Detroit Wheels for their 10th Birthday Party. Tickets were cheap, cheap, cheap, only $1.98. There was no way I was going to miss this show on Saturday, August 20, 1983.

Even though we were in the upper balcony, I have never had as much fun as I did at this show. There was a group of guys behind us who were definitely enjoying the beer sales. It was like we were like one big group of friends even though we'd just met that night. It was the most fun I ever had sitting in the upper balcony seats at a concert. These days an upper balcony ticket is basically nonexistent in my arena- and stadium-event world.

Sometimes I will see a KZEW shirt from that concert. The sight brings a flood of memories and a big smile to my face.

———o———

Entering my senior year also meant August rehearsals and my last year in marching band . I was looking forward to seeing whether the incoming freshmen were solid players. Obviously, I wasn't a squad leader due to my participation in the Great Computer Paper Caper. I was fine with that. That way I didn't have to worry about setting proper examples for the incoming freshmen.

There were several freshmen who were good kids. They were funny, quirky, and just all around great, impressionable kids. They knew that things didn't have to be so uppity in the band, especially if they were part of the saxophone family.

There was one freshman who was a good kid, and I took her under my wing. It was a friendship that was formed forty years ago and is still going strong today. Her name is Wednesday.

I claim proudly that I introduced her to Iron Maiden. She still enjoys their music.

During my senior year, she moved into my locker. The Bruce Dickinson photo that was given to me several years prior hung in that locker. That picture now hangs on the wall at her house. It belongs there.

With the school year underway, I was working by ushering concerts at Reunion Arena. Some of the shows I worked included the Moody Blues with Stevie Ray Vaughn as an opener and Loverboy with Zebra.

For the Loverboy show, I was more concerned with seeing Zebra. That's why it didn't bother me that I had to work one of the lower balcony sections. I was able to take in Zebra's full set with no visual obstructions.

In the fall, I only went to one show on a ticket. That was one of the three nights ZZ Top played on the Eliminator tour. Every rock music fan from Texas had to see the Little Ol' Band from Texas at least once, and I did.

Throughout my senior year, I secured decent seats to concerts, especially the ARMS Charity Concert. ARMS was an acronym for Action into Research for Multiple Sclerosis.

Originally, the ARMS Charity Concert was supposed to be a one-off show with plenty of legendary names set to appear. The show was billed as the Ronnie Lane Appeal for ARMS and was held at Royal Albert Hall on September 30, 1983. The show was such a huge success that dates in the US were booked. The first of those dates was at Reunion Arena on November 28 and 29, 1983.

Some of the performers included The Who's drummer, Kenny Jones; Eric Clapton; Jimmy Page, and Charlie Watts and Bill Wyman, both from the Rolling Stones.

My ticket connection was able to pull a pair of front-row tickets in section 12 on the floor at Reunion Arena. Section 12 was the front center section on the floor. Left to right, the floor sections went 10, 11, 12, 13, 14, with the seats running lowest to highest, left to right.

No matter how much pleading I did, I wasn't able to go. I sold the tickets at face value. It was a historical music event in Dallas, as only a handful of cities in the United States were selected to host the show.

The other venues were major markets as well. Three sold-out shows were held at the Cow Palace in San Francisco, two shows at the Forum in Los Angeles, and two shows at Madison Square Garden to wrap up.

I just shake my head at not being able to use those tickets. Missing events like that are one of the reasons I still actively support music and bands. That passion has never left my body. There's no midlife crisis in regard to music for me.

It's funny when I see people my age attempting to recapture and relive those moments and music from our teen years. They are just trying too hard. I never walked away; that's why it's easy for me to do it. The passion is real and not fabricated or a one-night affair.

———◆———

One important thing did happen for Christmas. I received a Kodak disc camera. It was nothing fancy, but I considered it to be a cool gift. I just didn't realize how fun it would be. I am glad I took a few photos here and there during my last semester of high school. I still have them.

I took the camera to the KISS's Lick It Up tour with Riot and Vandenberg in early January. I was more interested in seeing Riot than KISS or Vandenberg. I even made a Riot banner that said, "The Outlaw's Got the Deal in Dallas."

The song "Outlaw" is probably my favorite Riot tune and one of the reasons why their album *Fire Down Under* ranks as one of the top metal albums of all time. Add the opening track "Swords and Tequila," the title track, and "Flashbacks," and the songs only solidify the album as a personal favorite.

Getting the banner to the stage proved to be a little more difficult this time around. I was wearing a bulky winter coat. Even though I was on the third row, the coat hampered my attempted throw.

The banner fell between the stage and barricade. It's safe to say the band never saw my banner. I was bummed big time.

Somewhere I have a picture of the banner while it was being made. If I ever find it, I will scan it and send copies out to the surviving band members on social media.

EIGHTEEN

HELLO, SPRING SEMESTER CLASS OF 1984

THE FALL SEMESTER CAME and went. I left the record store and started working for a billiard supply company. I can remember stepping outside the downtown location during the Stock Show Parade in January. I said hello to the saxophone players. I really did miss them, but I didn't miss all of the band's nonsense.

If I would've attended the band trip as a senior, there's no telling what kind of shenanigans would have gone down. One can only imagine. Instead, I withdrew from the band and tucked away my saxophone in the closet. It remained there for thirty-two years. I spent many hours with that sax. Most importantly, it helped me create and cultivate lifelong friendships.

I was torn between two classes to take in place of band. On

one hand there was bowling, and on the other, there was an Introduction to Aviation class. I opted to take the bowling class. When I look back, I regret not taking the Introduction to Aviation course. I grew up in an aviation family and have taken a liking to photographing and plane spotting at DFW International when time allows. There's just something about airplanes, whether you're a little boy or an adult fast approaching sixty.

I was told some fun stories about times in the aviation class and the flying that occurred on weekends. Indeed, those would be great memories to have.

———◦———

One of the local radio stations, KEGL 97.1 FM, started promoting a heavy metal radio show that would be played on Saturday nights from 10:00 p.m. to midnight. My friends and I just laughed, thinking they were going to play Def Leppard, Quiet Riot, and bands like that.

The show was called Headbangers Heaven, and we were wrong, way wrong. At any given moment, you could hear bands like Slayer, Venom, Steeler, Mercyful Fate, Exciter, Raven, Bitch, Legs Diamond, Armored Saint, Metal Church, Manilla Road, Saxon, Metallica and a local act or two.

I would see these albums in the record store. Some of the covers had very intense artwork. These were bands that would never receive airplay during mainstream hours.

The first time I heard a Metallica song was on this radio program.

Every week they would play "Metal Militia" from Metallica's debut *Kill 'Em All*. What I remember the most was the fast tempo and tightness of the band. Now the tempo of "Metal Militia" doesn't even compare to the speed or thrash metal of today. Metallica received airplay every Saturday night on this show.

Eventually, other songs from *Kill 'Em All*, like "Whiplash" or the "Four Horsemen," were played. Even songs from their 12-inch singles, such as "Am I Evil" and "Creeping Death," were receiving airplay. For a while, "Seek and Destroy" was in regular rotation. That's when my interest in Metallica started growing.

The Saturday night before Spring Break of 1984, I was listening to the show. They were playing "Seek and Destroy." This time, though, I was really getting into the song. When the song finished, it was 11:50 p.m.

I knew the record store I frequented had the album when I was there earlier in the week. I also knew that I wouldn't be able to hit the record store before they closed at midnight. I would have to wait for Monday.

Sunday dragged by slowly, as in a minute-by-minute thing. I really wanted the album.

Monday morning, I went through my morning routine, but instead of driving to school, I drove to the record store, arriving at 9:30. I parked directly in front of the doors and waited for thirty minutes for the store to open. As soon as the doors were unlocked, I headed directly to the *M* section and pulled the album.

For the rest of spring break, if I wasn't working or hanging out, I was listening to *Kill 'Em All*. I soaked up every minute, rhythm, riff, and lyric of that album.

By the time Monday rolled around, I had a new, clean cover on one of my books. I had plastered the Metallica logo and name all over the cover in red marker.

In my psychology class, a fellow student asked, "Who's that?" My reply was simple and to the point, something along the lines of them being a really tight metal band that played fast.

His reply was, "They won't ever amount to anything."

------◇------

On a different Saturday night, I was listening to Headbanger's Heaven, and I heard this amazing guitar solo that led into a catchy song that instantly hooked me. It was a guitar solo and song I had never heard before. I needed to know who it was.

As soon as the song ended, I picked up the black rotary-dial telephone and called the radio station. I was praying that I would not get a busy signal.

My call went through and someone picked up. I asked who the band was. The answer to my question was very simple. He said, "They're Pantera, a local band from Arlington." I knew exactly who they were, as I would also see their album *Projects in the Jungle* but never purchase it. That changed the next time I was at the record store.

The guitar solo in question was "Blue Light Turnin' Red," and the song was "Like Fire."

Eight months after my Saxon experience at the Iron Maiden show in July 1983, Saxon returned by sailing to the shores of America. They were headlining a tour for their album *Crusader.*

Saxon was joined by Accept, a German metal band that was receiving solid airplay for their single "Balls to the Wall." It was an ideal billing for the fans of heavy metal in 1984. The best part—the show was at a great venue, the Bronco Bowl.

The Bronco Bowl was a sports-and-entertainment complex in Dallas. Besides having a midsize concert venue, it had a bowling alley, billiards, indoor archery, a pinball arcade, slot car racing, and a miniature golf course.

I didn't ask for permission to attend the show, nor would I have even considered it. I was not going to miss this show. I didn't want to risk not being able to go. This would be my third time seeing Saxon, and at this point, I lived and breathed Saxon and their brand of "Heavy Metal Thunder."

A fellow band member, Roger from percussion, who was one year younger, was my partner in concert crime that night. I just said I was going out for the night and would be back around midnight. No problem. Just standard for a Friday night in the spring.

We arrived, parked, and went directly to the merchandise booth. There I bought a *Crusader* baseball jersey and the *Crusader* tour book.

What was a plus for the Bronco Bowl was the seating layout. Directly in front of the stage was the dress circle. This was standing room for the people who enjoyed being on the barricade. Behind this section was the Golden Corral. The seats in this section were tiered theater seats. Each row was a step up from the previous row. They were great seats to sit back and watch a show if you didn't want to deal with the crowd.

As we were waiting for Accept to hit the stage, I thumbed through the tour book, looking at the live-action photos of Biff Byford. In the bottom portion of one photo, what did I see? I saw part of my Saxon banner that had been up on stage during their set with Iron Maiden eight months earlier. I flipped out. I just thought it was the coolest thing to see, and I had the banner in hand. It was an adrenaline rush I had never experienced.

A photo of Saxon vocalist Biff Byford standing on the drum riser during their set supporting Iron Maiden. The top left portion of the banner can be seen. Photo from the Crusader tour book.

I was sitting on the aisle passing the time, people watching while waiting for Accept. One row behind me and across the aisle, I saw four guys decked out in heavy metal attire. They were sporting white spandex, studded wristbands, black leather gloves, and bandanas on their legs, arms and white furry boots. Obviously, these guys were in a band.

The guy on the aisle had some serious frizzy dark hair. I looked at him and said, "You're Diamond Darrell Lance."

He looked at me, clenched his fist, and replied, "Rock on."

It was my first sighting of Pantera in the

wild.

I hit two major shows late in the spring and had great floor tickets. For Ted Nugent, I was on the fifth row in section 12. I was looking forward to seeing Nugent, but I was really excited to see the legendary Michael Schenker in a large arena from five rows back.

For the second time, I was seeing the Scorpions. Again, I was five rows back in section 12. The seats were great.

On the tour was a band called The Jon Butcher Axis that featured a guitar player named Jon Butcher. He was good, but in my opinion, there could have been a better band that fit the fan base.

Behind me was a guy who'd already indulged too much beer, shrooms, or something else. He was just swaying back and forth howling, "Jimeee, Jimeee, Jimeee."

The cool takeaway was that the video for the Scorpions single "Still Loving You" was recorded at that show. The opening shot is of silhouetted fans walking up to Reunion Arena as the sun is setting, casting that warm, golden hour glow across the sky.

Being such a music fan, I found it a huge deal to attend a show where a live video was filmed. Now, I just needed to be part of a live album at some point.

Paul had an older cousin who was a metalhead in his mid-twenties. In early January, he returned from a trip to Los Angeles, where he spent a healthy sum on heavy metal albums.

Paul invited me to go over to his cousin Robert's apartment to see and listen to some of the albums he brought back to Texas. These albums were not mainstream artists that one would hear in regular rotation on the radio. These were young and hungry heavy metal bands from the United States, throughout Europe, and other countries.

At the time, Metal Blade Records was still in its infancy.

The first record released by Metal Blade was *Metal Massacre Volume One*, a compilation album that featured upcoming bands such as Steeler, Malice, Bitch, and Ratt. There were five songs on each side, and Metallica's "Hit the Lights" brought the album to a close.

Robert showed and played us some of his favorite albums that he brought back. While looking at the albums, for the first time I was holding an opened copy of Venom's *Black Metal*. Honestly, I was a little skittish holding that record in my hands. I had goosebumps all over my body. Maybe it was just the imagery and song titles.

Right before we were about to leave, his cousin pulled an album out that he said was really good. It was Warlord's *Deliver Us*, their debut six-song EP. He then proceeded to play us the song "Black Mass" from chapter II. In standard album lingo, that's side two.

As soon as the needle dropped and the song started, my ears perked up. There was something about the song that instantly grabbed me. I was immediately captivated. I don't know if it was the soft keyboard sustained introduction followed by the steady beat of the bass drum beat and spoken world, but I quickly became interested. Then there were the varying time signatures in the song. The song quickly built into something different that I had never experienced song wise.

The album cover consisted of a lone woman in a long white gown or dress at the entrance of a mausoleum. Maybe it was "Mrs. Victoria."

The doors were cracked open, and a bright white light was creeping through the opening. Over the entrance was the band's red "W" logo.

Upon further inspection of the album and band, the five members' names were pseudonyms. Destroyer, Thunder Child, Sentinel, The Raven, and Damien King were the musicians that made Warlord. This mysticism only made me want to learn more about the band. I was on a mission.

Before leaving, I wrote down the band's correspondence address for the Warlord Battle Choir in North Hollywood. I was already a fan.

Within a day or two, I had written a letter to the band.

To my surprise, I received a reply from the band postmarked January 14, 1984. The envelope included the band's informational sheet and maybe a Warlord button.

Several days later, I called the phone number for Warlord Productions on the reply expecting to speak to a secretary.

Instead of a greeting that said, "Thank you for calling Warlord Productions, how may I direct your call?" a male voice answered. It was Mark Zonder, Warlord's drummer, aka Thunder Child.

I stumbled on my first few words of telling the person on the line who I was and saying thank you to whoever responded.

Besides my thank-you, I also mentioned the difficulty in finding the album. Mark said he would send me some albums. I was completely blown away by this gesture and concluded the phone call. Then I started thinking. I called back about ten minutes later and asked Mark if he would sign a copy of the album for me.

On January 23, I received another letter from Mark thanking me for the phone call. Taped to the bottom of the letter were several Warlord buttons that I passed out to my friends. I am sure Paul was the first to receive one of the buttons.

Mark also stated in the letter he would reach out to the distribution company that handles the albums.

True to his word, I received not one but four copies of *Deliver Us* within days, with one signed copy. It said, "Brian – Thank you for your effort in helping us conquer the southern regions! TC and D" (with a cross above).

A second message in cursive writing said, "Brian. Great to hear from a fellow Texan! DK II."

Damien King II was the second vocalist, who just happened to be from the DFW area. It was weird when I learned this.

I kept the signed album, gave Paul one, and sent one of the other two to Joe Anthony, the legendary on-air personality of KISS FM in San Antonio. He is considered the Godfather of Rock and Roll. Also, he's the reason why San Antonio still has a healthy population of hard rockers and metalheads.

The initial correspondence with Mark led to several years of exchanging letters and the reception of promotional materials, future releases, purchases of band merchandise, and privileged band news.

On a side note, it was in a letter from Mark that I first read and saw the term *poser* used in context.

Eventually Warlord disbanded and Mark joined American progressive metal band Fates Warning. I was still in contact with him. That's how I learned he joined the band.

When Fates Warning toured for their 1989 release *Perfect Symmetry*, the band played Dallas City Limits on November 26, 1989. I met Mark for the first time. He was very welcoming and invited me up on the tour bus. He put Rainbow's *Rising* on the bus turntable, and we just sat and talked. It was a memorable experience.

I was able to see and say hello to Mark on the following Fates Warning tour for *Parallels* in 1991. The next time I saw Mark was in 2003 at the Dallas Guitar Show when he was playing drums for Ronnie Montrose. At the time, I didn't realize that Ricky Phillps, who spent time in the Babys and Bad English, was playing bass.

I am fairly certain that eventually I will see Mark play live again and, of course, I will make every effort to say hello.

NINETEEN

SUMMER

1984

IT WAS AN ODD feeling in the days after walking across the stage to receive that coveted piece of paper that said "High School Graduate."

With the summer now in full swing, I was already hitting some concerts, whether I was working them or attending. Six Flags had some decent shows roll through. I was able to catch Missing Persons, Jefferson Starship, the Romantics, the Beach Boys and a two-band bill, Heart and Shooting Star. All of these were on my season pass.

The big concert news was that the mighty Van Halen was returning for three shows at Reunion Arena. I was very fortunate that my ticket contact secured me a pair of tickets on the floor, section 11, row E, seats 13 and 14. That meant seat 14 was on the left center aisle on Michael Anthony's side.

That week, I caught five shows in five nights.

The Beach Boys at Six Flags kicked off this five-night run of concerts. The next night was Stevie Ray Vaughn and Duke Jupiter at the Fair Park Band Shell. I saw the Romantics at Six Flags—night one of Van Halen and night two of Van Halen.

Flyer from the Stevie Ray Vaughn show two days before the first Van Halen show at Reunion Arena on July 15, 1983. Flyer from Brian McLean's collection of concert memorabilia.

I was on my way out the door for the third Van Halen show when my mother asked where I was going. I said I was heading out to see Van Halen. I should've just said I was going to Six Flags.

She said, "No you're not. You've been going to concerts all week."

That pissed me off. I recently graduated high school and just happened to love live music. I wasn't able to go to night three of Van Halen.

That third night of Van Halen was an historic one, actually. It was the last American show that David Lee Roth played with Van Halen until several decades later.

This experience is one of the reasons why I am the way I am to this day.

I just dealt with it, but the music passion would not be extinguished anytime soon, that I knew.

———

Throughout the summer, Six Flags was having local bands play Southern Palace, a two hundred- to three hundred-capacity theater-style seating venue. It was an ideal place for bands to play. There was one show that caught my attention when I saw the advertisement in the newspaper.

Pantera was booked to play Southern Palace on Thursday, August 9, 1984. I was excited about seeing this. I was familiar with some of their songs. The best part—the show was at Six Flags.

With my season pass in hand, I went to the show thinking I would get a great seat by arriving nearly three hours early. Unfortunately, many other fans were thinking the same thing.

I waited those several hours in the sweltering Texas sun, but I would not give up. Obviously, I was at the back of the crowd that had already gathered on the steps that led up to the doors.

Several attempts by park security to disperse the crowd were met with colorful language.

The crowd continued to grow, and the doors were still over an hour away from opening.

At one point, Darrell poked his head out from the left side of the building, looking over a white picket fence. Screams and high-pitched girly squeals filled the air as people rushed to get a closer glimpse or an autograph. Bras and bandanas were the impromptu items of choice for Darrell's signature.

The doors finally opened, and the mad rush was on. I was one of those who came in contact with the pillars and received abrasions on my chest.

Quickly, the seating was at capacity. The people working the doors were turning fans away.

Once inside, my feet became planted in the back half of the theater-style bench seating.

There was no opening band. This was Pantera's night to shine, and they shined as true headliners.

Southern Palace gave Pantera the opportunity to have plenty of stage room with no clutter. Amps for bassist Rex Rocker, as he was known at the time, and Abbott were strategically hidden.

Positioned at the rear and on each side of the stage and stage center were three individual hanging curtains that consisted of what appeared to be 1×1-foot sheets of Mylar. Behind each of these sheets of Mylar were colored lights. Imagine a 1970s disco dance floor hanging vertically.

The description may sound cheesy, but the effect was far from it. Square, vertical, diamond, and diagonal patterns of bright color lights would flash and pulse in rhythm with the music.

Pantera played material from the first album, *Metal Magic*, as well as *Projects in the Jungle*. They also played covers from Van Halen, Motley Crue and Accept.

Add a high-energy wireless effort from the band members along with a wild-and-enthusiastic crowd—and the results were nothing short of electrifying. Pantera's performance would put some major-label bands at the time to shame.

The show solidified the fact that Pantera was a band worthy of serious attention. It put them on another level, much higher than many of the other local bands playing the scene. Most importantly, their show added to the mystique of this foursome from Arlington that called themselves Pantera, Spanish for Panther.

I was speaking with vocalist Terry Glaze in late 1985 at a show in Muenster, Texas, at a place called The Ranch. I asked him about the Six Flags show. Glaze mentioned it was at that point one of their best shows. Unfortunately, the show was not filmed. You could sense the regret in his voice as he told me there was no footage.

At another point in 1985, I asked Vinnie Abbott, Darrell's brother, about the show and why it wasn't held elsewhere in the park.

Vinnie mentioned he told the people at Six Flags they were expecting a huge crowd, but it had all fallen on deaf ears.

"Everyone has told us that," he recalled the Six Flags people telling him.

It was an easy show to attend and well worth the wait. Most of all, it was my first opportunity to see Pantera live.

I can't say why I didn't take my Kodak disc camera. I guess I was thinking it would just be a cool local gig. I did take my disc camera several weeks later, though, when Zebra played Six Flags on the Friday of Labor Day weekend bringing August to a close.

I had been a Zebra fan from day one. When Zebra released their first single, "Who's Behind the Door," in the spring of 1983, I instantly became a fan. I added their debut album to my growing collection within a week of its release.

The show Zebra was playing at Six Flags was for the second album, *No Tellin' Lies*. I can't say for sure if the album was out or not at the time. In my attempt to find a specific date, the only information I was able to locate puts the release date in September 1983.

The first single from the second album was "Bears," and it quickly became my favorite Zebra song.

To express how excited I was about the show at Six Flags, I actually stepped out of my truck to take a photo of the marquee above the lanes where parking was paid. I then pulled up to pay.

Once I was in the park, I ran directly to the parking lot where the concerts were held, securing a spot at the front of the line. Like a true rock warrior, I was on the barricade for the show. The photos are not that great due to low stage lighting and the poor quality of the camera, but the memories are priceless.

TWENTY

OSSIE, LEE, CONCERTS AND FLIGHT 191

IT WAS THE FALL of 1984 and the first school year outside of public schooling. It would be my first year in junior college. I enrolled for twelve hours at TCJC (Tarrant County Community College) or, as people in the area would refer to the junior college, Taco Jaco. The repetition of the letters in TCJC is the only connection I can see for the origination of Taco Jaco.

Another name the campus was referred to was Harvard on the Hill or Harvard on the Highway. The school really wasn't on a hill but more off the highway. The names were still used, just not as much as Taco Jaco.

There's no specific reason that I am aware of why the campus was referred to by those two names. Maybe it was staking a claim name-wise for Tarrant County.

I don't really remember what I took that first semester, but I will digress for a moment. I did take English I in the first summer semester just to get a feel for the academics and campus.

Live music was still on my priority list. In the coming months, Reunion Arena would be a hot spot tour stop for major acts in the fall.

Bruce Springsteen played two shows on the Born in the USA tour. Elton John, Rod Stewart, and Neil Young all played one show at Reunion Arena as well. Something worth mentioning is that Neil Diamond played two shows at Reunion Arena in the fall, but his shows were at 8:00 and 10:00 p.m. on the same night. I worked all these shows.

The big show for me in the fall, though, wasn't any of the major shows. It was a show at the Bronco Bowl. I was able to see Motorhead, but not just Lemmy, in November 1984. The tour was one of those legendary tours that people still brag about to this day, including me. Supporting Motorhead were Mercyful Fate for *Don't Break the Oath* and Exciter, a thrash and speed metal trio out of Canada touring for *Violence and Force*. Mercyful Fate's album *Don't Break the Oath* is considered to be one of the top metal albums of all time.

I did take my disc camera to this show, but I am not certain if I have any images of Exciter. It's not like I can take the negatives on the small circular disc and get prints made.

———◄○►———

An extremely important event in my life occurred in the fall of 1984. Oddly, it went down at Sound Warehouse on Camp Bowie. As I was thumbing through the Motorhead albums, there was a guy several feet to my right who said to me, "Don't tell me you're a Lemmy Lover."

I said, "Yes, I am," and we started talking. His name was Lee. Our conversation quickly escalated to numerous bands, with the most important one being UFO. We had no problem talking about music. It was as if I had run into someone on the same hard rock and heavy metal wavelength as me.

Our conversation lasted about ten minutes, then we went our separate ways.

A few weeks later, I saw Lee sitting on a bench outside one of the academic buildings at TCJC, and I went up to him. We spoke for a few minutes. Again, we went our separate ways, but the friendship foundation was set, and it was starting to settle.

Sometime during the early fall, I started to work in Beverage at the Hyatt Regency in downtown Fort Worth. The beverage office was below street level. We handled the liquor and beer for the two bars as well as all banquet functions. Room service would restock their alcohol needs through the beverage department.

This was the same hotel where my father's city ticket office was located. It was a bit strange to see how much the ground floor of the hotel had changed compared to when I was a kid running around there ten years prior.

I recall one time receiving a haircut at a barbershop on the lower level. From what I could remember, the location was near where the beverage office was located. The storeroom could have been the area where the barbershop was. I am fairly certain some remodeling on that level occurred before I started working at the hotel.

For the first month or two, I worked in the Skylight, the daytime bar as a barback learning the ropes. Eventually, I would branch out, setting up and tearing down banquet bar stations with other barbacks.

During this time is when I learned how to carry a case of beer resting on my shoulder like a waiter carries a tray of plates.

One night, I was scheduled for my first night at the Crystal Cactus bar. This was the nighttime bar that closed at 2:00 a.m. It would take care of the drink and cocktail orders for the Crystal Cactus Cafe, the nighttime restaurant of the hotel. I was told the bartender was an older gentleman who was nice but a no-nonsense type of guy, which was no problem for me.

The bartender knew he had a new barback coming in, and when I arrived for my shift, I walked to the bar with the beverage department manager and was introduced to him. His name was Ossie.

We exchanged pleasantries, and he asked me to get a couple things for him before the bar opened. That included fresh garnishes for the night and replacement kegs. Once that task was finished, I helped him prep the bar. As we were doing this, we were just talking, getting to know each other. I wanted to make a good impression, as I would be working with him on a regular basis.

As we were talking and getting things ready, he mentioned how he had been working at the hotel for years under different hotel names, the Sheraton and Blackstone Hotels. Then it hit me.

I asked him if he worked at the 6666 or Four Sixes restaurant. He said that he did. I then asked him if he worked with a waitress named Corky. He said he did. He proceeded to tell me that Corky had passed away about seven years prior.

I paused and told him that I met him when he worked at the 6666. I was about eight years old. I mentioned that he knew my father. He asked who and I told him. He was so surprised.

From that point on, everything was smooth sailing. He told management he didn't want to work with anyone else. He wanted me to be his right-hand man.

While working with him over the two years I was at the hotel, I learned he was part of history. He had served JFK his last breakfast that morning before the president went to Dallas.

I am sad to say I don't remember what he told me the last breakfast consisted of, but I remember the next part.

He explained that when he was leaning over putting the breakfast on the table for the president and first lady, one of his back suspenders popped loose. He was afraid to reach back and reattach it while serving President Kennedy, as the Secret Service was right there. He waited until he was back in the kitchen area before he reattached his suspenders.

Ossie and I were a great team. I easily anticipated what he would need before he'd even ask. I was always ahead of the game behind the bar with him.

Ossie was very generous to me each night when he tipped me out. He would always tip me out $20 cash. Working four and five nights a week, that was decent money while in college. Then I would give him a ride home each night we worked together, and he would give me $5 for gas. I didn't want to accept it, but he insisted.

Sometimes I would give one of our waitresses a ride home as well. Since she lived a mile from the house, it was a no-brainer. She would give me $5 for gas, but I didn't want to take it since she lived nearby. Like Ossie, she insisted.

There were times that by the end of the night, I walked into the house with $30 cash. I am not saying I was banking, but this cash played an important part in my finances, especially in the spring of 1986. I would go weeks without cashing my paychecks.

A huge tour said goodbye to 1984 and hello to 1985 at Reunion Arena.

Prince played Reunion Arena on December 30 and 31 in 1984 and January 1, 1985, on the *Purple Rain* tour. I was fortunate enough to work the first and third show. I had to work at the hotel on New Year's Eve, so I wasn't there to ring in the New Year at Prince.

I secretly always wanted a 35mm camera but never really pursued it. One of the main reasons was finances. Also, I thought I just wasn't "cool" enough to have one. All that changed on December

30, 1984.

Barry's Camera store in Fort Worth was having an after-Christmas sale. I pulled the trigger and purchased a Canon AE-1 Program with a 50mm f/1.8 lens for $199. I finally felt as if I had a real camera. In a way, I did.

I learned the basics from a friend's father who was a photographer. He was my guide for questions and answers related to photography.

Within a month of purchasing my camera, Deep Purple played Reunion Arena for *Perfect Strangers*. That was the first show I smuggled my camera into. I had a way of doing it so I would not get caught upon entering. Once in, it was no problem from there.

By this time, I had purchased a 70-210mm f/4.0 zoom lens. That's the setup I took to concerts.

Another show that I was able to get my camera into was KISS for their *Animalize* album. Queensrÿche was supporting and touring on *The Warning* album. It was the band's first full-length studio album after their impressive four song EP released in 1983.

Several important things worthy of mention occurred that night. First, I was able to see Queensrÿche for the first time. Their *Waning* album was and is still amazing. Queensrÿche is one of those bands that the first time I heard their music, I was instantly hooked. The song that hooked me was "Queen of the Reich" from their EP.

The second notable thing occurred while KISS was on stage. Gene Simmons had a large white towel that was knotted on one end. The knot in the towel allowed him to securely fasten it between the strap and his bass.

I was watching the show as normal. Out of my peripheral vision, I saw something white land on the floor several chairs away to my left. I glanced at the chairs and quickly realized that Simmons had thrown the towel into the audience.

I quickly jumped off my chair and scooped up the towel. It's one of those things people want to catch at a concert. I just happened to have a quick reflex and was at the right place at the right time. I finally had a cool concert memento from a show. Sure, towels get tossed out at shows all the time, but to come home with one of those towels is a rarity. I need to look over my negatives and see if I have a photo of Simmons with the towel.

The third and most noteworthy takeaway from the concert involved my camera.

Maybe two or three chairs down on the same row where I was sitting were the Pantera boys. This was the second time I was in close proximity to the four members in a concert setting. And unlike at the Saxon show at the Bronco Bowl ten months earlier, I had a camera in hand.

I am not sure why or what prompted me to do so, but I put the camera up and took a photo of Darrell Abbott three seats away. He was just watching the show like everyone else, but a deep, strange feeling prompted me to take the photo.

The picture has never been published. Only maybe two or three people have actually seen the image. I have never posted it on the internet. Actually, I have been very protective of the print and negatives, especially since 2004.

It's just a photo of a young Darrell Abbott watching his heroes. KISS wasn't in makeup, but I am sure he still looked up to them even without Ace on stage.

Darrell Abbott watching KISS on the Animalize tour at Reunion Arena in Dallas on January 29, 1985.

It's one of those things that happened. The importance of me snapping a quick photo of him has been only magnified years later.

Could I have made some quick cash on that photo twenty years ago? Probably, but it wouldn't have been right.

I treasure the photo and still have the original that was printed by 60 Minute Photo back in the day.

It was only the shows at Reunion Arena where the front door people were concerned about cameras.

Besides the Deep Purple show, I was able to get my camera in Triumph on the *Thunder 7* tour at Reunion Arena.

As I was walking into the arena for Triumph, I had the camera around my neck but under my shirt. I also had my winter jacket zipped all the way up. A ticket taker at the door told me to unzip my jacket. I immediately thought I was busted.

I did as she asked, but my camera with the 70-210mm lens was under my shirt. I sucked in my stomach and leaned back a bit. That removed any bulk in my shirt. She thanked me for unzipping the jacket, and I proceeded through the doors.

Another show I was able to get my camera into was AC/DC's *Fly on the Wall* tour. I was hanging out around the barricade and taking photos. I noticed roadies off to stage right watching me. I kept my camera hidden for the rest of the night and casually disappeared to my seat a few rows back from the stage.

Several years ago, two box sets of live radio broadcasts of AC/DC shows were released and available. Since I favor more of the Bon Scott era of AC/DC and Brian Johnson material through the *Blow Up Your Video* album, I purchased both box sets. The Bon Scott shows are on the *Hell's Radio* box set and the Brian Johnson shows are on the *Radio Lucifer* box set.

When the box sets arrived, I looked at the shows included. To my surprise, the AC/DC show I attended in October 1985 at Reunion Arena is on one of the discs in the *Radio Lucifer* box.

It's just a cool feeling having a disc of a show I attended several decades ago in my collection.

Where I had the most success as an inspiring photographer was from shows at the Arcadia Theater. The venue didn't care about a camera being brought in. I took my camera to Metallica on *Ride the Lightning*, Raven on *Stay Hard*, and Uli Jon Roth on his solo tour.

It was Uli's show that I walked away from with my best photos up to that point. There wasn't a large crowd, so my spot on the orchestra pit railing wasn't compromised. Also, I used the nifty 50, which captured the rainbow of the stage lights.

Two of those shows, Metallica and Uli Jon Roth, still rank as two of my All-Time Top Five Shows that I have attended.

The run of Metallica, Raven, and Uli Jon Roth shows play an important part in this chapter of my life, especially the Raven show.

———✦———

By this time, my concert partner was Sammy. We would hit many of the shows that came into town. Our first rock concert outing was Motorhead in November of 1984. Then we started hitting the shows at the Arcadia theater— the aforementioned Metallica, Raven, and Uli Jon Roth dates.

The Raven show was just another show. I had my camera and was ready to take some photos of the band. They put on a crazy, high-energy show. Bassist John Gallagher even busted a wine bottle on the drummer Wacko's goalie helmet. I captured the moment in time—pieces of glass were flying everywhere. It was a nice stop-action photo.

Years later when I met John Galagher for the first time, I mentioned the photo. He said that was the first and only time he did that.

After the show, Sammy and I went across the street to 7-Eleven to grab some sodas and snacks for the trip back to Arlington. While we were standing in front of the pay phone, a guy that was obviously at the show came up to me and complimented me on my sleeveless Warlord shirt. He was caught by surprise to see a Warlord shirt out in the wild. My shirt was the perfect icebreaker.

We started talking, and all of us introduced ourselves. His name was John, and his car had broken down on the highway. He and his friends were determined not to miss the Raven show no matter what. With the help of a guy dressed in some fly threads in a purple Cadillac and a pack of smokes, John and his friends had made it to the Raven show.

They would address having no mode of transportation after the show. My Warlord shirt provided that opportunity for discussion.

After a few minutes of talking and learning John and his friends lived in Arlington, it was a no-brainer for them to hitch a ride with us back to Arlington. John rode in the cab, with Sammy sitting between us. That night was the foundation of a more than four-decade friendship that is still ongoing to this day.

For the spring semester, I continued taking the basic core classes at the junior college. Lee and I would run into each other here and there more often. Little by little, a friendship started to form.

He was a writer already majoring in journalism, and I was a photographer with a few live rock photos.

One afternoon, he invited me over to his house to see his music magazine that he wrote during his senior year. The magazine was called *The Rocker*, and he wanted to write future issues. The plan was that he would write, and I would supply the photos. The team of Ed Banger and MaccaM was born. MaccaM is the combination of the original spelling for the Scottish Clan MacLean and the first part of camera. We had dreams and aspirations of covering music.

Around February of 1985 I started attending live rock clubs. Pantera was the first live band I saw in a rock club. I soaked everything up. I would see them as much as I could when they would play Savvy's or Joe's Garage.

In April, Pantera would play the Bronco Bowl with two other local bands. This was the same venue where I'd attended the Motorhead and Saxon tours a few months earlier.

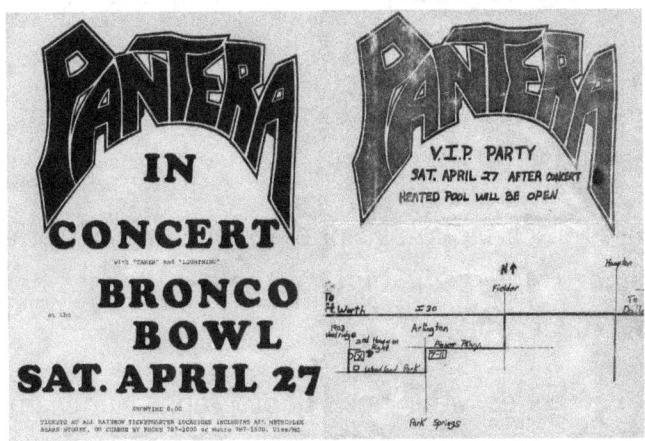

Oddly, a year and three weeks prior, Pantera was playing the same venue where they sat watching Saxon and Accept on March 31, 1984. Now, on April 27, 1985, Pantera was playing the same stage in a midsize 3,500-seat venue. There was a decent turnout, but it wasn't a full house show.

Even though I had only been photographing for a few months, I was able to secure a credential to shoot the show. Obviously, I was out of my league. I did what I could do. More importantly, it was a definite learning and networking experience.

Photos from the show a photographer shot were used as live images on the *I Am the Night* album that would be released at the end of the summer. The photo of Vinnie was shot in the garage/practice room at the "party house."

It was at this show that I met a true photojournalist for the first time. He was a staff photog at the *Star-Telegram* and was very kind and helpful to this young, inexperienced photographer. His photos were the images used for the *I Am the Night* release.

I want to add that the term *photojournalist* is overused these days. So many people with a camera now consider themselves photojournalists. Not even close.

A photojournalist is a photographer who tells news stories mainly through images for media outlets. The key phrases being news stories and media outlets.

There are categories within news photographs. For example, spot news, general news, local news, national, and international news can fall under hard news or breaking news.

Then there are features or lifestyles such as people, food, travel, arts, and entertainment. Obviously, one of my preferred or favorite categories is entertainment and having the media accreditation to cover a show at a major arena or a theater size venue.

Add this to NCAA D1 athletics such as the Big XII or SEC. There's just something about a nice fall day in a football stadium or basketball arena filled with people watching fast action.

International soccer, whether the match is friendly or competitive, also makes for a great adrenaline rush atmosphere with thousands of people cheering for their country in an NFL stadium.

The not-so-glamorous side of things, business, finance, education, and politics.

The photographer needs to write the captions and input metadata for the photos being submitted or transmitted, collaborate with reporters if applicable, and research the event being covered.

These last three components I consider to be very important. Those are being prepared, ethical behavior, and etiquette. It's amazing how many photographers new to the game don't understand the etiquette part of being behind a camera.

The photojournalist I met that night would give me true words of wisdom a year later. Those words are still applicable to this day.

Throughout the summer, I would hit the local rock clubs on a consistent basis with camera and flash in hand.

Around this time, bands that toured the regional club major market circuits would play six nights a week with four sets each night. The sets would include mainly covers and some original material. There were no other bands on the bill, just the one act.

Monday was the travel day. Sundays were dressed-down days. Bands that normally wore stage clothes Tuesday through Saturday would wear jeans and T-shirts for the more informal Sunday shows.

I was rooted in the trenches of live music and wanted to experience as many nights as possible throughout the week.

If a band was fortunate enough, they would have an album for purchase at their merch table. Some bands would have a crude cassette or demo to be sold along with the other merchandise staples such as promotional photos, buttons, and shirts.

Photography-wise, I would dedicate one roll of 24-exposure, Kodak 400-speed film for each set from the headliners. The only band I did this with was Terry Glaze era Pantera.

The following day, I would take the film to be developed at the 60 Minute Photo lab on Hulen St. It was nice having images in hand so quickly.

The person who developed my film was the person who taught me the basics of ISO, shutter speed, and f stop/lenses when I first purchased my camera–in other words, the exposure triangle and how each component interacts with each other.

As odd as it is, twenty-two years later, this specific commercial spot where I would have my film developed played a major role in a life-changing event for me.

Little quirky instances like this have occurred more than just once or twice in my life. This was just another. Maybe it should be called fate.

At one point, a second band started showing up on the bills as a warm-up act. These bands normally were local bands trying to get their foot into the door. The goal: to start working their way up the club circuit ladder, eventually becoming a regional touring act.

The addition of this second band changed the dynamics of the night. The headliner would play three sets, and the local opener would play one set.

Eventually, a third band would be put on the bill. That put the headliners at two sets and one set each for the opening bands. At times, there were four bands billed for the night. That left the headliner with one set, longer than the standard forty-five minutes on stage.

These multi-band shows normally occurred on the weekend. Sometimes there were two different bands for the Friday and Saturday night shows.

There were times when two local bands with established followings would share the stage on a weekend night. The band with the larger fan base would headline.

That was the case for Pantera and Warlock (Texas) on the first weekend in August. The bands played two nights, August 2 and

3, at Rascals in Arlington. Each band played one set respectively.

The summer gigs at Rascals were unforgiving. The temperature inside Rascals easily became stifling as Mother Nature showed no mercy in August.

On that Friday, my family drove to Bossier City in Louisiana for the horse races at Louisiana Downs. We had a stake in several racehorses, so we went to see one run in the early afternoon. My parents called him Mr. Personality, but his formal race name was Mr. Sync.

After the race, we went back to the hotel for dinner. I came down from the room and walked into the hotel lobby. I saw my father staring at the TV, his eyes glued to the screen. He was not alone. There were other guests who had their eyes fixated on the TV as well. All were frozen as they stood as the live TV news feed came in.

From what I quickly gathered, there was a major and tragic news event that occurred. I asked my father what was happening. He said, "We had one go down."

A Delta L-1011, Flight 191, had crashed at the northeastern end of DFW International Airport on approach to runway 17L. Seeing those images and live coverage sent a sinking feeling throughout my body. I was in a Delta family, and it hit me hard. It was at that moment I vividly remember deciding that I wanted to be a photojournalist.

The first newspaper photographer on the scene was the *Star Telegram* photog I met at the Bronco Bowl in the spring. Since he lived closest to the airport, the photo desk called him to see if he could head to the crash scene.

Several years later I would be in a position to look at those negatives he shot.

———◇———

During the summer, I worked more shows and attended them as well. By this time, I had introduced Lee to Pantera's music. The band would release their third album in August of 1985. Pantera once again played a local show at Six Flags, but this time at the Music Mill Theater. The people at Six Flags learned from their previous year's experience with Pantera playing the Southern Palace, and the band played in the larger outdoor amphitheater.

Darrell Abbott tuning his guitar backstage at the Music Mill Amphitheater prior to their show at Six Flags over Texas in May 1985. Photo by Brian McLean

Photos from this show would be used for the cover feature story on Pantera in issue number 16 of *Metal Forces* magazine in early 1986.

Meanwhile, Lee and I were doing some basic stuff with a local magazine called *Texas Entertainment Magazine*. Nothing really would start kicking in journalism-wise for us until the 1985 fall semester.

With the release of Pantera's third album, *I Am the Night*, in August, many locals thought the band would be swooped up at any given moment by a major label. The album was that strong and was able to stand on its own against any major label release at the time.

I enrolled in Photography I and learned how to process and develop black-and-white film, as well as how to make black-and-white prints in the darkroom.

Lee was taking Reporting I, and we both were spending more time in the newsroom of the school paper, the *Reflector*. Several times we covered concerts for the *Reflector*, as I was able to smuggle my camera successfully on more than one occasion. If I was caught, normally I would be recognized, as I would still work shows here and there.

Near the end of December, the band John had pieced together with Walt, Darrell's guitar tech, and two others needed a band photo. The band was called Rotting Corpse and was one of the first pure thrash bands in Texas, if not the first.

Walter is a guitar player I befriended by following Pantera on the local circuit. There was an ironic twist and a small-world bit tied in with Rotting Corpse. The vocalist Mo and drummer Dave went to my high school. Mo was a year ahead of me, whereas Dave was a year behind me.

Many times during high school, I would have lunch with Dave and several others. Actually, Dave was in our group of friends that went to the Scorpions, Maiden, and Girlschool show in August 1982.

I also credit Dave with introducing me to UFO's music by walking

171

from his house to mine with *Strangers in the Night* in hand. I don't remember what side of the album he played; I just knew as soon as I heard the first few riffs of the first song he played, I was on board. My immediate reaction was, "This is the ideal hard rock band." UFO had great vocals, solid guitar sound, and cool music. Everything I'd heard in those first few moments was perfect hard rock to my ears.

Slo Mo photo bombing a photo of Darrell during a set at Matley's in Dallas, circa 1985. Photo by Brian McLean

Then, I was shooting my first band promo photo to be used in the first Rotting Corpse demo tape. The photo consisted of John, Walter, Mo, Dave, and number 75. He was a bass player whose inclusion in the band was very short-lived. To this day, no one remembers his name or, as a matter of fact, any details about him.

The location was behind Rascals in north Arlington. Later on, many people called it "Thrashcals."

During the coming months, classic underground metal bands would grace the crude stage. There was Nasty Savage from Florida, to name a national act, and Militia and Watchtower, both from Austin, played the north Arlington sweatbox.

Rigor Mortis entered the conversation, but at this point, they were only hanging out in the parking lot.

TWENTY-ONE

A BIG YEAR OF CHANGE AND PHOTOGRAPHIC GROWTH

LEE AND I WENT our separate ways academically, but in regard to our friendship, nothing changed. He traveled south to San Marcos and enrolled at Southwest Texas State. I stayed local, enrolling at TCU. Lee would continue his pathway in journalism, whereas I would pursue photojournalism.

I was welcomed with open arms at TCU and by the student publication, the *Daily Skiff*. I quickly learned several things from the photo editor who was an older student and a Vietnam vet.

The first thing he told me was that I didn't have to major in photojournalism to be a photojournalist. People don't realize that and complete a major in photojournalism. The degree becomes completely useless when that path is not followed.

He was totally correct, and those words are still 100 percent accurate today, thirty-eight years later. Now you can take the photojournalism classes, but there's no need to declare it as a major. Select something else that gives you a backup plan in case you don't follow the photojournalist path.

Second, he told me it doesn't matter what you shoot; it matters what your stuff looks like. This also is 100 percent accurate thirty-eight years later.

I find this a lot with people who want to shoot major concerts or major sporting events. These people want to jump right in and land the big credentials. They should spend their time crafting their skills and experience, learning things like properly understanding the exposure triangle in photography and how to properly adjust the settings for the shooting environment.

New photographers should learn as much as they can to have a solid understanding of composition and what helps to make great images. Editing, culling images, metadata, meeting deadlines, white balance, color balance, and etiquette are a few things that also play major roles.

An analogy that can be used is that not all baseball players who turn professional immediately start playing in the majors. Yes, there are the standouts, but then there are many who work their way through the minor league systems. Eventually these players step up to the plate in a MLB stadium, after crafting their skills and level of play over time.

The final thing he told me during my first semester at TCU was editors don't care about your GPA; they care about your portfolio. That's true to a point, but it's a bit worrisome for those who may leave the journalism field. Keep that GPA up, but also continue shooting away.

Within a day or two of being at TCU for the spring semester in 1986, I was assigned to cover a basketball game at the former Daniel Meyer Coliseum. Now the coliseum is known as Schollmaier Arena.

Those first few days were mind-blowing. I felt completely lost as to what I actually wanted to do and accomplish at TCU. Second, suddenly I was covering Southwest Conference basketball. It was crazy. I was amazed with SWC basketball. I was told to just wait until football season.

————◦————

During the last home basketball game of the regular season, I learned my first big lesson as a photographer with less than two months' experience.

TCU was hosting the University of Texas for an afternoon basketball game. With five seconds remaining and down 54–53, TCU inbounded the ball to Jamie Dixon. He was immediately swarmed by three UT players trying to foul him. Dixon wouldn't let it happen.

He made his way past midcourt, roughly thirty-five feet out from the basket. He stumbled forward, launching the ball toward the net. As the clock expired, the ball dropped in the basket. There was nothing but net on the perfectly placed shot, giving TCU a 55–54 win over UT.

It needs to be noted that this was the year before the three-point line would be put into play.

The crowd stormed the court. It was an amazing sight to witness. The funny part is that I can see myself in footage posted on YouTube. I was wearing a blue and white striped, long sleeved rugby shirt and entered the court from the bottom left of the screen.

I was following Dixon and watched him launch the ball toward the basket through my camera. I didn't press the shutter button. I became too involved in the game. It was a valuable lesson learned early on.

Nobody from the *Fort Worth Star-Telegram* captured the shot. Their photo desk was calling the student paper staff to see if anyone had captured it.

If I would've just pressed the shutter button and captured the moment, I would've had a front-page cover shot as an aspiring photojournalist only six weeks in.

After the UT game, TCU dropped their last two games, which were on the road of conference play.

The first of the two games, TCU lost to Texas Tech, 62–52. The second game, which was against Houston, went into OT; and TCU came up short, 85–83. Just one win in either of those two games would have given TCU sole possession of the SWC Men's Basketball title.

At the end of conference play, TCU, Texas, and Texas A&M all went 12-4. That meant all three teams shared the conference title.

Every time I step foot onto the basketball court at Schollmaier Arena, I can't help but think of that moment, especially with Dixon as the head basketball coach at TCU.

This game occurred in late February. The first week of March, I was assigned to cover the SWC Basketball tournament at Reunion Arena.

All the teams in the conference were present for the tournament except Baylor. In conference play, they went 3-13, and that's why they were not there. Now, Baylor has a powerhouse basketball program.

TCU lost to Texas Tech 71–67 in the second round, but my experience of the tournament as a whole was something new. I was experiencing basketball with multiple teams on a higher level.

Texas Tech beat Texas A&M 67–63 in the finals, thus winning the tournament.

I was still working at the hotel pulling the late shifts in the Crystal Cactus, but only on the weekends. With school in full swing, I spent a lot of time working banquets. Cash tip outs allowed me not to cash my checks. I was at a point of having ten to twelve checks that were not cashed. Cashing those checks allowed me to take my shooting to the next level.

It was time to up my gear to the professional level. With all the money I received from cashing the checks, I went back to the camera store and made the switch to Nikon. At the time, Nikon was the gear of choice. All the major daily staffers shot with Nikon gear.

At the guidance of my photo editor, I needed a Nikon F3 body and drive. That was the camera at the time. I also needed three lenses, a telephoto, wide angle, and portrait lens. Most importantly was the 180mm 2.8, 28mm 2.8, and 105mm 2.5. Eventually, I would need to add a fourth lens for football in the fall.

The spring semester was rough, but I did survive. I admit I was lost, not really having a plan as to what I would pursue academically. All I knew was that I was at TCU, and I wanted to cover rock bands. That really wasn't going to work, but I was making things happen.

———◦———

Just like remembering the first album I purchased with my earned money, I easily remember the first photo pass I was approved for. It was Anthrax.

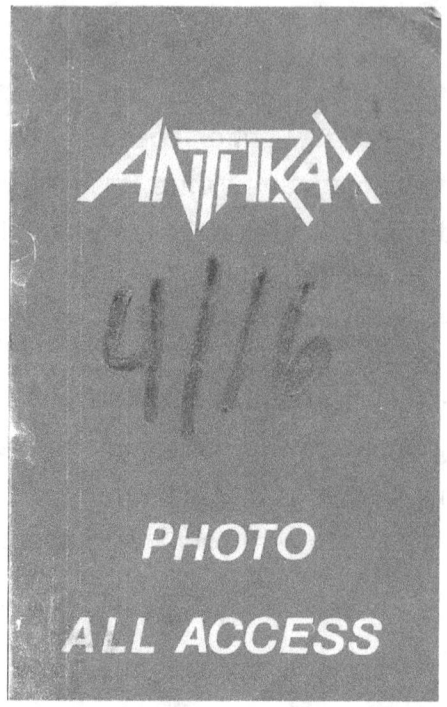

*Brian's first photo pass for Anthrax
at the Arcadia Theater in Dallas
on April 16, 1986. Pass from
the media credential collection of
Brian McLean.*

With Metallica's *Ride the Lightning* being picked up by Elektra Records in 1985, thrash bands and heavier bands over all were being looked at. Anthrax was one of those bands.

The first Anthrax album, *Fistful of Metal*, was released through Megaforce Records, the same label that released the first two Metallica albums. The band's second album, *Spreading the Disease*, was released by Island Records/Megaforce Records in October 1985.

Anthrax toured for the album in the spring, and securing a pass to photograph them wasn't difficult at all. I think the publicists were very accommodating to photographers at this point.

Anthrax played the Arcadia Theater in April, and my friend John conducted an interview on the bus with them. I was present for the interview. It was a unique take on things. I am not sure if John had the interview already set up.

I had the band sign my ticket, but unfortunately, I left the ticket on the bus after the interview.

Upon arrival at the venue, we were just hanging out in the parking lot. I saw Anthrax guitarist Scott Ian milling around. No one was around him. I pointed this out to John, and we went up to speak with him. At this time, Pantera was either on the cover of the current issue of *Metal Forces* magazine, or they'd been on the cover of a recent issue.

What I do know is that I asked Scott Ian if he saw Pantera on the cover and asked him about the band. For the summer of 1986, he wasn't too impressed with their look, as Anthrax was totally anti "that look."

Anthrax was out on their first national tour under the major label debut album. Metallica's third studio album, *Master of Puppets*, hit the streets several weeks prior.

Metallica hit the road as support for Ozzy's *Ultimate Sin* album. The tour stopped at Tarrant County Convention Center on Saturday, May 10, 1986. As soon as they hit the stage, Metallica quickly won the crowd as "Battery" kicked in.

I didn't get approved for credentials, but I was put on the list with a plus one. I felt very fortunate that I was able to see this tour. Being on the Ozzy tour was a good move for the band even though they only played seventeen dates.

Several weeks later, Metallica swung back through on Monday, June 3, and played the Bronco Bowl. For this show I did get approved for credentials. Eventually, I made my way to the photo pit. Crazed and rabid fans were already jockeying and positioning for a spot on the barricade.

As I was in the photo pit area, I saw a familiar face fighting for one of the coveted spaces.

A more perfect story couldn't have been written. It was my friend from high school who had asked me who Metallica was after spring break my senior year. This is the same person who then concluded his inquiry with the following words: "They won't amount to anything."

Believe me, I told the story to those holding on for dear life at a barricade spot as he was trying to work his way in. They all booed him and wouldn't let him join. I am thinking they actually started to push him back.

While in the photo pit area, security explained they were anticipating some craziness down on the floor, such as stage diving, bodies coming over the barricade, and things like that. Eventually, they cleared the photogs out. We had to shoot from the walkway between the upper and lower level.

The summer wasn't even in full swing, and I already witnessed two shows that would become legendary. A third was just sixteen days later at a venue on Commerce Street in Dallas called the Circle A Ranch. It was more of an underground heavy metal/punk club.

The band was Celtic Frost with support coming from Voivod. Running Wild was listed as part of the tour but was not at the Dallas show.

I am not exactly sure who went to the show with me, but I think it was my friend John, or I went by myself and met him at the show.

What I do remember was John and I talking with the three members of Celtic Frost. From magazine photos and album artwork, I was under the impression that vocalist/guitarist Tom G. Warrior was this person who appeared to be as his name implies—a warrior covered in leather and spikes and towering in height. In actuality, he wasn't all that massive; he was more slender and not towering in height at all.

All three were super nice and cordial, taking time just to talk with us. John was more engaged in the conversation than I was, as he was really into and familiar with European metal.

Years later when Tom G. Warrior's autobiography *Are You Morbid?* was released in 2000, he referenced the Dallas show quite a bit.

The venue was three floors: the bottom was obviously the entrance, the stage was on the second floor, and the dressing rooms were on the third. To get to the stage, bands had to walk down the fire escape on the outside of the building and make their way through a small door on the second floor. I can't even picture the members of Celtic Frost climbing down the fire escape above Commerce Street in Dallas.

As I read through Tom G.'s book, I really enjoyed his perspective on the Dallas date. He also talked about other shows in Texas that played a major part in his life at the time.

——◇——

The summer of 1986 music scene was very strong in DFW as well as in Hollywood, on the Sunset Strip and in all the legendary rock clubs.

There was a band that relocated from Ohio to Dallas and quickly established themselves as a major player in the scene. The band was Sweet Savage. They independently released a five-song EP that hit the number one Import Charts in the UK.

Sweet Savage had no problem pulling in six hundred people on a Saturday night at Savvy's in Fort Worth. I photographed this band quite a bit during the summer. Like Pantera, we—as in the local music scene—thought they would be signed very soon and record their major label debut.

They would pack up and head to Hollywood for six weeks in search of a record deal. Labels were seriously looking at them.

One label, a major independent label called Enigma Records, offered Sweet Savage a deal, but the band turned it down. Their thought process was why should they sign with an independent record label when the major labels were looking at them?

Chris Sheridan, guitarist for Sweet Savage, once told me it was the biggest mistake they made. He added it just showed how unpredictable the music industry is.

I was still working at the hotel when AC/DC played the Tarrant County Convention Center supporting the *Who Made Who* album. Queensrÿche was the opener on their *Rage for Order* album.

Since I was still working at the Hyatt Regency, I heard the rumor that the bands were staying at the hotel.

One of my high school friends and regular concert partner, Paul, went with me. I told him that the bands were staying at the hotel and we should stop by. He was hesitant and said we wouldn't see anybody. To him it would be a wasted trip. This would be no more than 150 yards north of the convention center. I had to convince him. He finally gave in.

As we approached the valet station near the front doors, I saw a guy with long hair walking toward the entrance telling a female, "I promise, I will call you."

He was about to enter the hotel when I said, "Chris DeGarmo?"

He swung around and said, "Yes."

And with that quick it's-now-or-never sense, we stood around the valet station in front of the Hyatt Regency Fort Worth talking with Chris DeGarmo. I don't recall any of our dialogue. As two college-age fans of hard rock, we just wanted to have a nice conversation with DeGarmo and not fanboy out on him.

What I do remember the most about our encounter was he was very cordial and super-nice. At one point, someone came up to him and told him the final edit of the "Gonna Get Close to You" video was on the bus.

He apologized and said he needed to go watch the video.

We thanked him for his time. We didn't even ask him to sign our ticket stubs. We wanted to give him a break from that and just have a normal conversation.

As we were walking away, I turned to my friend and said, "Now aren't you glad I kept asking you to go to the hotel?"

The obvious answer was a yes.

Several years later with the release of *Operation Mindcrime*, I would learn that DeGarmo had family ties in DFW.

It was a great way to end the summer before having to return to TCU and start the grind of being a staff photographer.

Twenty-Two

Summer Flood

1986

ONE SUNDAY IN LATE August, my friend Bryce and I went to the high school to "toss a Frisbee around." We selected the practice field as the perfect spot. What was best about the area was, no matter how errantly the Frisbee flew, there was plenty of room for it to land safely and not lose it. The area was wide open, and it's where the marching band would have morning practices in the fall.

While we were out there, I stumbled across part of the in-ground sprinkler system. The whole reason for us being out there immediately changed. Now, we were on the hunt for the other in-ground sprinklers. Ironically, we just happened to have a can of spray paint with us.

With the location of that one outlet, we set out to find more. With a little thinking in a grid-like fashion, we went to work. We found a second outlet, but it was forty paces west from the first one. With this information, we started locating more sprinklers in this line by walking east of the first location.

While we continued to search, I ran across an outlet that wasn't in line with the others, north and south. It was located twenty paces in, east and west, and twenty paces north and south from the original sprinkler.

Once we realized the pattern was in a zigzag, we quickly located others. By the time the sun was setting, we found, in total, maybe ten or twelve sprinkler outlets. Each one was marked with orange fluorescent spray paint.

Once we were done, we went to the baseball field. Up against the field house were ten or twelve sprinkler heads. The jackpot was just way too convenient. We temporarily borrowed those sprinkler heads for six weeks or so.

Fast-forward a bit, and the fall semester was in full swing at the high school. That included morning marching band practices.

In the early fall, one of the competitions for the marching band was the City Contest. Strange as it sounds, Bryce and I decided to head back up to the marching field and toss the Frisbee. We had the sprinkler heads in tow.

The marching field looked a tad bit dry, so we decided with the available resources, we would irrigate the field starting at 6:00 p.m. that Sunday.

Unfortunately, we were unable to return to the field, so irrigation continued through the night and into the next morning. I am not sure who turned off the sprinklers, but I was told there was plenty of standing water the next morning. Ironically, this just happened to be the morning of the City Contest. The marching band was forced to practice in one of the parking lots. The band and their fearless leader adapted.

Later in the fall, I went to a football game and had access to the field due to my media credentials. I went back to where the band members were having their break following their performance. I said hello to a lot of my former saxophone friends and squad members.

As I was leaving the area, the band director was walking in my direction. As we passed, he said, "Mr. McLean, I just want to thank you for watering the marching field."

I replied, "I have no idea what you're talking about."

———⚙———

When I returned for the fall semester, I was on staff with the student daily paper. My photo editor made the comment that he could see improvement in my shooting even though I'd just photographed bands all summer long.

As previously mentioned, the highlight for fall was Southwest Conference football. Honestly, I don't remember the first football game I shot. The schedule from the 1986 season showed Kansas State as the first home opener. It was the SMU game that I remember the most from my first season since it was at the Cotton Bowl, and I associated the Texxas Jam with that stadium. I will say it was a cool feeling being in the Cotton Bowl press box and looking out over the field.

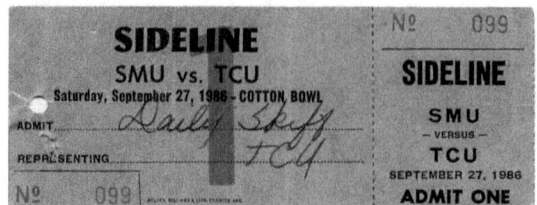

Brian's first sideline pass for the TCU vs. SMU football game at the Cotton Bowl in Dallas.

All the other games I shot were at Amon G. Carter Stadium. There was and still is just something about making a road trip to another stadium to shoot a game, just like road tripping to another city to catch a concert.

The fall presented another photographic opportunity outside of TCU football. Along with shooting TCU football, I started working as a stringer at the *Fort Worth Star-Telegram*, the major daily. I was mainly shooting high school football, which is huge in Texas. The opportunity afforded me to be around names I would see in print and start learning from them. I was able to speak with other photographers and pick their brains at times.

I recall a very important conversation on one overcast day when I was photographing TCU women's soccer. The photographer that I'd met at Pantera's Bronco Bowl show was shooting the same game. Since he photographed the Bronco Bowl show, he'd started shooting a lot of the music for the magazines. In the 1980s that was a photographer's dream gig.

After the game he wanted to show me some Queensrÿche slides he'd shot. I am fairly certain the images were from when Queensrÿche opened for AC/DC at TCCC several weeks prior.

As we were sitting in his black Honda CRX, he told me he was moving to Seattle. He was ahead of the curve on that move. I was totally bummed, as I looked at him for guidance, but he did say one thing. I don't remember his exact words or how he phrased it, but he told me to just shoot "newspaper" for a few years: "You'll understand."

At the time, it was something I didn't want to hear, but I continued to do so.

When I look back, those words are so true and are the most important words ever spoken to me in regard to photography. I have realized for years how profound his words are, and they are still relevant today.

Shooting for the major daily newspaper in college and after graduating gave me the skill set to look at and approach things differently photographically. Those years definitely have given me an advantage when it comes to shooting sports and entertainment. Grinding it out via the editorial route made a huge difference.

In late October, TCU hosted the Baylor Bears on the last Saturday of the month. It was an early game, maybe 2:00 kickoff at the latest. With that, my Saturday night would be free to catch

Motorhead at the Longhorn Ballroom in Dallas. It's a legendary venue. The Sex Pistols played there in January of 1978.

Wendy O. Williams, or W.O.W. of Plasmatics fame, would be main support with the Cro-Mags, a New York City hardcore punk band, and Scratch Acid from Austin.

I don't recall seeing the first band, but I do recall watching the Cro-Mags. Whether it was the full set or not, I am not able to say. I can say that I did watch the entire set of W.O.W. and shot some interesting images.

Williams was in a black leather two-piece bikini-style outfit. She would face the drum riser, bend over backward, and stare at the crowd. This made for an interesting photo from my point of view. I was able to frame the band logo on the bass drum. Recognizing that small detail with the logo was part of shooting the editorial route.

Of course, she would stomp around and just do her thing vocally. Her presence on the stage made for an interesting set to watch.

As for Motorhead, it was great to see Lemmy a second time. There was no real photo pit barricade at all. It was just banquet tables that sectioned off an area in front of the stage. The area was never breached even though it would have been easy to do so.

The one thing I remember the most about the set was the white leather boots Lemmy wore with his black outfit. Lemmy was throwing down some fancy footwork throughout the band's set.

Afterward, I was behind the venue with a friend from the scene. I was standing to her left as she and Lemmy spoke. I was so nervous to be back there, a few feet from Lemmy, I just froze.

The only thing I can say is that I stared at his left nipple and nipple hair, afraid to say anything.

This would not be the first and only time I would freeze up in the presence of a legendary figure. It would happen again eight months down the road.

There was big entertainment news in Dallas-Fort Worth. A Hard Rock Cafe was opening north of downtown Dallas. In an effort to drum up publicity, the Hard Rock Cafe held a press conference one cold afternoon early in the spring semester.

High schools and colleges throughout the DFW area were invited to attend and have lunch. Afterward, the attendees received a tour of the Hard Rock Cafe, viewing the cool pieces on display before they opened to the public.

To encourage the visiting journalism students to write stories in their respective student publications, there was a contest. It was called the Hard Rock Cafe Journalism Contest. There were two categories, high school and college.

The winners in each category, writer and photographer, would receive a Hard Rock Cafe Dallas denim jacket. At this point in the 1980s, the Hard Rock Cafe brand was *very* trendy and in major international markets. Also, denim was popular at the time.

Since I was the photographer, I snapped a few images during the press conference. The reporter who I went with was actually the editor of TCU's daily student newspaper. She took it a step further like any inquiring editor would.

She set up a one-on-one interview with Steve Routhier, who at the time was the general curator of all the Hard Rock Cafes. He was responsible for collecting, cataloging, and displaying the music memorabilia worldwide. In other words, Routhier's job was supercool.

The story ran on Friday, March 6, 1987, and the tear sheet was submitted for the contest.

I wasn't surprised the feature on Routhier won for the college-level entries. We were invited back to the Hard Rock Dallas for the presentation of the jackets.

I knew the photographer who took the presentation, and a year or two later, he gave me the negatives of the two of us receiving our jackets.

I wore that jacket so much when chilly weather gave me the opportunity to do so. I even had several Motorhead pins on it. I put plenty of wear and tear on that jacket, made many road trips with the jacket, and spent many hours in the darkroom wearing it. To this day, the jacket hangs in one of the closets at the house with darkroom chemical stains still present.

TWENTY-THREE

THAT ONE CLASS, BON JOVI, AND SPENT

I MADE IT THROUGH the fall semester and was definitely looking forward to the break. I was a bit more excited for the spring semester.

My photo editor on the student daily was stepping down and passing the torch to me. That meant I was photo editor for the spring semester. It was a big change for me. I can't say I wasn't nervous.

The deal with working on the student daily was, as soon as class was out, I went straight to the newsroom. I needed to see what was going on. If nothing was happening, I would retreat to my little hideaway, the darkroom at the end of the second-floor hallway. After that, I would start cruising the campus to capture the daily feature photo. That's a photo of somebody out and about doing something.

The most common place new photographers go in an attempt to find a feature photo is the park. Those photos are so common that they are referred to as "People in the Park" photos. That's always a last resort for me.

Eventually, I started walking a certain path or "beat" in search of the feature photo. Some days I would have great success; other days, not so much.

———◇———

The one class that impacted me the most during the spring semester was Religions of the World at 10:00 a.m., Mondays, Wednesdays, and Fridays.

We would learn about the major religions of the world. At the time, those were Christianity, Judaism, Hinduism, Islam, Buddhism, and Sikhism. I am fairly certain there were more that we learned about.

Our professor was a huge Texas Rangers fan and an amazing educator. Not only that, but I am certain he's still the amazing person he was when I took his class.

In this class, an analogy was presented: a year becomes a smaller and smaller percentage of a person's life as they grow older. I think of that moment quite a bit and have used the analogy in conversation many times, especially when I was an educator.

I remember the first exam. It was on a Friday.

The exam would be 100 points total; broken down, that would be seventy 1-point multiple-choice questions, a 5-point essay, and a 25-point essay.

I sat in my bedroom the Monday night before the exam. I really didn't want to start studying. After a few moments of just sitting there thinking, I thought to myself, "I don't want to disappoint my professor."

That Monday night, I studied for two hours. It was the same on Tuesday. I stepped things up a bit for Wednesday, studying four hours, and did the same on Thursday.

Since my class was at 10:00 a.m., I arrived on campus two hours earlier and studied for another ninety minutes. In total, I spent thirteen and a half hours studying for my first Religions of the World test.

I felt good about the test. Unfortunately, I went blank on the 25-point essay question. I just couldn't pull it out; I was stumped. Maybe that's why the question was worth 25 points.

The exams were graded and given back to students on Monday. I remember when the professor handed my test back to me. The best way to explain the expression on his face was, "How?"

I'd earned a 73 on the test. Needless to say, I was disappointed with my results. I wasn't able to answer the 25-point essay question and missed two multiple choice questions at one point each, thus the 73. I did answer the 5-point essay question.

I read the look on his face as, "How did you miss the essay question but get so many multiple choice questions correct?"

If I looked at everything overall, I'd answered 68 multiple choice questions correctly.

What I took away from the class besides the knowledge about major religions was learning how to study. Some of the study habits I used remained with me for the rest of my time at TCU and two other universities.

No other class at TCU impacted me the way this class did. I walked away with so much from his class.

In 1988, I took the Cult and Sect Religion class offered by the same professor during the spring semester.

———◦———

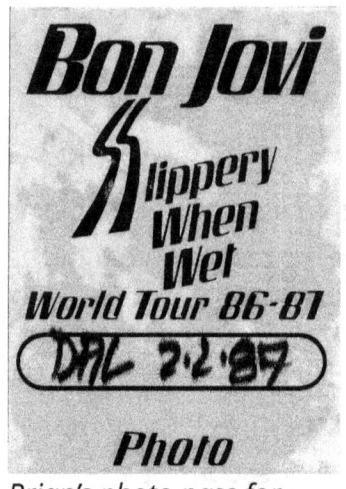

Brian's photo pass for Bon Jovi's Slippery When Wet tour. Pass from the media credential collection of Brian McLean.

One of the albums that was burning up the charts in 1986 was Bon Jovi's *Slippery When Wet* album.

Suddenly, Bon Jovi was rocketing to arenas and rock stardom. The tour came through on February 2, 1987. At the time, *Slippery When Wet* was sitting at number one on the Billboard 200. The album spent seven weeks sitting at the top of the charts.

Opening the show was Cinderella. Their debut album *Night Songs* peaked at number three the week of February 7, 1987.

I was pumped to photograph two of the hottest bands in the country on the same night. I entered the barricade to get ready for Cinderella. The head of security or tour manager said I couldn't photograph them. I am not sure why, but I only shot Bon Jovi's set. I was a bit disappointed.

When a photographer is shooting a major show, there's a three-song limit. As Bon Jovi was blowing through the first three songs in front of twenty thousand crazed fans, I felt as if I wasn't capturing anything.

Then it happened. Jon Bon Jovi jumped up on the drum riser, sporting a Texas flag as a cap. There was ample light, and smoke was falling from above. This was the moment and photo. It needed to be captured and it was.

The next day, the photo ran full color on the bottom half of the front page. When the paper was rolled up in its paper bag, the picture was visible through the plastic. I saw one such example as I was walking across the street from the newsroom at TCU to the parking lot. For some reason, though, I believe that it ran on the bottom of local/state.

It was a true feeling of accomplishment. To say seeing it made me feel like a lottery winner would be a good indicator of how I felt.

Several weeks after Bon Jovi, Iron Maiden came through Fort Worth and played Tarrant County Convention Center for their *Somewhere in Time* album. Pete Way of UFO fame was out with his band Waysted as support.

This would be the fifth time I'd catch Maiden, but this time around,

I was on a credential for the daily. It was a genuine "Is this happening?" type of feeling as I was heading up to the photo pit. I ran into several sets of friends seated on the floor. I even assisted one friend by loading his camera with film.

As anticipated, Maiden delivered a great set with serious production and great stage lighting from the photographer's standpoint. The standard three songs was the photography protocol for the night.

Maiden's vocalist, Bruce Dickinson, was sporting a sci-fi-themed black leather outfit that consisted of tubes with blinking lights. He was the showman who never disappointed with his enthusiasm, stage energy, and command of the crowd.

Dickinson came out to the center of the stage and placed his left foot on one of the monitors. His left arm was resting on his thigh with microphone in hand. There was a single spotlight on him and a single spot behind him. This created a cameo lighting effect with everything else around him going black. The backlight was highlighting several stray long hairs with a rim light.

The photo looked great in black and white once printed. The picture was cropped down to just a headshot with Dickinson looking off to his right.

Needless to say, I was pleased with the final print. I thought to myself that if I ever had an opportunity to meet Bruce Dickinson, I would get a 16×20 signed with a silver paint pen and framed.

The spring semester did present some challenges since I was now the photo editor. As spring break approached, I was mentally spent. I was so spent that I didn't even want to cover the SWC basketball tournament at Reunion Arena. Instead, I opted to hop a flight to Austin a day or two later.

From there, I hung out in San Marcos for five days with good friends, including Lee.

I attended a photography class at Southwest Texas State with one of my friends, Christy. I even ran into a fellow classmate from high school. He was surprised to see me there and asked what I was doing down at Southwest Texas State. I told him I was hanging out during my spring break.

I stayed until Friday. That's when I caught a ride with Lee, and we came back to Fort Worth. That night, the aspiring Ed Banger and MaccaM team would catch Saxon at the legendary Longhorn Ballroom in Dallas.

Brian at the counter of Dunkin Donuts in Austin. Lee and Brian made a stop to get road munchies before heading back to Dallas for the Saxon show that night at the Longhorn Ballroom.

The most memorable part of that night was not seeing Saxon, but meeting and talking with Biff Byford after the show. It was something that wasn't even on my radar several years earlier when Biff put my banner on the drum riser in 1983.

Still to this day, I am not a fan of being in front of the camera; I belong behind it. However, I made an exception. I had to get a photo of myself with one of my high school heroes.

There we were, Biff and I, in front of the bus. Lee was ready to take the photo, but the camera malfunctioned. There was Biff, pointing at the camera while waiting for it to fire, ready for the photo. This happened several times. When I think back on this encounter, it's hilarious. It was a camera *Spinal Tap* moment. The vocalist for the mighty Saxon had been kind enough to take a photo with a camera that kept malfunctioning.

Saxon vocalist Biff Byford and Brian patiently wait for the camera to work. Lee took this photo in front of the Saxon tour bus.

It needs to be mentioned that my concert partner, Sammy, was also attending Southwest Texas State. I made sure I gave her contact information to Lee when he arrived for his first semester. Their friendship remains solid to this day.

When I reflect upon it with John, it's amazing how a simple gesture of kindness—giving people who were, at the time, complete strangers a ride home from a concert—birthed an incredible circle of friends. These friendship bonds are unbreakable.

I am sure John and I would have eventually run into each other out and about in the local scene, but whether the friendship would be in the same place is an important question, a deep thought.

It's the same for Lee and me. If I wasn't thumbing through Motorhead records on that day at that hour at the record store, would Lee and I be as close as friends as we are? That's another deep thought. I was also the in-between for Lee and Sammy's friendship.

———◇———

Besides photographing concerts for the major daily, the spring semester also presented additional photographic opportunities at TCU.

Every semester, the student TCU magazine *Image* was published. I don't think it was published more than once a semester when I was a student.

Being part of an issue for *Image* was a special opportunity for students to be published in a glossy magazine format, not a newspaper. That meant having tear sheets from a magazine for the portfolio, not just newsprint tear sheets.

For the March 1987 issue, I was assigned to photograph the story art for a feature. The story was about TCU students in the School of Education. The students were student teachers working in the field. Their student teaching experiences were one of the last things on the checklist before graduation.

I was asked if I wanted to shoot the assignment. It sounded fun and had the potential of producing some nice photos. I accepted without hesitation.

I phoned the contact in the School of Education to see where the education majors were doing their student teaching. When I was speaking with the contact, I was told there was a math student teacher at Paschal High School and a PE student teacher at Arlington Heights High School. There was also a social studies student teacher at Wedgewood Middle School. I really liked that choice because I attended that middle school.

During our conversation, she said, "Oh, this sounds good. We have a student band teacher at Southwest High School."

I have never had such a sly grin on my face while on the phone. I said, "That's the one."

The education department contact said she would let the band teacher know someone from TCU was coming out to photograph the student band teacher; she just didn't say who.

Back in the day, security at schools was minimal. If I went to a school now, I would need to check in at the office, present my driver's license, get a sticker, peel off the back, and stick it to my shirt.

The class was maybe a 10:00 band class. It was not the symphonic band class. More likely, it was the concert band.

As I walked through the outer doors, the band director was exiting the inner doors. Our eyes met.

I said, "Hello, Mr. Denison. I am here to photograph Mr. Angler, the student band teacher, for *Image* magazine." I was very pleasant and professional and kept walking. Obviously, I'd walked through those doors hundreds of times as a high school student.

The look on his face was priceless, like, "I can't believe this is happening."

I still laugh at the moment I walked into the band room.

As soon as I walked through the doors and was visible, I heard several voices at the same time say, "Brian!"

I nodded to the student band teacher, did a quick introduction of myself, and found a vacant seat that was ironically located near the saxophone section.

I behaved. I had to hold back on any laughter or slight giggles during my visit with the most intense straining of my facial muscles and gestures. I was professional about everything, but the thoughts running through my head were so funny. I made sure I didn't cause any distractions even though members of the saxophone section were so happy I was in there.

The deal with the student band teacher was that he always pushed his glasses up because they would slide down. I took one photo of that happening. The saxophone section snickered, so I decided not to take any more photos of him doing that.

Unfortunately, Wednesday wasn't in this particular band class. She was in the higher-level band. That would've been the cherry topping of the whole experience.

I was told at one point after I graduated that younger saxophone section members considered me legendary. I was just one of those different types of band students—a cool kid in the band who liked to have fun, lots of fun. At the same time, though, I was a solid sax player from start to finish or from low B flat to high F. I was even able to get my instrument a half step higher to F sharp, a note that is in what is known as the *altissimo range*.

These days, saxophones have a key that allows for that extra half note to F sharp, and some even have a second key that allows for a high G.

I did not use any of those photos for the story. I just wanted to go up to my old stomping grounds in the band hall and see some old friends.

As for the story about student teachers, I went to a middle school in the eastern part of Fort Worth and photographed an English teacher. Actually, it was on Valentine's Day of 1987. The classroom was on the second floor and had great natural light coming through the window. I captured some nice images but didn't realize how nice until the *Image* magazine photo editor looked at my negatives and pointed one photo out.

Once the image was printed and I was able to finalize a print, we looked over it. We discussed all the details that made the picture a great photo. His words, not mine. I secured a portfolio photo in a magazine. To this day, that story and my photo on glossy magazine paper is still in my photography and writing samples book.

Years later when I was working on my M.Ed., I presented an enlarged photo of that picture to one of my professors as part of a semester project. I felt at that point that I had come full circle, but in reality, the M.Ed. was just a stop in my orbit.

The two issues of *Image* magazine, spring and fall of 1987, were entered into competition in 1988. I had no idea this happened until one day around February 1988.

I was informed that my photo of the student teacher had won third place, Best Feature Photo, in the Southwestern Journalism

Conference.

I had my first award-winning photograph, and I had only been shooting seriously as a student for one year. It blew my mind how much I had improved—enough to win an award for that territory.

TWENTY-FOUR

WILD ART, THE TEXXAS JAM, AND WILLIE

THE SUMMER OF 1987 saw Sweet Savage still searching for the elusive record deal. At one point, the vocalist, Joey C. Jones, went to LA and formed a band called Pal Joey. The band was turning heads pretty quickly and was offered a four-album deal with Warner Brothers. The four band members couldn't agree on the percentage split, so the band was dissolved, and Jones returned to Sweet Savage.

As for Pantera, they landed and settled on a new vocalist. It was shocking to me that Glaze departed the band in late 1986. There were reasons circulating as to why he left, but I don't want to speculate.

Three vocalists came and went through the Pantera camp after Glaze's departure. Two had a prior history as a vocalist with the band, and one, Matt La'Mour, was a fresh face.

La'Mour didn't step away from the stage. He now fronts the

respectable Zeppelin tribute act Zoso.

For the fourth and final candidate, word was they had this eighteen-year-old vocalist from New Orleans, and he was a beast on stage. The "Kid," as people referred to him, had to be seen. His name was Phil Anselmo. It was evident from the get-go that with the new vocalist, the band was heading into a heavier direction. Songs like "Start the Fire" and "Ton of Bricks" by Metal Church became set staples. One new addition that caught me off guard was "Stellar Masters" by Malice. That was something I wasn't expecting.

Eventually, Slayer songs started creeping into the set.

———◇———

I was shooting more for the major daily during the summer. Cruising around for weather features and "wild art" was a normal daily routine.

One photo that sticks out was a kid, about ten years old, sitting in one of the chairs on his front porch. He was crocheting with his hands. As he was doing this, he continued to wipe the sweat off his forehead.

Even though he was sitting in the shade of the porch, he had a large golf umbrella attached to his chair. This only made the photo more interesting and a bit different.

The following day, the photo ran as the cover photo for the local/state section. It was always a nice feeling and a sense of accomplishment, seeing my work front and center of a section.

Somewhere in my collection of tear sheets is the local/state section from the day this photo ran. Today, the boy would be in the neighborhood of forty-seven years old.

For the rock fan, summers in Texas meant one thing—the Texxas Jam.

The official title of the annual summer music event was the Texxas World Music Festival, and it was held at the Cotton Bowl in Dallas. The term "Texxas Jam" was just a nickname.

There was one year, 1981, that the Jam was held in Houston at the Astrodome and the headliner was REO Speedwagon.

The next three years, 1982, 1983, and 1984, saw the Jam splitting time between Houston and Dallas with one day off between the dates.

It was 1985's Jam that saw the event returning for the final three years. In 1988, there was a stadium rock event at the Cotton Bowl, but it was the Monsters of Rock.

I have many fond memories of sitting around the pool at the YMCA with friends and listening to the radio broadcast of the Jam. Throughout the day, disc jockeys would do a live spot while a band was playing in the background. The rock concert-craving kid in me during my middle school days always enjoyed those live spots.

As a high school student, the thought of attending the Texxas Jam was a pipe dream. It was something that I really wanted to do.

When I was working in the record store as a junior in 1982, I can vividly recall vacuuming the carpet after closing while listening to the radio when Journey hit the stage. Steve Perry's voice just soared as he greeted Dallas.

If in 1982, someone would have told me that five years later I would be photographing the Texxas Jam, I wouldn't have believed it. Yet it happened.

I was assigned to photograph that coveted mecca for me—the Texxas Jam. It was a bizarre feeling, driving to Dallas and picking up the credentials several days in advance.

The day before the Jam, one of the local rock radio stations held a charitable softball game with radio station staff and members from several of the bands. Brian Wheat from Tesla took part, as well as a member or two from a band called Farrenheit. I don't recall any others but Robert Englund, the actor who played Freddy Krueger, was out and about on the field. He was the emcee for the Jam.

He wasn't in costume with full makeup, but he did have the finger blades for his right hand.

Since I was photographing the Jam and was shooting for the major daily, I had access to the field. I stayed back and out of the way. The 300 mm 2.8 lens I was using helped to get some nice photos from a distance.

I do have a photo of Englund pointing at me with his left hand, but he didn't have the blades on that hand. At one point, I caught a photo of him scratching his right butt cheek with the blades. I found that amusing.

Later in the game, one of the more visible jocks was up to bat. He was sporting bright-colored, flashy board shorts. As he was positioning himself in the batter's box, someone came out from the dugout and "pantsed" him in front of the crowd. His board shorts were yanked down to below his knees, revealing his Texas flag men's bikini briefs. After the game, he came up to me and said in a firm voice, "Nobody sees those photos."

It was like, "Whatever."

I still have the negatives and still laugh when I look at them.

The following day was the Texxas Jam. It's something that I had dreamed about attending for several years. I was going to be there as a member of the working media, properly credentialed. It was hard to believe.

The lineup for the Jam consisted of Boston, Aerosmith, Whitesnake, Poison, Tesla, and Farrenheit.

The protocol for us was to hang out in the press box during the bands' sets. As standard, we received the first three songs for each band. A representative, or media liaison, would walk us down from the press box and through the back end of the Cotton Bowl, behind the stage, and down the ramp.

I had told one of my friends, Jimmy, that I was going to be there shooting. He told me he was going to make it to the barricade for Tesla.

Sure enough, he did.

Along with other photographers, I was in the barricade area waiting for Tesla to hit the stage. Then I heard someone yelling, "Brian, Brian, Brian."

I looked over, and who did I see but my friend Jimmy.

He then shouted, "I told you I would make it."

Unfortunately, I do not have a photo of this moment. I was situated more toward the stage left of the barricade, whereas he was more toward the center of the crowd. There were too many obstacles and obstructions to capture a clear photo.

To say I wasn't nervous about being there would be false. I was petrified, to say the least. The last thing I wanted was to do something that would get my pass yanked.

After shooting one of the bands—maybe Poison—I was walking up the ramp, away from the stage.

When I looked up the ramp, I saw Steven Tyler waltzing down. He was bebopping, jiving, moving, and grooving as he was walking toward me. He was wearing the outfit from the "Dude Looks Like a Lady" music video. I froze, and my eyes locked on him as he walked past me.

I wanted to say hello or something. I wanted to tell him that Aerosmith played an integral part in my formative middle school years. Unfortunately, I didn't. Why? I was afraid of doing something to get my pass yanked.

When he passed and I watched him walk down the ramp away from me, I felt a huge sadness drape over me. I'd just missed my chance to meet Steven Tyler, one of my middle school rock star heroes.

It was an experience I never forgot and still regret to this day, as I wasn't assertive enough just to say hello.

———— ❖ ————

Besides photographing the Texxas Jam in June, I would cover another music festival two weeks later. This time it wasn't a huge rock festival; it was more of a gathering of country folks. The event—Willie Nelson's 4th of July Picnic.

It was held at stadiums in previous years, but this Willie's picnic was held in a big open area thirty miles north of Waco at Carl's Corner, a local truck stop. On top of the roof covering, the fuel pumps near the entrance were six 10-foot dancing frogs. The frogs were nicknamed the Tango Frogs.

I was expecting a huge turnout and actually went down the night before, found a pasture to park in, and slept in my truck. Not far from my truck was another truck. This guy had his radio playing all night on some AM station. It was very annoying, and honestly, I didn't get much sleep.

The turnout wasn't as large as I was expecting. I do know that I needed to leave early to bring the film back for processing and printing. I missed Willie Nelson's afternoon press conference. It was something I had actually been looking forward to.

Willie did play a mid-morning set, and I was able to grab some images of him that were published the following day.

TWENTY-FIVE

THE SEIZED OPPORTUNITY

THE FALL OF 1987 marked the tenth anniversary of Lynyrd Skynyrd's plane crash. Looking back at that time frame, it was hard to believe that ten years had passed. In that time, I had gone from being a kid in sixth grade who was discovering music to being enrolled at TCU. Along with that, I was now a working media member, photographing a few concerts on media credentials.

It was announced that the surviving members of Skynyrd would do a Tribute Tour. That would include Gary Rossington, Billy Powell, Leon Wilkenson, Artemus Pyle, and Ed King. Fronting the band would be Johnny Van Zant, Ronnie Van Zant's youngest brother.

The show was scheduled for Sunday, November 1, 1987, at Reunion Arena. There was no way I was going to miss this. At this point, Skynyrd's music still had a huge impact on me.

With my ticket in hand, I was heading out the door to the show. My father asked me where I was going, and I told him. He expressed displeasure that I was going to a concert on a school night even though I was twenty-two at the time. I said that I wasn't going to miss this show as I walked out the door. I felt a bit of guilt for flatly defying my father for the first time.

I made it to the show and was walking around the concourse area. I purchased the tour book from the merchandise booth, as I wanted something more than just a shirt.

After this, I ran into a fellow photographer, Mike, who's name I'd seen in print many times and vice versa. This was the same photographer who took the Hard Rock Cafe jacket presentation photos.

He asked how I was doing, and I said, "Okay." He sensed something was up and asked what was going on. I explained to him how I'd defied my father for the first time. I was a little bummed about it.

He looked at me and said, "You need this more than me," and with that, he pulled off his VIP pass and handed it to me. He then walked me to the elevator that would take me to the tunnels and dressing rooms on the floor level of the arena.

The Lynyrd Skynyrd VIP pass that was given to Brian that allowed him to meet the band prior to their show.

The reason he had the pass was that he photographed a lot of the backstage fan meetings for the record companies. His business partner at the time was already down there.

In the VIP meeting area, I met Billy Powell, Leon Wilkenson, Artemus Pyle, and Ed King, the man who wrote "Sweet Home Alabama." I had those members and another individual sign my tour book.

As Artimus was signing my book, he got called away for a huge group photo, so I only have his first name, but I was fine with that.

Gary Rossington and Johnny Van Zant were not there, nor was Allen Collins.

On January 23, 1990, Allen Collins was involved in a car crash that paralyzed him from the waist down. The accident had limited the mobility of his arms and hands. He would no longer play guitar on stage. The wreck also claimed the life of his girlfriend. It was a sad incident all the way around.

During their set, Allen Collins was wheeled out on stage in his wheelchair to make an appearance. It was truly a heartbreaking sight.

It was strange hearing those classic Skynyrd songs being played with the youngest Van Zant singing them. The most surreal part of the night for me was when the band played "Free Bird," but there were no vocals. Adding to the emotional impact of the song, Ronnie Van Zant's black hat with the rattlesnake headband was placed on the microphone. It was the audience that sang "Free Bird."

A double live album from this tour was released in March of 1988 called *Southern by the Grace of God*. Of the eleven tracks, six were recorded at the Reunion Arena show. There was the show opener "Workin' For MCA," which followed the introduction by Lacy Van Zant, the father of the Van Zant brothers, and then "That Smell," "Comin' Home," "You Got That Right," and "What's Your Name?" The cherry on top, "Free Bird," with the audience singing on the album, was from the Reunion Arena show.

It's just crazy when I sit and think about it. "Free Bird" was my first seriously favorite song, and to see it performed by several of the members who recorded the song was magical. Add on top of that being part of the audience that sang the lyrics to music that night at Reunion Arena, and it was something I couldn't even imagine.

By this time, I was getting a decent collection of photo passes that I was attaching to my mirror. One afternoon, my brother came into my room to ask me something. He was looking at the passes, paused, and asked, "Did you meet Skynyrd?" I said yes and showed him the tour book. He couldn't believe his eyes and immediately called one of his friends who was a huge Skynyrd fan and told him.

I never showed my father the tour book, as I didn't want to cause any friction from flat-out defying him by attending the show.

It's crazy when I hold the album in my hand and know that I am part of the audience on some of the tracks. If there was only one live album I could be part of, Skynyrd's *Southern by the Grace of God* was it.

Now, the Skynyrd album wasn't my first live album to be part of. That distinction goes to Molly Hatchet's *Double Trouble Live* released in 1985.

I have been to shows where videos were recorded, but there's just something about claiming with certainty that you are part of a live album. It puts the passion for music on a whole different level.

I really don't give *Southern by the Grace of God* album very much attention. I think I have listened to it once since adding it to my collection. I really can't give a reason why the album is not part of my regular rotation of music selections. Maybe it has something to do with what occurred leaving the house before the show, but I can't put a finger on it.

I will say that hearing another Van Zant singing those classic Skynyrd songs doesn't appeal to me. The only voice that belongs on those songs is Ronnie Van Zant's voice.

Sadly, all of those members, Gary Rossington, Billy Powell, Leon Wilkenson, Ed King, and Allen Collins, who were at Reunion Arena that night have now passed. The only surviving member of the classic Skynyrd lineup is drummer Artemus Pyle.

Besides being blessed with the opportunity to meet these musicians who were a huge part of my rock music discoveries early on, my lack of assertiveness was no longer lingering over me. That cloud of shyness was gone.

The fall semester of 1987 saw me dipping my toes into education by enrolling in the class Psychology of Teaching and Learning.

Somewhere deep in my soul, there was a lingering desire to be an educator. Unfortunately, this class quickly diminished it.

In all honesty, the professor's delivery of content to the class was a big failure. Instead of presenting the material in lecture format with students taking notes, material was presented in the form of "graphic organizers" on an overhead projector. This is an approach I saw twenty years later in my first year as an educator in 2007.

At the time, the presentation of the class material in this manner was so foreign to me. It's not like we were learning content such as science or language arts. To this day, I still can't figure out why the material in this entry-level education course was being presented that way. Just lecture the students and let us take notes and enter into a class discussion.

I did not learn one thing from that course. It made being an educator toxic to me for twenty years.

There was one funny thing from the class that came from watching and observing a high school journalism class. It's not that the kids thought I was a narc. It was a football coach who thought I was a student.

One morning I was wearing straight legs with high tops, a sweatshirt, and my denim Hard Rock Cafe jacket. As I was walking through the parking lot at an odd time, a football coach approached me and asked me where I was going.

I told him I was going to class.

He then asked me why I was late, and I told him because I got out of class. He asked if I had a pass, and I told him that I didn't need one.

He started to get a bit agitated. At this point I told him I was a TCU student heading to the journalism class for my weekly observation.

I then mentioned to him things weren't looking great for TCU football-wise and rattled off their record. That convinced him, and he let me go.

I became a mentor to a photographer in this journalism class. He now shoots for Live Nation in DFW. When I photograph Live Nation shows, I see him. If there's someone new in the group of photographers for the night who does not know the story, he will tell it. There's always a laugh or two when we revisit those days.

In October 1987, Tipper Gore brought her PMRC campaign to TCU for an evening presentation at Ed Landreth Hall on the TCU campus. The PMRC was still in its early stages, but I really wanted to see this presentation for myself.

I covered the press conference she had prior to her presentation. I just had no idea what direction or angle or presentation would go. She based her speech on her book, *Raising PG Kids in an X-Rated Society*, released in early 1987.

Gore talked about how violence is portrayed against women in the entertainment industry and how the media represents women as objects of violence.

She had a slideshow to help hammer her point home. On a large projection screen behind her, she clicked through images of sexually explicit and violent album covers, as well as pictures from concerts and magazines.

My take from the presentation was that Gore was a bit misleading. I recall the thought that a high percentage of her images and album covers were from European metal bands and magazines. The albums and publications were imports and difficult to find. Maybe in a large metropolitan area, there might be one or two stores that would carry those items.

The best example I remember was Mercyful Fate's *Nuns Have No Fun* album. In 1987, I had only seen that vinyl release once before, and that was in 1984 at Pipe Dream Records in Arlington. That's it.

Her concern was that all this imagery was aimed at young children fourteen and under. Her terms in regard to young children and age fourteen really haven't aged well over the years. Kids fourteen years old then and now are at opposite ends of the spectrum.

Twenty-Six

Road to Speech Comm

By the end of the fall semester, I declared a major in speech communications with a target date to graduate in December of 1989. I would continue to spend the majority of time in the Moudy Building, but instead of being on the second floor surrounded by journalism majors, I would now be camping out on the third floor surrounded by speech comm majors.

With that being said, I would begin the lower-level speech comm classes. Now, all my classes for the spring semester would not be for my major. I would take a class that I deemed a perfect fit as an elective.

Introduction to Production was the weeding out course for the radio, TV, and film majors. It dealt with the basics related to Radio TV Film, or RTVF for short. The edge I had taking the class was my photography background as well as hanging out and being involved in the local music scene.

I was actually looking forward to taking Introduction to

Production. A lot of my interest in stereo equipment, music, tape, photography, live music audio, and other things related to this class. The only content that posed a bit of a challenge for me was related to microphones and the different types. Everything else was smooth sailing.

A week out from the first exam, the professor warned the class not to wait and start studying the night before. Even though I was familiar with and knew the content being covered, I started studying that night. As elementary as it sounds, I made flashcards from index cards, not just for the first test but every exam during the semester. A week out from each test, he would provide a review sheet, with the majority of information being terms and definitions. There was a lot of technical terminology taught in the class.

When it came time for the final in the spring, the review packet for the exam consisted of seven or eight pages, double-sided with terms, definitions, and other technical material. It took me several days' worth of work to complete all my flashcards for the final. My stack of cards sat at four inches in height. That's quite a bit.

I can't say why I didn't keep those cards just to have for reference, but I do regret not doing so. It would be something to look through them years later and see how the technology has changed.

I walked away with a B in the class. I was a bit disappointed, as I thought I could earn an A.

After taking that class, I realized that I wanted to major in RTVF, but time was not on my side. With all the labs required for that class, I would not have been able to bang out that major and graduate by December 1989. Logistically, it wasn't possible.

One of our early assignments was to watch Super Bowl XXII. We were tasked with making a diagram of the various camera angles used during the broadcast. If I remember correctly, this was before the camera above the field was used.

The number of camera angles used for that broadcast, maybe eight, ten, or twelve is archaic per today's standards. The only way to be certain was to watch the game again.

With a quick search, I found the broadcast. I would just need to block off nearly three hours of time to rewatch the game.

For those curious, the Washington Redskins defeated the Denver Broncos, 42–10. Denver jumped to a 10–0 lead by the end of the first quarter. Unfortunately, that was it. Washington opened a can of beatdown and posted 35 points in the second quarter. Denver never recovered—not even a field goal for the rest of the game. To add insult to injury, Washington posted an additional 7 points in the fourth quarter.

These days, it's normal to see numerous camera angles at the Super Bowl. Things have seriously changed in regard to TV production and broadcasts of sporting events.

On a sad note, my brother's cat, who we'd had for nineteen and a half years, passed away one night that week while I was studying for the RTVF final.

When you're twenty-two years old and the cat has been in the family for that long, it's difficult. All her little quirks and routines were normal feline behaviors to me. I would always ask friends if their cat did this or that. Many times, the answer was no.

She was a great tabby cat named Tiger, but that night sucked.

———◇———

I was still shooting for the major daily. Probably the best assignment I had for the entire spring semester was covering the NHRA Winter Nationals at the Texas Motorplex forty-five minutes south of DFW.

As the assignment was explained to me, the teams involved were the "big boys" of racing. This was serious stuff.

When I arrived at the track, I needed to check in at the media building. As I made my way to check in, I heard deafening roars from the engines of cars on their quarter-mile run. With each race, I wondered if I'd made a mistake taking the assignment.

The assigned media credential allowed me inside the fence. I was against the concrete barrier that separated the grass from the track. If I had Go Go Gadget arms, I would be able to reach over and touch the track.

When a race occurred, I would get blasted with soundwaves from the vehicle. This was not a one-time deal; it would be for each race, one after another. Ten to fifteen feet separated me from the vehicles on the track. These were not mom-and-pop garage restorations; these cars were the real deal Top Fuel and Funny Cars with big-time sponsors.

My 180mm 2.8 and 28mm 2.8 and the F3 body were the pieces of gear for this unique assignment. Of course, fresh sets of earplugs were in my camera bag as well. The equipment allowed me to get close or capture a nice overall of the track. The gear also allowed me to keep a safe and respectable distance.

By the end of the day, I was literally exhausted from being hammered on a consistent basis. Plus, my clothes had black soot on them, and I smelled of racing exhaust and fuel.

———◦◦———

I continued to photograph for the major daily during the summer. Again, there were two big assignments I covered, the first of which was the Monsters of Rock Festival on July 3, 1988. It was a big outdoor touring music festival, but it wasn't the Texxas Jam.

Van Halen was the headliner. The other bands were the Scorpions, Dokken, Metallica, and Kingdom Come. The first band on stage was Kingdom Come followed by Metallica. I shot those two bands before I had to leave with the film.

Prior to the start of the Kingdom Come's set, photographers were granted ninety seconds to photograph the band in the backstage area. The only thing I recall was the vocalist Lenny Wolfe eating grapes off the stem like some Greek or Roman VIP. The only thing missing was the toga. Honestly, I thought it was a bit silly.

I have never been a fan of Kingdom Come from the first single they released. I still feel that way.

When Metallica hit the stage with "Creeping Death," they were a whole different beast to be reckoned with. They tore it up.

After Metallica's three songs, I had to leave and take the film back for processing and deadline submission. I missed the rest of the Metallica set, Dokken, and the Scorpions. I did make it back out there, but Van Halen was on stage. I didn't stay very long. I just wanted to say I saw Hagar on stage with Van Halen. That's the extent of it.

———•◦•———

The second big event was the opening night of the Starplex Amphitheater on July 23, 1988. It's located in Fair Park where the Cotton Bowl sits, as well as the grounds for the Texas State Fair that's held every year in the fall.

Over the years, several corporations have had naming rights. Originally, it was called the Coca-Cola Starplex. After that, naming rights became a revolving door. Other names included Starplex Amphitheater, Smirnoff Music Centre, Superpages.com Center, Gexa Energy Pavilion, Starplex Pavilion, and Dos Equis Pavilion—the current name.

I would come to have a love-hate relationship with the venue. It's been roughly twenty years since I last walked through the gates for a show.

Rod Stewart headlined that first night. I don't recall an opener. What can I say about Rod the Mod? He's a smooth entertainer who just glides across the stage while delivering an outstanding set.

Obviously, I didn't stay for the entire night, as photos were needed for the show review.

Since I had declared speech comm as my major, I needed to start chipping away at the classes if I wanted to graduate with my target date of December 1989.

The first class I needed to take was a basic speech class, Introduction to Speech or something along those lines. TCU wasn't offering this class during a summer session, so I enrolled at the junior college to bang out the class.

I basically slid through the class with little or no effort. Everything that was being taught was the same content I'd been taught in my high school speech class. I didn't blow off the class even though I could have. I took the class very seriously and did my best with each speech we had to present.

I was amazed at how many people were truly terrified about getting up in front of the class and speaking. Their nerves would get the best of them. They would stumble over their words, look down, giggle. I was amazed at how many students would use the phrase "you know" during their speech. It's actually crazy how often people do that. It's something about verbal communication that has never really gone away. Just like in high school, the first experience to get up in front of the class was Introduction to Speech. Each student basically had sixty seconds to introduce themselves to their classmates. When I look back at the students introducing themselves, no student really stood out for me to remember to this day.

I do have a vivid memory of one student listening to me and

looking right at me as I made a comment in a class discussion. I just remember she had this fixated look in her eyes. She just smiled at me when I was talking. I remember she told the class at one point she worked for Cheddar's Restaurant in Arlington.

If I am traveling westbound on I-20 through the west part of Arlington, the restaurant is visible from the highway. Each time I see it, I am reminded of my classmate in my Introduction to Speech in the summer of 1988.

In the fall at TCU, I would start loading up on the speech comm classes. These included Business and Professional Speaking, Interviewing, Listening, Instructional Communication, Interpersonal Communication, Oral Interpretation to Literature, Reader's Theater, Organizational Communication, and the Intro to Speech I took in the summer. There may be several other classes, but I am not able to actually recall them.

As for shooting for the university daily, I passed the photo-editor torch, as I needed to concentrate on my classes and stay on track to graduate on my target date.

It was a different vibe. I was becoming more of a news hound, chasing down news or whatever needed to be done, and others weren't at that point.

Images I captured during the fall semester were entered into competition without my knowledge. One of my images earned first place, Division II, Newspaper News Photo, 1989. The photo was shot during the 1988 presidential campaign.

George H. W. Bush had come to TCU on a campaign stop to jog around the track with the College Republicans. All the photographers had to stay inside the track as the president and his security detail jogged around the track; they were not allowed to be anywhere else.

I knew that photographing from the top southwestern end of the Amon G. Carter Stadium would produce some nice images of everyone running on the track, as well as the press people inside the track.

Prior to running with the College Republicans, President Bush was stretching, and a reporter asked him a touchy question about Vice President Quayle. Bush didn't take too kindly to the question. He pointed directly at the reporter and responded in an agitated manner while he was still stretching.

I was on the ground at a low level on Bush's right side, and the reporter was off behind me to my left. I had perfect framing of Bush in my camera. I didn't think the photo was all that great, as it was a bit soft for me, but that didn't seem to matter to the judges.

The second award was for a feature photo I'd shot while cruising the campus on my beat.

Part of my route when I would look for feature photos around the campus included walking the hallways of the music building. This was the building that students majoring in music did a lot of their practicing in.

As I was heading toward the front doors, a member of the

janitorial staff was cleaning the windows on one of the front doors from the outside. I took a camera reading for the light on the woman cleaning the window. When I took the photo, the huge difference between the outside light and indoor light caused the doors on the inside to go solid black. The lady was framed perfectly in one of the two vertical windows. Everything came together for the photo, and the final image turned out fantastically.

During the fall, I noticed that my shooting was starting to change and evolve. I was paying attention to the surroundings in the photo as well as the subject. I considered this to be the turning point for me photographically.

As it was stated to me in the fall of 1986 at the TCU's women's soccer game, "Just shoot newspapers for a few years. You'll understand." I was starting to understand.

The point when it all clicked was during the TCU Basketball Media Day. A player was stretching or just lazing on the court to the side of the basket. I shot a wide-angle photo and included the "FROGS" painted in white on the end baselines in the photo. That's the exact moment when it clicked with me photographically about shooting from an editorial aspect. I now understood.

Twenty-Seven

Final Countdown

I HAVE READ TWO very powerful messages out in the world. The first is one of those quotes that will make you stop and start reflecting. It's an anonymous quote, but it's very deep. The quote reads as follows: "At some point in your childhood, you and your friends went outside to play together for the last time and nobody knew it."

Kids these days may not even begin to understand the significance of that quote. I think it's a rarity if kids actually meet up outside, play, or explore at all.

The time for me to move on had arrived. At some point, I would develop my last roll of film and print my last photo in the darkroom at TCU. I just didn't realize it at the time.

Academics took front and center when placed next to my camera. Yes, I still shot, but it wasn't at the point or to the extent I had been doing over the last year or so. I did miss photographing, but I needed to make that sacrifice so that I would be able to graduate.

Then I would be free of the academic chains for several years.

The second quote comes from Uriah Heep's song "Circle of Hands," and a line from this song is deeply thought-provoking. Late in the song, the lyrics say, "And today is only yesterday's tomorrow." The song comes from Uriah Heep's 1972 album *Demons and Wizards*. It's just brilliantly poetic and absolutely true.

I made it through the spring semester, but—me being me—I always had to go above and beyond.

There was one class I had, Instructional Communication, whose major project consisted of a fifteen-minute presentation. The parameters stated the presentation needed to be evenly split between an oral presentation and a presentation with visual/audio aids, which was no problem for me. I am the type of person who likes to make a mind-blowing statement when I present. This project may have been the birth of that trait in me.

As society approached the 1990s, there was a "major" concern in the United States best described as the "Satanic Panic." That's what my Instructional Communication project would be on, heavy metal and this panic.

I had access to vintage European metal band albums such as the first three Venom releases, Mercyful Fate's EP *Nuns Have No Fun*, Slayer's *Hell Awaits* and *Show No Mercy*, Demon, and many others. These things would be the foundation of the visual presentation portion. Along with the album covers, another component of that portion would be audio recordings I would acquire myself.

Radio evangelists such as Bob Larson helped to fuel this Satanic

Panic. He would have guests on his radio show who, according to him, would manifest into demons when he was trying to reach them with the word. I recorded these so-called manifestations.

To add a more sinister atmosphere and dark element to my presentation, I cut the lights to the classroom. Only window light from the end of the hallway and artificial light from the commons area illuminated the class. It wasn't much at all.

It should also be mentioned that the class wasn't set up like a normal classroom. Instead of desks, there were big comfy couches that, when joined together, formed a circle.

I actually recorded this presentation on cassette, but if only there was video—not of me, but of the little bubbly college girls. The looks on their faces said it all. They were terrified when the audio of these manifestations came over the classroom intercom. The whole classroom was dead silent except for the audio they were hearing.

Add to this the photos of these European metal albums and then photos of me and several metalhead friends wearing black concert shirts, and you had quite the show. By design, my presentation made a shocking statement, earning high marks for my efforts. A high five was in order for heavy metal.

With the speech comm major fully underway and December 1989 being the target date for graduation, I needed to take a summer school course. Whether it was a three-week or six-week course, I am unable to remember.

The class was Oral Interpretation to Literature, with the major grades coming from a group project as well as an individual project. My individual project consisted of my interpretation of Jeff Wayne's *War of the Worlds* album soundtrack.

I obtained my copy of the album after our band trip in 1982. Included with the album was a booklet with the story. That booklet was a tremendous help when it came time for me to analyze and interpret the narrative and dialogue of the soundtrack.

When my project was complete, it was somewhere in the area of being a twenty-three-page analysis. Some students in the class said I spent way too much effort and time to produce a paper of that length. What I learned from that project is that I had taken the task very seriously and was proud of what I'd created. Somewhere I still have the analysis.

Also during the summer, I had to take a step back and look at things. I was asked to shoot as a staff member for three weeks during the summer for a suburban daily. I really wanted to, but I was at a point where I wanted to perform the best I could academically.

I was able to contribute to the daily, but not to the amount they were hoping I would. My takeaway from shooting that summer for the daily was a front-page photo spread of the city's 4th of July Parade. I was really proud of that, as the photo package made for a great inclusion in my portfolio.

There was one semester left—the fall of 1989. Then it would be all over. It was hard to believe that a college degree was a mere three months away.

———◦———

As mentioned, academics were front and center. Music was unfortunately pushed to the side. It was something difficult to do, but this may have been one of those first lessons in adulting. Missing a show here or there was severe punishment to the music lover in me.

There was a show on Sunday, September 17, 1989, at the Starplex in Dallas. There was only one band I wanted to see that day—Bad English—but academics took precedence over live music. It was a day our group in Reader's Theater had a study session for our major semester project.

The band, to me, was a supergroup. It featured three members of The Babys, John Waite, Jonathan Cain, and Ricky Phillips; Neal Schon from Journey; and drummer Deen Castronova. It needs to be noted that Cain was in Journey after The Babys and is credited with writing "Don't Stop Believin'." With the lineup, I wasn't surprised by the strength of the material on the debut album. To this day, I still think it's one of the strongest debut albums, but others may not agree. Some may say the music was too polished and slick.

I never was able to see the band live even though they came through town a few more times. Unfortunately, I have yet to see John Waite live, the voice of The Babys. Schedule-wise, it just has never worked out for me.

We had a great group of people in our Reader's Theater one-off troupe.

As I have mentioned, I like to do things in a big way. Fortunately, the other four members in our Reader's Theater group were on board with a big idea.

The class as a whole was divided into groups. I think there were five in total.

The semester project consisted of a major assignment that would have to be presented to the gifted and talented school of elementary kids on campus at TCU.

It was a given that every group was very nervous about having to do this project. When I look back on it, the project itself wasn't that big of a deal. The anxiety came from how much the project counted toward the class grade.

The hardest part of the project was coming up with what the group wanted to present. As a group, we decided that we would present a selection of *The House at Pooh Corner* in Reader's Theater style.

We also decided to be the first group to present at the end of September. Not only would we present to the elementary kids, but we would also present to the class. We knew as a group that since we were going first, Dr. Hall would go a bit easy on us. We also had the mindset that we were in a position to set the bar high, and that's what we did.

Instead of just sitting on stools and reading from our scripts, we were out and about with the kids. Not only that, but we also added costuming to our presentation. The other groups had no idea, as we kept our ideas and upgrades a tightly guarded secret.

The characters portrayed in our group were Pooh Bear, Tigger, Eeyore, Piglet, and yours truly as Christopher Robin.

Each group member fashioned their costume, as primitive as they were. We wanted to help the listeners, whether kids or adults, visualize the story we were telling.

There were times when instead of going to class, we could go off to a vacant room on the third floor of the Moudy Building and rehearse. If only we'd had tape rolling that one time when the *House at Pooh Corner* turned into the *House at Pooh Corner* rated R. It was so funny. I still laugh when I look back on it. To this day, the other two I am still in contact with still laugh about it as well.

The night before our presentation to the class, we had a study session. It wasn't a dress rehearsal but a meeting to make sure we were truly familiar with the script. The dedication of every group member was off the charts.

While we were rehearsing, we ordered two large pizzas to be delivered from a local, smaller pizza delivery place. I think one was Italian sausage and the other was pepperoni. Both pizzas were delicious, and we devoured them.

I must point out that when we left for the night, we were extremely anxious, and our nerves were rattling off the charts. They could have gotten Richter scale readings. Our marks from this one presentation would be 40 percent of the final grade, if memory serves me correctly.

Serious nervousness and stress for the delivery of a major project along with spicy Italian sausage pizza is not a great combination, especially when the project is set for a 9:00 a.m. presentation, and at 8:50, the Italian sausage hits.

Yes, minutes before showtime, this happened. Pooh Bear and Christopher Robin were unloading in stereo, side by side, with only a metal stall partition as separation.

We were literally counting down how many minutes until we had to be there.

Even though this Reader's Theater bonding between Pooh Bear and Christopher Robin occurred thirty-four years ago, the story still brings tears to our eyes from laughter.

As for the presentation, let me just say our group killed it. I remember a look on some faces of disbelief from fellow classmates as to how high we were setting the bar.

Some classmates could not believe what they were hearing and seeing. Our presentation was strong, smooth, and flawless. Each person knew their script.

Oddly, the rest of the presentations for the remainder of the semester all included costumes and, to a degree, some production. Our group had set the standard, and the other groups had to put in a lot of effort and time to reach our level. The best part was that since our group presented first, our project was done. We didn't have to worry about it at all. The only thing the group needed to do was to present it to the elementary kids. They loved it.

As an added bonus, the presentation was filmed on VHS. I should get the video transferred to DVD so I can watch it with Pooh Bear over a cheese pizza.

After everything was said and done, I swore off that pizza shop. I have not had a slice of their pizza since that fateful day in September 1989.

———◦———

One of my other memorable classes in my final semester was Organizational Communication. It was a Monday, Wednesday, and Friday class, and I sincerely enjoyed it. There were two sides to the organizational classes offered at TCU—the communication side and the business side.

The class was on the communication side of things. Each student needed to have a subscription to the *Wall Street Journal*. Articles would be assigned to read, and class discussions would occur on these articles.

There was one class session I specifically remember, not topic-wise but for another reason. I can't even tell you what the class discussion was that day. What I can tell you is that our professor split the class and had all the girls move to another room. He gave the topic and parameters for the discussion to each group.

The room wasn't set up like a standard classroom. It was more of a square-shaped discussion room with narrow tables placed together in a square. There were no windows. The room was small when compared to standard classrooms and lecture rooms. The arrangement of the tables allowed a roundtable format discussion. I think there may have been eight tables total.

Having gone to their rooms, the girls left the guys in our class. Even the professor was gone.

It wasn't even a full minute after the girls left that a rank, rotten, foul-smelling, warm cloud of butthole-burning methane started wafting through the air of the tightly sealed classroom. Anything that would make future NFL players gag was serious, and this was a serious release. The lone door to the discussion room was quickly opened to allow fresh air to enter.

One of the students near the door started opening and closing the door very quickly to bring in any amount of fresh air from the hallway and vacuum out any floating rankness.

Honestly, if fresh air could verbalize; I wouldn't have been surprised to hear an audible, "Nope, not going in there."

Guys pride themselves when it comes to their contribution to the 1 percent of the atmosphere which includes methane and other gasses. This contribution exceeded what any human should be able to contribute with a one-time release. The climate change people would have been mortified.

Our final consisted of reading eight *Wall Street Journal* articles, but only one was selected for the short-answer response. Two of the articles were back-to-back. I cut one article out and butchered the other on the backside; thus, I didn't read that article. The article I didn't read just happened to be the one on the final. That one little gamble cost me an A in the class. I should've just kept both with the whole page of the paper intact, but I really did not plan ahead.

Not even my perfect attendance in the class would sway the professor to award me that quarter of a point needed to earn the A.

Since there were no commencement exercises in December, I would walk in the May 1990 graduation ceremony.

TWENTY-EIGHT

HELLO, 1990 AND BEYOND

EVEN THOUGH I GRADUATED in December 1989, I enrolled in a class at Tarrant County Junior College to get the business side of Organizational Communication. As expected, I thoroughly enjoyed that class. I approached class discussions and studying as I did in my final semesters at TCU. I aced every single test, actually.

At one point in the last twenty years or so, I started downsizing clutter in my life, and college textbooks were on that list. I vaguely recall getting rid of the actual textbook from the Organizational Communication class. I regret tossing the book, but I had images of an additional textbook, the book for the TCJC class.

I went to a storage tub of books I have in a container and spotted an Organizational Communication book on top. This textbook was not from TCJC but from my Organizational Communication professor at TCU. I am not sure how I ended up with it and have a bit of guilt seeing his name written on the inside.

That spring semester of that one class came and went. From

that point, I just concentrated on shooting and carving a path for myself photographically.

It was becoming apparent that I would not be able to land a staff position at the major daily, or any other major daily, as a matter of fact. I did a lot of freelancing as an editorial photographer—covering bands, shooting corporate headshots, model portfolios, and anything else. I still continued shooting for the major daily as a freelancer but not as a staff member.

This period of photographing continued for a bit, but things started to change photographically in May 1992. I digress back one year, specifically to the NHL playoffs in the spring of 1991.

My good friend Jimmy played hockey as a kid at Will Rogers Coliseum in the 1970s. This is the same Jimmy who worked his way up to the barricade for Tesla at the Texxas Jam, shouting my name.

It needs to be mentioned that the sight of NHL games on TV in Texas at this time was basically nonexistent. Actually, hockey in Texas itself was a rarity at the time.

Jimmy told me I should come over and watch the NHL playoffs. He was able to get a pay-per-view special for the entire playoffs and Stanley Cup Finals for $35.

I only knew a few things about hockey. That would be recognizing logos for the Philadelphia Flyers, Boston Bruins, and Montreal Canadiens.

There was an additional recognizable feature for the Flyers. It was their curly-headed team captain and his two missing front teeth. His name—Bobby Clarke.

That was the extent of my hockey knowledge besides the object of the game, the puck, and playing the game on ice. I didn't even know which team to favor. As mentioned, I recognized the Boston Bruins logo, but Jimmy suggested I pull for the Pittsburgh Penguins. The Pens had a young Czech player named Jaromir Jagr with a flowing hockey-hair mullet. So I did pull for them, and I quickly became a faithful follower.

If broken down into the rounds, there would be the division semifinals, division finals, conference finals, and Stanley Cup Finals. If every matchup went the distance of seven games, there would have been 105 games for $35. Obviously, that didn't happen.

In total, 92 games were played from the start to the Cup being raised. That broke down to thirty-eight cents a game. Not a bad deal, actually.

In the division semifinals, three matchups went the distance. The matchups were Pittsburgh and New Jersey (4-3), St. Louis and Detroit (4-3) and Calgary and Edmonton (3-4). Teams that didn't go seven games and moved on included Boston, Montreal, Washington, Minnesota, and Los Angeles.

For the division finals, only Boston over Montreal (4-3) went the distance. As for the others, Pittsburgh over Washington (4-1), Minnesota over St. Louis (4-2) and Los Angeles over Edmonton (4-2).

Up next were the conference finals, which saw Pittsburgh and Boston facing off with the Penguins moving on after taking the series (4-2).

On the other end of the playoffs, the Minnesota North Stars with a young Mike Modano defeated the reigning Stanley Cup champions, the Edmonton Oilers (4-1). With the North Stars defeating the Oilers, that brought Edmonton's dynasty run of five Stanley Cups from 1983–84 through 1989–1990 to an end. Now my newly discovered favorite hockey team was in the Stanley Cup Finals.

I was at his house every night the Penguins and North Stars played. It was insanely exciting watching each of the six games that were played in the finals. When all was said and done, Mario Lemieux, Jaromir Jagr, Tom Barrasso, Kevin Stevens, Paul Coffey, and many others led the Penguins to their first Stanley Cup.

It was a magical experience to watch. I was hooked. September 1991 couldn't come fast enough for the 1991–92 NHL season to start.

I was a hockey fanatic and avid supporter before hockey came back to Texas.

———◦———

In the spring of 1992, I entered into a photography swimsuit competition. All I needed to do was to submit photos of a model sporting the company's swimwear. I took it a step further, and with the model's approval, we submitted a lumberjack-themed photo shoot.

The submission was selected, and both of us were invited to the finals in Redwood City, an area outside of San Francisco, for the week-long event.

Photographers were tasked with setting up sessions with the numerous contestants throughout the week. Once a session was completed, the images shot on slides were submitted for processing. The swimwear company would look through the images, make notes of the contestants, photographers and their ratings.

At certain times throughout the week, there would be "physical challenges" for both contestants and photographers to participate in. Upon completion of these challenges, additional points would be added to the ratings of participants.

I befriended a fellow photographer who had a vehicle. He asked if I would like to go to the mall and just get away. I accepted, as it was something different. While there, I saw a sportswear store that sold pro-team shirts, hats, jerseys, and anything else related to major league teams.

I went to a rack of hockey jerseys and started browsing through them. Something caught my eye that caused me to just stop flipping through the jerseys. I saw a black Pittsburgh Penguins hockey jersey. This is what the team would wear while on the road. I couldn't believe what I was looking at. It was a euphoric sight. I just stared for a minute or two. This was the first time I'd ever had a hockey jersey in hand, and it left the store with me.

At the front counter, there was a point of purchase set up. Under the front counter glass, there were San Jose Sharks hockey pucks. Again, I was frozen in a stare. At the time, the San Jose Sharks jersey was the hottest-selling logo. Many logos of minor league teams followed suit with a new logo that included a stick or another piece of equipment vital to the sport.

Not only was I walking out of the store with a Pittsburgh Penguins hockey jersey, but I would also be leaving with a hockey puck. I can't explain how something so basic just blew me away, but it did.

Those two things I purchased were my cool items from the trip to Redwood City. In fact, I still have them. The funny thing is, earlier in the week I had been approached by the film crew that was documenting the entire week. The production manager of the crew told me that they were instructed to get footage of me and to keep an eye on me. The owner of the company was watching me closely.

I arranged a time with the production crew to capture footage of me. I had found a contestant to photograph—actually, the mother of the contestant found me and asked me if I would do a photo session with her daughter.

I have a photo from the session of the production crew filming me as I was photographing the contestant. I am actually in the VHS tape that documented the week-long event.

After our session, I spent the majority of my free time with the mother and daughter. They were so nice.

The final night showcased a talent contest for the contestants. At the end of this finale for the week, the winner would be announced for the aspiring models as well as the photographers. The winners would fly out with the company for a catalog shoot at an exotic tropical location ideal for swimwear.

I placed second overall and missed out by a point or two. I did not participate in the physical challenges, as I was used to shooting all day. That point or two made the difference between me not walking away with the photographer title. Not placing first wasn't a career blunder or anything of the sort.

Maybe six weeks later, some serious news hit the Dallas-Fort Worth area. The announcement was front and center on the major daily. It was announced that the Central Hockey League was returning in the fall. I could not believe my eyes. That announcement superseded anything I'd ever experienced. My excitement reached a level I'd never experienced before.

Not even the yes that I could attend my first rock concert topped the return of the CHL. One thing was certain: I wanted to be the photographer for the Fort Worth team.

At the same time, the Pittsburgh Penguins were back in the Stanley Cup playoffs. The Pens would eventually defeat the Chicago Blackhawks in a four-game sweep. Pittsburgh would raise the Stanley Cup for the second year in a row.

As a Pens fan, life was grand while I watched another round of Stanley Cup playoffs. I was starting to devour any hockey literature

I could get my hands on, as the sport was returning to Texas.

One of the first hockey books I purchased was Tod Hartje's *From Behind the Red Line, An American Hockey Player in Russia*. Hartje was drafted by the Winnipeg Jets in round seven, 142nd player overall in the 1987 NHL Entry Draft.

Hartje, a Minnesota native, was the first North American–trained player to play in the Soviet Championship League in 1990 with Sokil Kyiv. His book is an amazing read, and an avid hockey fan would have a hard time putting the book down. I highly recommend it, and to this day, it's still one of the top hockey-related books in my library.

TWENTY-NINE

IT'S HOCKEY TIME IN TEXAS

THE REVIVED CHL WOULD have teams in Fort Worth, Dallas, Oklahoma City, Tulsa, Wichita, and Memphis. These cities had teams in the old CHL. The rivalries of neighboring cities would resurrect, reignite, and be on full display—in other words, full-on gloves-off hockey.

The old CHL ceased operations after the 1983–1984 season, the year I graduated high school. I am unable to explain why I never went to a Fort Worth Texans game as a high schooler. Their last season of play was 1981–1982.

As for the new team names, there would be the Fort Worth Fire, Dallas Freeze, Oklahoma City Blazers, Tulsa Oilers, Wichita Thunder, and Memphis RiverKings. The geographic locations of these teams definitely played a part in agitating the bad blood between teams.

At some point during the summer, I sent my portfolio over to the team's front office. I wanted to wait a month or two for the front office to be put in place before submitting my work. Positions like the GM, ticket manager, public relations manager, and receptionist needed to be filled. It was a small staff.

Instead of mailing the portfolio, I paid a courier to hand deliver my portfolio to the public relations person and waited for a response. I don't think the wait time was very long before I was invited for an interview. Several days later, I received the answer I was hoping for. It was a yes to the team photographer position.

Brian's media credential as team photographer for the Fort Worth Fire hockey team. Pass from the media credential collection of Brian McLean.

One of the first things I did after being told I was now the team photographer was to set up a black-and-white darkroom at the house. I already had the knowledge of mixing chemicals, developing film and printing photos. I knew what equipment I needed for a fully functional darkroom.

I purchased a commercial-grade Beseler enlarger, contrast filters, a grain focuser, developing trays, tongs, film reels, canisters that would hold four reels, a film changing bag, chemicals, printing paper, and an easel. All these things allowed me to immediately start processing and printing photos.

Leading the team from behind the bench would be former NHLer Peter Mahovlich, who had a sixteen-year career in the "show," which is lingo for the NHL. Mahovlich's hockey resume is fairly impressive. He was an important part of the Montreal Canadiens and their Stanley Cup Championship teams in 1971, 1972, 1976, and 1977.

Mahovlich was also a member of the legendary 1972 Summit Series, where he netted a shorthanded goal in game two, and a member of the 1976 Canada Cup team.

One of the first orders of business once all invited players arrived in October was training camp. During this time, ice rinks for hockey were few and far between in DFW. There was ice at local malls for ice skating, but options were limited for hockey rinks. To have a rink for hockey, there needs to be glass, dasher boards, benches, penalty boxes, and the scorer's box.

There was one rink, the North Texas Ice Arena. It was located in the Valley Ranch area of Irving. At the time, the Dallas Cowboys called Valley Ranch home. Their offices were located just a short walk south of the rink.

The ice arena itself was surrounded by open land and was a one-building, a poorly lit facility. Upon entering for the first time, I went to the glass and just stared at the rink. I couldn't believe I was standing at the glass of a hockey rink. It felt like a dream, but I knew it was real.

Since I was the team photographer, I had access to areas the ordinary public was not allowed.

I was introduced to the equipment manager, Steve Sumners, aka Sudsy. He spent four years with the Adirondack Red Wings of the American Hockey League before making his way down south to the Fort Worth Fire. From day one, he was totally cool and very helpful, just an all-around good person.

I made my way to the bench as players started walking out from the locker room on the rubber runners to the ice and started skating. Their freshly sharpened blades cut into the ice while they slapped pucks against the glass. It's a distinct sound specific to hockey warm-ups.

Ever since being introduced to hockey, I've thought the goalie masks have always been cool just to look at. Now, standing in the bench area, staring at Roch Belley's goalie mask, it was my first "whoa" hockey moment. The mask had a Chicago Blackhawks paint scheme to it. It was big news for Belley to come and play for the Fire.

He'd been selected by Chicago in the fourth round of the 1991 NHL Entry Draft. He was Chicago's 11th pick overall in the draft and was the big name on the Fire's roster.

Even though this was AA Minor League hockey, the experience was one of those first hockey experiences I've never forgotten.

Another thing I quickly noticed was the temperature while standing in the bench area. It was very chilly. I was told to dress warmly, which I did. Then I heard the players talking in their Canadian accents.

This was a new world, and I was devouring every moment. Just seventeen months prior, I had been introduced to the sport. Now, here I was, front and center behind the lens with a hockey team.

At one point during training camp, headshots of all the players needed to be taken. I set up a studio in a small conference room at the hotel where the players were housed. I don't recall how many hockey players were invited to training camp, but I had no problem banging out headshots of each player.

The season opener for the Fire would be a road game in Wichita on Wednesday, November 4, 1992. The Fire lost that first game of the season 6–4. Two days later, the home opener would be November 6, and the Fire lost that first game against Dallas 6–4 as well. My dedication to this new chapter in my life would be tested that night.

Ronnie James Dio rejoined Black Sabbath, and the band released 1992's *Dehumanizer*. Dio era Sabbath is my favorite era of Black Sabbath. I remember in high school missing the tour for *Mob Rules* on May 13, 1982. It had been a school night, and there was no way I could convince the concert gatekeeper to let me go.

Now, ten years later, the legendary Ronnie James Dio was back with Sabbath. I would finally be able to see the lineup live, or so I thought.

The tour for *Dehumanizer* wasn't a massive tour, but there was a date at the Bronco Bowl in Dallas. Unfortunately, it was on Friday, November 6, the same night of the Fort Worth Fire's home opener.

I would just switch to a backup plan and catch the tour in Houston, Austin, or Oklahoma City. That wasn't going to happen.

I phoned the record company to get tour dates. The show before the Dallas date was on November 4 in Milwaukee. The band had a day off and then Dallas. Following Dallas, the band would have the next day off and then play Mexico City with the following day off.

The band would then play four dates straight, Mesa, San Diego, Sacramento, and Oakland. The Oakland date would be Dio's final date with Sabbath until the 2000s, when he rejoined the band. Eventually the band would be forced to change their name to Heaven and Hell, Sabbath's 1980's album and Dio's debut with the band.

Seeing Dio fronting Black Sabbath or Heaven and Hell was never meant to be. It didn't happen even years later.

In February, one of the local universities in the North Texas area was hiring a University Photographer. I thought to myself, "This is it. This is what I have been waiting for. I have the editorial experience that will allow me to shoot whatever the school needs me to shoot." It all went back to what I was told that afternoon in 1986 at the TCU Women's Soccer field: "Just shoot newspapers for several years; you'll understand."

I submitted my resume with a cover letter. Within a day or two of delivery, an interview was set up for Wednesday, February 24,

1993. I was very excited and happy, so much so that I finally cut my hair to a more professional look. My shoulder, same-length hair with cool spiral curls was gone. That's how badly I wanted this photography position.

The day before the interview, I loaned a photographer my studio gear so she could do a studio session with Mercyful Fate for *In the Shadows*. The album would be released several months later in June 1993 on Metal Blade Records. In the credits, my name is Dave.

———

At this time, King Diamond was still a very mysterious figure. He was actually living in DFW.

The studio was located at the back of a camera shop in Dallas. To get to the studio, you had to walk down a hallway with standard household white linoleum tile.

As we were setting up the studio, we heard footsteps. With each step, it was obvious that the person was wearing boots. Each time a boot heel struck the floor, chains would strike the floor.

The photographer and I just looked at each other and said, "King Diamond." It was a chilling feeling, hearing those sounds, knowing that King Diamond was approaching.

Everybody in the Mercyful Fate camp, including Metal Blade Records' owner, Brian Slagel, was super nice. I knew Slagel was a huge hockey fan, so we talked a little bit about hockey.

That afternoon, after the studio was set up and ready to go, I witnessed something that ranked high in my music-related experiences.

I would always look at the back covers of the Mercyful Fate albums *Melissa* and *Don't Break the Oath*. I even attended an in-store signing with the band in 1984 when they were on the Motorhead tour. I never thought that one day I would watch King Diamond apply his makeup.

Sitting on a stool off to his right, I watched in amazement as he put it on. Every now and then during the process, he would make various facial expressions in the little mirror with round bulbs on each side. It was just mind-blowing to experience this unique part of heavy metal.

When all was said and done, he took his makeup off, and everybody was very grateful.

I had my copy of *Fatal Portrait* with me. King Diamond signed and put "Poor Molly." Bassist Timi Hansen and Michael Denner signed as well. On the back Hansen wrote a thank-you note with the date and then ended by writing, "and good luck with the interview."

I truly appreciated that and his kind words. Even thirty years later, I still appreciate the sincerity and time he took to write that, more so now since he passed away from cancer on November 4, 2019.

Brian with Mercyful Fate after the photo session for the In the Shadows album.

The following day, the interview went well. The experience I had to offer them was ideal. There were several other photographers, all portrait and wedding photographers, but I was the only one with editorial experience. What the university photographer job would need.

About a week later, a letter of rejection was received, thanking me for applying and interviewing. I couldn't understand what had gone wrong.

Then a day or two after that, I received a call from the person who interviewed me, wanting me to shoot at the university for a day rate of $400. This happened not once but twice. I cruised the campus, doing what I used to do at TCU. It was a day of photographing features.

During these two days, I learned how the university had hired a student assistant for the job. I remember being in the photo workroom and seeing a contact sheet from a headshot session.

Headshots are just that: photos of the subject from around the shoulder area or a little below and up. These headshots had people sitting on a stool, shot at the waist. I couldn't understand how somebody with no basic knowledge had landed the job.

I had worked so hard to get to this point and was left speechless. I only shot twice for them and did not follow up again on a third phone call for the $400 day rate. I was done. The idea of freelancing started to become a thorn in my side. That was strike one against the continuation of being a freelancer.

THIRTY

THREE BIG PHOTOGRAPHIC EVENTS

MY LONGTIME FRIEND JOHN's musical landscape evolved over the next few years from Rotting Corpse thrash. He moved into a heavier and slower direction called doom metal. John was influenced by Candlemass, a Swedish band whose debut album *Epicus Doomicus Metallicus* helped in defining the genre epic doom metal.

Eventually, John formed the American doom metal band Solitude Aeturnus in 1987. The band released six albums from 1991 through 2006. Their debut album, *Into the Depths of Sorrow*, was released through Roadrunner Records in July 1991 after several delays. By this time, the band had already written enough material for their sophomore album, *Beyond the Crimson Horizon*, which would be released through Roadrunner Records as well.

Since John and I had an established personal and working business relationship, he asked if I would shoot the photos for the second album. I was beyond honored.

Eventually, an idea was hatched based on the artwork for the album cover. Along with the group picture, another photo was taken that ended up being used.

During the shoot, vocalist Robert Lowe was wearing the Solitude Aeturnus cross around his neck. The cross was a piece of band merchandise available for purchase, but only fifty crosses were made and available globally.

The editorial photographer part of me kicked in. I decided to shoot a close-up of the cross chains wrapped around Lowe's right hand with the cross dangling. One light was used in front, and the backlight had a blue gel that provided a rim on Lowe's black clothing, hand, and cross.

Everybody from the record label to the band were pleased with the results. I remember walking into the record store for the first time and seeing the CD in the blister pack. Of course, I bought the CD. What I should have done was picked up a second copy but left it sealed. Today, it would be a really nice conversational piece.

The whole photo shoot meant a lot to me. I now had photos on a worldwide distributed release. Not only was the photo on a CD and cassette insert, but it was also on an album that would have a limited pressing.

The vinyl was difficult to find in the United States, so I reached out to the UK office to inquire how I could purchase a copy. Instead of allowing me to purchase, the office sent me a free copy, which I was extremely grateful for.

265

About a week later, I received notice to pick up a parcel from the post office.

As I stood in line waiting my turn to be helped, an old acquaintance walked into the post office. We locked eyes, and I smiled and greeted this person with a polite hello and, "How are you?" This person was my high school band director—yes, *that* band director.

I told him I was at the post office to pick up my first album that I'd photographed. I basically did this to let him know I'd turned out to be a productive citizen.

Of all the days of the week and times during that day, our paths had crossed in those few minutes. I still laugh to this day about that encounter.

The next time our paths crossed was in a church hallway in 2007. He didn't notice me, and I was so tempted to stop and say hello. I even wanted to ask him if he ever thought we would be colleagues for one year, but I didn't.

At ProgPower in Atlanta 2005, I found a sealed copy of the *Beyond the Crimson Horizon* cassette at a vendor's table and immediately purchased it. I was actually surprised to find it and had no problem pulling out the cash to take it home.

To this day, the cassette is still sealed and sits with the other releases I have acquired over the years.

In 2022, the album was re-released on pink vinyl. Obviously, I purchased a copy as well as the CD release.

On a Sunday afternoon in the spring of 1992, I was out on a photoshoot, and a call came into the house.

The brief phone call went like this:

Caller: May I speak with Brian?

Father: No, he's not here. He's out on a shoot. Can I take a message?

Caller: Yes, tell him Tony Dorsett called. Here's my number.

With that, my father hung up the phone.

This was a turning point photographically for me. My father had finally seen that things were happening with my photography.

The 1976 Heisman Trophy winner and 1977 NFL Offensive Rookie of the Year wanted to hire me to shoot some photos for Da Boys Sportswear. This was a line of clothing endorsed by Dorsett. There were shirts, tank tops, hats, and visors in various colors.

I was tasked with taking studio photos of Dorsett and a few other people wearing Da Boys swag.

One night in April, a photo assistant and I went out to his house in Dallas for the shoot. We surveyed the interior and decided to set up the studio in his living room. It was a strange feeling, looking at his trophies. Then we needed to move them. Some of the trophies were a bit on the heavy side. Up close, the trophies are beautiful pieces of crafted art.

We set up a basic studio with a large, marbled gray muslin and several lights. Everything we needed was shot within an hour. Tear down didn't take long at all.

After the shoot, he thanked us for our time and was very kind. He was a super-nice individual, and it was a pleasure to do the shoot.

I explained I would turn the slide film in for processing the next day and that I should have images by three in the afternoon.

Later the next day, as expected, I had images in hand and phoned Dorsett. After rush hour traffic died down, I once again headed back to Dallas with the processed slides, lightboard, and magnifying loupe.

As we were looking over images and discussing the keepers, a Houston Rockets game was on the big-screen TV. I don't recall who they were playing though.

At the same time, a serious spring lightning storm was blowing in and dumping heavy rains with high winds. It was one of those serious Texas storms in April. The weather was getting intense, and knowing that I drove from Fort Worth, Dorsett extended the offer for me to stay in the guest room. It was a very thoughtful gesture for him to do that.

As we were wrapping things up, he said that he was going to go get a picture. Phonetically, I heard "pitcher" instead of "picture." I was thinking, "I don't really want to drink a beer or two."

He came back and handed me one of his publicity photos. He was in the Dallas Cowboys blue road jersey with two thick white stripes on each sleeve and white pants. His #33 was visible, and the iconic

Cowboys silver helmet with the blue star sat on his head, his hands on his waist.

On the photo he wrote in gold paint pen:

Brian, the photos came out fantastic—thanks for a job well done.—Tony Dorsett

The number 33 was in a loop at the end of his signature.

Along with the photo, he signed two Da Boys hats and gave them to me.

The photos we shot were used for a full-page ad in the *Dallas Cowboys Observer*, a printed publication with the sole content being on the Cowboys.

I had to wait for several weeks, but when the next issue came out, I picked up a few copies and had the Da Boys advertisement framed with the photo. It's hard to believe that I've had the framed photo and ad for thirty-one years now.

My brother's country band had been gigging and playing some impressive shows, the majority of them private corporate events. One such event was even for a prince of Saudi Arabia. That was an impressive booking.

My brother's soundman, Phillip, was heading out on the road with Iron Maiden on the *Fear of the Dark* tour as a monitor engineer.

This was it. This was the opportunity I had been waiting five years for: possible access to Bruce Dickinson. I let my brother know with advance notice Maiden was coming to town and asked if he could get us on the list.

On tour with Maiden was Corrosion of Conformity and Testament, but I had one goal in mind. That was to get Dickinson to sign the photo I'd shot in 1987 on the *Somewhere in Time* tour.

After picking up our tickets and passes from will call, we met up with Phillip and were escorted to a covered backstage area with picnic tables. One by one, band members arrived in taxies. Nicko McBrain was the first and waved at the small group of people flashing one of his trademark goofy smiles. He was followed by Dave Murray and Steve Harris. Then Dickinson showed up. He and Harris were the band members that greeted everyone in this area and signed stuff.

Suddenly, both were surrounded by people wanting to bend their ears with never-ending conversations. I stayed back and watched, being respectful of their space.

First, I had Harris sign a Maiden 12-inch "Be Quick or Be Dead" picture disc. Unfortunately, over the years, his signature in Sharpie has deteriorated.

Now, it was time to approach Dickinson with my 16×20 black-and-white photo I'd shot in 1987. The whole time, the photo had been rolled up in a tube for secure-and-safe keeping. I kept priming the paint pen, so when the moment came, the silver paint pen would be ready to go for his signature.

Then my moment came.

I placed the large photo in front of him and held it down so the picture wouldn't roll back up. Dickinson put a huge signature on the photo with the silver paint pen. It looked incredible and still looks incredible to this day. The best part is how clean the signature is and how the signature pops out on the photo.

I must have kept the picture unrolled for ten minutes to allow enough time for the ink to dry. As I was allowing the signature to dry, I couldn't believe that I'd actually completed a bucket list item.

After everything was all said and done, I put the photo back into the tube and placed it back in my white CRX Si, or as other people called it, my little skateboard.

We watched the Testament set from stage left. It was funny seeing the reaction of friends who spotted me on the stage.

The following day, I took the newly inked Dickinson picture, my photo pass from 1987, the complete ticket from the show the previous night, and the VIP pass to a frame shop. I had a custom frame put together of those items. To this day, it's still one of my favorite pieces tied to my photography.

It's displayed proudly as a centerpiece in my game/music/man cave room.

THIRTY-ONE

STRIKES 2 AND 3

DURING THE LATER PART of the Fire season, chaos was happening in Waco at the Branch Davidian compound. A stringer for the major daily was venturing down there on a daily basis. It was a big news event just ninety miles south of Fort Worth.

One evening at a game, I was speaking with a photographer from the major daily and inquired what it would take to become a staff member. The reply was a shocking brutal truth, but most of all, very discouraging. I was unable to check a specific box. In doing so, I would be eliminated from the pool of candidates in the first round. That was strike two.

With the CHL in full swing of its first season, it was becoming apparent that hockey was thriving in Fort Worth and Dallas. Both teams were experiencing healthy attendance figures, and a fiery rivalry had reignited between the two. People were taking notice, especially a businessman named Norm Green.

At the time, Green was the owner of the Minnesota North Stars, the NHL team in Minnesota. Even though the team made a run at the Stanley Cup in 1991 against the Pittsburgh Penguins, Green wasn't pleased overall.

There were rumblings about the North Stars moving to Dallas, and Green even attended a Fort Worth Fire game. Fans were happy to see him at the game, giving hope to an NHL team that may be calling DFW home. A fan even sent a box of popcorn down from the upper balcony to him in the lower-level seats.

Minnesota North Stars owner Norm Green showing his appreciation for the box of popcorn that was sent down from a fan in the upper level at Tarrant County Convention Center. Photo by Brian McLean

With talks of relocating the team, I was already planning, researching, and preparing to apply for the team photographer position. By this time in the season, the major daily had lit TCCC. That enabled color photos to be shot with strobes. Those images were used for editorial purposes but also given to the team.

Since I was just mainly shooting black-and-white images, my photography and services were now at a disadvantage.

As the season came to a close, I was looking forward to the possibilities for the second Fire season and the Dallas Stars as well.

When the time came, I interviewed for the team photographer position but wasn't selected. The position paid a $12,000 retainer for the season. The photographer that was selected had prior experience shooting indoor sporting events with strobes set up. At one point, he was at a Fort Worth Fire game with strobes for the sole purpose of capturing lighted hockey action.

As a backup plan, I was looking into being able to photograph for a hockey photography outlet that shot for magazines and card companies. With the Dallas Stars going with another photographer, I reached out to the hockey studio to inquire about photographing the Stars. After they reviewed my portfolio and we had a couple of phone conversations, I was told that I would be photographing NHL hockey in the fall. I couldn't believe what I was hearing. It was amazing news.

—◇—

As the second Fort Worth Fire season neared, I was informed that the team was going with the major daily photographer. He had access to resources that I did not, mainly color processing and printing at low or no cost. I couldn't compete with that.

That was strike three.

The public relations person did give me a credential for the season, as he felt bad for how everything went down.

At least I was photographing the Stars for their first season in Dallas, but there was a shift in my mindset. I was looking at my future differently now, especially how it would relate to my photography.

Prior to the first Stars season, I was sent a set of lights that were to be attached to the catwalk above the ice at Reunion Arena. The strobes would illuminate the ice from the blue line and attacking zone to the corner. I would be photographing from the goalie's right.

The second Fire season was underway, as well as the first Dallas Stars season. I didn't shoot opening night, and actually, it took a few games into the season before I had a credential for my first game.

Upon arrival at the arena, I had to meet up with a union person who would escort me to the catwalk above the arena floor. I wasn't allowed to go alone; I had to have an escort, and it was the same person each time. They actually got paid to do this.

The entrance to the catwalk was actually a small door at the top of the stairs of one of the upper balcony sections. If I was looking at the pressbox, the small door was over to the right several sections. To access the catwalk, you actually had to crawl through the door. This puts you outside the arena. Then another door had to be accessed. On the other side of that door was the catwalk and the zone of the ice that my lights covered. I would switch the lights on for the game. After the game, I would be escorted back to the catwalk to turn the lights off.

Photographing the Stars that first season was cool, but at the same time, I wasn't just photographing just the Dallas Stars. I also shot other things that year.

I shot the first and second seasons of the Stars.

I would be assigned games to cover teams mainly within the central division. Detroit, St. Louis, and Winnipeg were the teams I seemed to photograph the most. Some of the other teams I shot with less frequency were Buffalo, Calgary, Chicago, Edmonton, Ottawa, San Jose, St. Louis, Tampa Bay, Toronto, and Vancouver.

When I look back on those two seasons, it was a great experience. I was published in various formats, but there is one published piece that I am extremely proud of. One of my photos of Bob Essensa, goalie for the Winnipeg Jets, was used as a pullout, four-page panel poster in *Pro Hockey*, a magazine in Sweden. It's framed and hanging up in the game room with the credential I shot it on. This poster was a huge accomplishment for me, and I am very proud of it to this day.

As for the Fire's second season, I wasn't photographing them at all even though I was provided a season media credential. I was helping every so often with the public relations and media people if an extra pair of hands was needed. Basically, I was running errands in the arena if I wasn't watching the game.

During the two seasons with the Fort Worth Fire and the first season photographing the Dallas Stars, I utilized any opportunity to network, no matter who the person was. By the end of the Fire season, I started to re-evaluate things photographically. I would continue to shoot the Dallas Stars as the season progressed. I would not put my camera down in the coming months, but changes and a transition career-wise was on the horizon—I just didn't realize it at the time.

Thirty-Two

A New Chapter

DURING THE SUMMER, I decided that a change was needed. I enjoyed all aspects of editorial photography—news, sports, and entertainment—but I grew tired of the roadblocks I was encountering.

As a member of the media, I enjoyed dealing with working professionals in the media. I also enjoyed dealing with those who worked on the other side of the media line. Those working professionals were publicists, PR people, and media-relations people.

My foot was already in the door of the Dallas-Fort Worth sports market. The direction I wanted to go only made sense. I just had to do a few things academically and make a few sacrifices. I was ready to do so.

I decided to start making a transition from being a photographer to being a public relations professional in the sports world. The first order of business—I needed to re-enroll in school to take a few writing classes, and that's what I did.

As a speech communications major, my degree plan didn't include writing classes. I knew the basics; I just needed to build upon those basics.

———◦———

At the end of August, I had what I thought was my "last hurrah" related to music. It was a banging experience, to say the least.

The band Type O Negative on Roadrunner Records was a hot act receiving quite a bit of airplay on their single "Christian Woman." They were out on a summer tour with Mötley Crüe, who were, at the time, fronted by vocalist John Corabi.

I consider the 1994 Mötley Crüe album, simply titled *Mötley Crüe*, with Corabi on vocals, to be their best. The album had a heavier, more aggressive sound. Songs such as the first single, "Hooligan's Holiday," "Power to the Music," and "Misunderstood" saw the band departing from their prior lyrical themes of rebellion and rock and roll debauchery. On top of that, besides Corabi being a vocalist, he was a guitarist, which added another dimension to the band's music.

In the end, I think people were having a difficult time accepting Corabi as the vocalist despite him being in the band for four years.

For those who have never heard it, I highly recommend giving it a spin.

The summer tour was coming to an end in late August at the Oil

Palace in Tyler, 132 miles east of Fort Worth. I reached out to the publicist at Roadrunner Records and asked if she could put me on the list. This was the same person I worked with when the Solitude Aeturnus album art was shot.

When the Dallas Stars came to town, I hooked her up with a personalized authentic Stars jersey. She had no problem putting me on the list. I was instructed, once there, to ask for Neg, the tour manager.

Jason, a very good friend, made the Saturday road trip with me. When we arrived at the Oil Palace that afternoon, we walked to the back by the buses. I saw a guy with jet-black hair with the Type O Negative logo on his bicep. Obviously, I knew he had to be in the TON camp. It was Johnny Kelly, the drummer. I asked him if Neg was around, and he immediately took us to Type O's bus.

Suddenly we were on the bus, and the other three members were in the front section. We took a seat, and everybody introduced themselves to each other. The first thing I noticed when I saw vocalist and bassist Peter Steele was the size of his biceps; they were massive. His voice had that low baritone range accompanied by a thick Brooklyn accent.

While we were there hanging out, just chilling, someone went to the back of the bus and returned with a shopping bag. Inside was a large variety of complete matching lingerie panties and bras in peach, baby blue, and black.

What I didn't know at the time was that this date for Type O Negative was their last night on tour. Normally, when that happens, the headliner sabotages the support band's set with cake, silly string, and other crazy pranks. Oddly, that didn't happen to TON. Instead, Type O Negative was plotting how they would prank Mötley Crüe's set.

Besides the women's lingerie sets, catfish stink bait, canned tuna fish, silly string, fresh produce, and other items would be utilized.

To see the members of Type O Negative in the women's lingerie was quite a sight. Not only did they wear nothing but the silky garments with their combat boots, but members also put on blush, gaudy eyeshadow, and bright red lipstick. Peter Steele even put his long hair into pigtails.

"F*ck me, Vince" was completely spelled out in red lipstick on his back.

Type O Negative didn't come out on stage during the Crüe's set until the acoustic unplugged portion. In 1994, being unplugged and delivering an acoustic set during a show was common.

Mötley Crüe was seated on stools at the front of the stage. The band invited a lot of female fans on stage for this part of the show. Obviously, the invited fans took the band up on their offer. Once the girls were on stage, Type O Negative decided to hit Mötley Crüe with their pranks.

For starters, the stink bait and tuna were dumped into the high velocity industrial ventilation fans. That meant chunks of the stink bait and tuna fish were blown onto the stage, creating a very smelly situation. The TON members went around spraying silly string on anything and anybody within reach.

Keep in mind, each of the four members in Type O Negative were in silky garments.

While guitarist Kenny Hickey was running around, he would periodically stop and start helicoptering a large, flesh-colored, floppy sex toy in front of the seated fans or Mötley Crüe.

Bassist Peter Steele had several pieces of the fresh fruit tucked into the back of his peach-colored panties. The funny part was he would reach to his backside, grab a peach, and toss it out into the crowd. Just imagine, whoever caught the pieces of fruit had no idea they were snuggled up against his crack just moments earlier. In total, three to four peaches were launched into the crowd.

After all the chaos came to an end, Type O Negative went back to the hospitality room, and we took a band photo. I shot maybe five or six photos of the band in lingerie. Afterward, Peter Steele came up to me and said in his deep voice, "No one sees those photos."

I kept my word for twenty-nine years before one image was supplied for a video interview I took part in with guitarist Kenny Hickey. The interview was for the anniversary of Type O Negative's *Bloody Kisses* album. During the interview, the guitarist was surprised to hear that I was there, and not only there, but also there with the band before and after all the craziness. When I started sharing details of the incident and things that were tossed to the fans as well as him running around with the dildo, he knew I was there.

After the show, we continued to hang out with Type O Negative, and my friend Jason was able to hang out with Nikki Sixx of the Crüe. That was a dream come true event for him.

I am so glad I was able to do that for him. I never knew the importance of that night to him until years later. Melanoma took him in May of 2011, and his mother said he always talked about that night.

Both Jason and I were invited to ride the tour bus into Dallas that night, as the band had Sunday off. They were starting a small venue headlining tour on Monday, August 22, 1994. We declined as we drove from Fort Worth to the show.

On Monday, the band was playing a radio-station-sponsored show for KEGL 97.1 FM, a rock station in Dallas-Fort Worth. The show was a promotion called a Low Dough Show, and tickets were $4.97 at The Basement in Dallas. Obviously, with that ticket price, it wasn't surprising to see the line wrapped around the building waiting for the venue doors to open.

All the photos I shot in Tyler were taken on color slides. E-6 processing only takes an hour, so when I went out to the venue for the show on Monday, I had images in hand. I saw several friends from the local scene I knew as I walked to the bus. I spoke to them for a few minutes, and then I knocked on the bus door, and Kenny answered. I was immediately welcomed back on the bus.

Everybody was getting a good laugh from the photos taken two nights earlier in Tyler.

I was able to spend some time with the band again. I even played a game of chess with Kenny. It's something he really enjoyed doing.

That night, I hung out on stage left and shot more photos of the band. I can tell you it was very hot in the venue, especially with the number of people in front of the stage. At least I was standing near the load-in door and could get some fresh, cool air compared to the stifling temperature inside.

After the show when people were clearing out, I was able to witness the formation of a friendship between two bands. Darrell and Vinnie from Pantera were there and met the members of Type O Negative for the first time. Eventually, the two bands toured together.

If there was a mic drop moment to walk away from music and start concentrating on a sports public relations career, that night with Type O Negative in Tyler was the ultimate curtain call.

In the fall of 1994, I enrolled at the University of Texas at Arlington and started my journey as a public relations professional. The first class I took was Media Writing, which taught the basics of news writing. After a few days, I realized that I was on the right path.

Besides the standard professor introduction and welcoming of students, the first thing he said to the class was, "Forget about everything you learned in high school English."

Writing for news outlets is a bit different, as there's a thing called AP Style that writers in the media follow. Within a day or two, I had already purchased my AP Stylebook. It went with me everywhere. The book became an extension of me. Actually, I still have the original copy I purchased.

I was photographing the Dallas Stars for the second season, and as for the Fort Worth Fire, I crossed over the line and was working in the public relations department. I was learning the ins and outs of tasks related to this other side. I was able to relate to the things I saw due to being on the photographer's side of things previously.

Instead of photographing from the penalty box or through a hole cut in the glass, I was upstairs in the press box. There were so many different things I would do on game days, things like running tape to the local network affiliates, updating stats, calling in scoring updates throughout the league, delivering game notes, tasks that involved writing, and countless other things.

The most important skill was not knowledge of hockey, but having strong writing skills. Yes, knowing the game was important, but being able to write was the biggie.

Throughout the season, I made several road trips with the team as the public relations contact. I went all the way up to Wichita and down to San Antonio, which was the first expansion team in the league.

On the trip to Wichita, we watched *Field of Dreams*. It was a surreal experience, watching that movie while on a road trip with a hockey team.

I even provided color commentary on several games. These were broadcast via cable TV when the Fire played the Dallas Freeze at the Fair Park Coliseum.

I was able to walk away with several writing samples that were published, but there was one thing I did that generated a lot of publicity for the team.

Early in the season, I pitched, created, and put together a High School Media Day campaign that concluded late in the season. The purpose was to give high school journalism students a taste of covering a minor league hockey team for a day.

This campaign wasn't something that was just thrown together; it involved extensive planning, research, development, and phone calls and letters that all started on October 31, 1994, for a game on February 17, 1995.

The day of the game, the students were granted access to the pregame morning skate. They were able to interview the coach and players. The students would also attend the game that night as credentialed members of the media.

That afternoon, there was a media luncheon with presentations from the Fire team photographer, Fire beat writer, Fort Worth community cable broadcaster, radio play-by-play broadcaster, and "Class Acts" print media correspondent. This luncheon allowed the media students to have informal dialogue with members of the working media.

Tips and suggestions for the students were even provided to make their experience more enjoyable. For example, photographers should wear a heavy black shirt for warmth and glare reduction on the glass while shooting at ice level. The photographers were not allowed to use flashes on their cameras, which is standard procedure.

For writers, it was suggested they bring notepads, several pens/pencils. and a mini tape recorder for post-game interviews with players and coaches. It was highly recommended that the writers dress in professional business casual, but no T-shirts or shorts. We wanted the students to experience the real deal, not just a fun casual night of hanging out and watching a hockey game.

Friday, March 3, 1995, was the deadline for stories and photographs for judging. That was two weeks after the initial game day coverage.

The end goal was for the Fort Worth Fire to receive publicity in ten or more high school newspapers. The campaign was also a journalism contest like the one I'd participated in for the Dallas Hard Rock Cafe. That's where my campaign idea came from. I just took it a few steps deeper to give aspiring journalists in high school real-world experience.

The winning reporter was able to trade places for a half a day with a writer from the "Class Acts" section of the major daily. The winning photographer was able to shoot a game from the penalty box with the team photographer.

Overall, the campaign was a success, and publicity beyond the high school newspapers was achieved. Feedback from the journalism sponsors of several high schools was very positive, and the campaign was an encouraging experience for the students.

———◇———

In minor league sports, game-day promotions are a must to entice people to buy a ticket for the game with the promotion. One such promotion during the season was sumo wrestling. One of the wrestlers was Emanuel Yarbrough, a six-foot, 620-pound athlete. At the time, he'd recently competed and placed second in the World Amateur Sumo Championship in Japan. He was touring the nation to promote the sport. That's why he was at a Fort Worth Fire game one night.

During the afternoon prior to the game, he made an appearance at an elementary school in Arlington. I went to the afternoon appearance as a PR representative for the hockey team. Two different media outlets were present. One just ran a wild art feature photo, whereas the other wrote a small story and had a two-photo package.

It really didn't matter what ran or how much publicity the team received. The bottom line was the team received press coverage in local print media.

The elementary students had so much fun at Emanuel's appearance. A group of kids even volunteered to go up against him in an attempt to push him back.

Sadly, Emanuel passed away in 2015, but he was a really super-nice and soft-spoken gentle giant. He even held a Guinness World Record for being the heaviest living athlete at one point.

The promotion that was probably the biggest hit of the season wasn't the Famous Chicken formerly known as the San Diego Chicken, the godfather of whacky sports mascot antics. Simply, he's a 1970's sports legend that paved the way for crazy behaviors of team mascots today.

Instead, it was the Hanson Brothers from the 1977 classic hockey movie *Slap Shot* with Paul Newman. The fictional Hanson brothers are based on the Carlson brothers, who were actual hockey players in the 1970s. They provided plenty of humorous and funny moments during the film. The brothers were known for starting fights and verbal outbursts while the coach was delivering pregame speeches. They were iconic with their thick, black-rimmed, medical-tape-patched glasses, foil-wrapped fists, and affinity for playing with toy race cars and trucks in their hotel room. In hockey lore, the Hanson brothers are legendary.

After the Fire game, the Hanson brothers took photos with fans, office staff, and players. One Fort Worth Fire player actually stayed in uniform to get his photo taken with them.

———

During the season, I was still photographing the Dallas Stars while I was a public relations assistant with the Fort Worth Fire. It was my second season to photograph the Dallas Stars, but it would also be my last.

THIRTY-THREE

THAT LAST STEP

SEVERAL DAYS AFTER THE end of the Fire's season, I called the front office to speak with Jason, the public relations person who'd given me the opportunity to work during the season. The GM answered the phone, and I asked for Jason. I was told that I could reach him at his house. I knew what that meant: he was let go, and no time was wasted after the season before doing so. That forced me to look at things a bit differently and be a bit more cautious of the people around me.

In this new "career" chapter I experienced during the season, I was all in on the media-relations aspect of things. I did whatever I could to network and handle duties. I wanted to absorb any and everything related to public relations that I could. The Fort Worth Fire wasn't the only organization I would learn from.

As a kid growing up, I always saw the name Bobby Bragan. I never really paid attention to it, I just knew that my father had a working relationship with him and dealt with Mr. Bragan a lot.

Many times, my father would come home with items related to the Texas Rangers or just baseball in general. Many times, these items were signed by Mr. Bragan.

In April 1993, my father gave me a book that was gifted by Mr. Bragan to me. The title of the book was *You Can't Hit the Ball with the Bat on Your Shoulder.* Inside the front cover, there was a personalized inscription followed by "Keep Swinging, Bobby Bragan."

He spent many years in baseball, rising up through the minor league system to the major leagues where he not only played but managed as well.

Mr. Bragan was always a generous person, and in 1991, he established the Bobby Bragan Youth Foundation (BBYF) Scholarship Program. The organization awarded scholarships to students in eighth grade. BBYF put forth an effort to encourage students to stay in school and pursue their educational and career dreams. BBYF is still going strong, awarding scholarships to those outstanding eighth grade students across the metroplex.

More recently, BBYF has created the Bobby Bragan National Collegiate Slugger Award for the Most Outstanding Offensive Division 1 College Baseball Player In America. The potential recipients are judged under athletics, academics, and citizenship.

To help fund these recognitions, the foundation has several fundraising events, including the BBYF Gala and the BBYF Golf Tournament.

Prior to the 1995–1996 hockey season, I jumped on board with BBYF as a public relations assistant and started working on those two events. The first event occurred in the fall and was the Gala. The 1995 Gala would honor TCU alumnus, sportswriter, and author Dan Jenkins with the Bobby Bragan Lifetime Achievement Award.

I approached the Gala as a project for a Public Relations class I was enrolled in. I created a complete action plan with situation analysis, targeted publics, action play with short term- and long term-goals, objectives, methodology, organizational impact, evaluation, timetable, budget, media list, pitch letters, radio interview information sheets, news releases, and PSAs. I put forth a lot of work into putting information out for the event, and I had some results.

The *Fort Worth Star-Telegram* came out, and the Texas Rangers put the news release in their On Deck Community Bulletin Board that's part of the *On Deck* team newsletter.

The second event I worked on was the Bobby Bragan Golf Classic that was held in the springs of 1996 and 1997. I wrote news releases and updated literature such as the brochure informational booklet, newsletter, and entry forms.

For the 1996 golf event, I was on-site at the golf course and served in a media/public relations liaison capacity throughout the day.

There's a gap time-wise, but that information will be cleared up with later passages.

———◇———

With the 1994–1995 Fort Worth Fire hockey season in the books, it was time to take that final step. Since I had been photographing the Dallas Stars for the '93–'94 and '94–'95 seasons, I had a working relationship with the PR department. Ironically, at the time, the public relations manager was a PR intern with the Fort Worth Fire the first season, 1992–1993.

I vaguely remember him. I think we may have interacted once or twice during the season. He was upstairs while I was rink side during the games.

With the shake-up of the Fort Worth Fire front office, I needed to look beyond minor league hockey on the path I was now focused on. I sent a resume and cover letter to the Dallas Stars' Public Relations department. This was a leap of faith over that line separating the working media and working with the media. I felt that with the network I had established and relationships I had built over the past three seasons locally, I stood a chance of landing the PR internship with the Dallas Stars.

I already knew the director of public relations for the Stars from my time photographing the previous two seasons. I had already been through an interview with him for the team photographer position two years prior.

During the interview, I concentrated on the things I handled with the Fort Worth Fire. Even though this was for the NHL, I made connections between the two leagues and the duties I had. The main emphasis was how I handled the press box for the Fire and other things such as delivering game notes to the locker rooms, for example. It was mentioned in the interview that writing skills and not knowledge of the game was one of the important skills.

If I landed the Stars gig, the press box on game night would be my domain as well as other duties. It was basically the same as with the Fire, just on a larger scale.

Several days later, I received a phone call offering me the position, and of course, I accepted. My mind was racing. I couldn't believe it.

Just three years earlier, I had been watching the Pittsburgh Penguins win their second Stanley Cup, and just four years earlier, their first. Here I would now be, behind the scenes working in a professional capacity with the Dallas Stars Public Relations department.

If someone would have said back during those two years I was watching the Pens in the playoffs that I would be working and interning with an NHL team, I would've never believed it.

At that time, the NHL in Dallas wasn't even on the radar for DFW sports. It was mind-blowing how quickly things changed.

The road map, the plan I had, was working out. I couldn't have been happier.

Within several days, I was meeting up with the Stars' public relations manager to go over the duties, expectations, and locations of items that would be needed. Most importantly, I was given the key to the press box of Reunion Arena.

This was the arena that I'd craved to see rock concerts in as a high school student. Reunion Arena to me was the mecca for Dallas-Fort Worth rock concerts. Now, I had the key to the press box. I recall when I had attended shows at Reunion Arena, I would look at the press box and just stare. I would be looking down from the press box now instead of looking up at it.

My normal game day routine consisted of driving to the front office where I would pick up the game notes, media guides, and game programs.

The game notes consisted of rosters for each team and biographical information for each player that included fun facts, current streaks, winning percentages, summaries from a previous game, and other information. These notes are vital to the broadcasters, but also to the writers covering the game.

A set of game notes could easily consist of fifteen to twenty-plus pages of information, front and back. The game notes I would pick up would be in a box that would hold ten reams of paper. The box was always filled to capacity, and it was extremely heavy, seriously heavy. There were times when the box was beyond capacity when high-profile teams were in town.

I would also pick up ten to fifteen media guides of the visiting team for the local media, as well as a box of the game programs for that night. A media guide is an information book on the team with every piece of information from franchise history and team ownership to players and statistical records. The media guide is in a bound book form, and every team on the major league level creates one. Media guides are distributed to members of the media prior to the beginning of the season as well as throughout.

The programs I picked up were the same as the ones the fans would be able to purchase the night of the game.

After picking up all these things, I then drove to the arena. It was very weird those first few times, walking in the empty concourse and hearing the sound of my dress shoes echoing throughout it. The arena where I'd seen concerts with twenty thousand screaming fans was quiet, very quiet. Only my shoes broke the silence.

Unfortunately, when Reunion Arena was constructed, there was not an elevator for the press box. That meant I had to schlep everything up the stairs from the concourse to the upper level. That was only half the journey. Then I'd go straight up the stairs to the press box at the top of section 201. It was definitely what one would call *sweat equity*.

Seating in the press box remained consistent for the local media members from season to season. Visiting media seats remained the same as well. This was before the cell phone; thus media members supplied their own phone. I would connect their phones to the landline jacks. To make sure I was being consistent, on that first day of being in the press box, I created a seating chart cheat sheet where each member of the media sat and what phone jack they used. I would even set up the TV for the off-ice officials to view when tracking or to review when a goal was scored. This ensured the proper players were credited with the assist or assists and the goal.

After several games, I knew all the locations and seating arrangements.

Once the press box was prepped—that included distributing all the game notes and media guides to all the broadcast booths and connecting the phones—I then exited to hang the huge radio station banner to the right.

At that time, during the '95–'96 season, the radio station that broadcast the games was WBAP 820 AM. This station has a rich broadcasting history in North Texas to this day.

The vinyl banner itself was twenty to thirty feet in length and at least three three to four feet in height. It was a large piece of advertising for the radio station.

There were other duties besides the press box. I could end up gathering stats for visiting media or broadcast production.

There was one specific duty, though, I was responsible for at the end of the game. That was pulling the players for the Three Stars of the Game. It didn't matter what team—I just had to notify the players and attempt to have them stop as they were coming off the ice.

For those who are not really familiar with the Three Stars of the Game, they are the three best players of the game, the first star being considered the best of the three.

After everything related to the media and press box was taken care of, I then delivered game notes to each locker room. As I was making my way down to the locker rooms, I was walking the hallways or tunnels with blue-and-green decor that I had seen in music videos and home video VHS tapes, such as Mötley Crüe's *Uncensored*.

I would place ten, twelve, or fifteen sets of game notes on the table in the middle of each locker room. The first time I delivered notes to the locker rooms, I just took a moment to take it all in. By this time of the day, all the locker rooms were prepped and ready to go.

Normally, just the equipment staff was taking care of things. Typical duties included sharpening skates, stitching up jerseys, and sewing name plates for a player acquisition or new arrival being called up.

I will admit it was a sight to truly see a few hours prior to the puck dropping. It wasn't until I stepped foot into an Original 6 team's locker room for the first time that it really hit.

The Original 6 are the first six teams in the NHL: the Boston Bruins, Chicago Blackhawks, Detroit Red Wings, Montreal Canadiens, New York Rangers, and Toronto Maple Leafs.

The first Original 6 team locker room I went into was Boston's. When I walked into the Bruins' locker room with all the game equipment ready for the players, I thought, "This is serious hockey history." It was an incredible sight, seeing the iconic *B* logo on the black jerseys hanging up.

I wouldn't even know it at the time, but the game between Dallas and Boston would eventually prove to be a very memorable event.

The eighty-two-game regular season schedule saw the opposing conference teams play one road game and host the opposing conference team for one game. Due to the shortened season of forty-eight games the previous year, neutral-site games had been eliminated, which brought the regular season to eighty-two games. This is still in effect as of 2024.

Of the Original 6, that meant Boston, Montreal, and New York would visit Dallas once and host the Stars once.

Sometimes players were already at the arena but not in the locker rooms. With a quick glance around, I would see personal effects such as Stanley Cup rings from prior years in the cubby of a player's stall.

Once the game notes were dropped off in each locker room, I would head back to the press box just to double-check everything. From there, I would walk back down and grab dinner in the cafeteria where the media ate, the media being beat writers and broadcasters for both teams. We would all sit at these large round banquet tables and talk shop.

Thirty-Four

NHL Season Part I

Boston Bruins vs. Dallas Stars

Saturday, October 14, 1995

As previously mentioned, Boston was the first of the Original 6 teams that came to Dallas for the season. It was the fourth game of the regular season but the third home game.

Boston wasted no time putting the puck in the net at 1:38 of the first period. Dallas tied the game 1–1 at the 13:45 of the first. The Bruins netted their second goal in the closing minutes of the first period at 17:11. Boston went ahead with their third goal, the first of the second period at 6:04, putting the Bruins up 3–1.

Dallas closed the scoring gap at 14:55, cutting Boston's lead to one goal, 3–2. The Bruins answered with a short-handed goal at 16:36, bringing the score to 4–2, and that's how the second period ended.

Just 1:16 minutes into the third period, Dallas netted their third goal, cutting Boston's lead to one goal, 4–3.

Several minutes later at 5:44, Boston extended their lead to 5–3 with their fifth goal of the game.

The Bruins continued to stay strong, holding off Dallas into the closing minute of the game. Dallas scored at 19:11 of the third period. The score was 5–4.

Boston still had a one goal lead with forty-nine seconds remaining in the third period. Then it happened.

At 19:44, Dallas scored again, tying the game at 5–5 with sixteen seconds remaining. It looked as if the teams were heading to overtime until at 19:55, Dallas scored again with five seconds remaining on the clock to take a one-goal lead over Boston with a 6–5 score.

Boston was pissed. The Bruins gave up three goals in the last forty-nine seconds of the game and lost to Dallas.

Of the Three Stars of the Game, the third star was a Boston player. I don't recall who, but looking at the box score, Cam Neely and Todd Elik both had two goals each. I would think one of them was the Third Star.

As the Bruins were skating to exit the ice, one player smashed his stick on the red goal frame. There was no way in hell I was going to even attempt to pull the Third Star of the game.

The home schedule was only three games into the season, but it was a memorable one.

New Jersey Devils vs. Dallas Stars

Saturday, November 25, 1995

The New Jersey Devils would be the sixth Eastern Conference team of the season to visit Reunion Arena. Any time a team from the Eastern Conference played in Dallas, I looked forward to the experience. Eastern Conference teams just had this air of royalty about them, whether they were a Stanley Cup contender from day one of the season or not.

Just like any other game, I approached the daily tasks as normal and took care of my responsibilities. I was very meticulous about having everything set for all media.

As game time approached, the PR manager informed me that I would be sitting in the broadcast booth with Mike Emrick doing stats. He asked me if I knew who Mike Emrick was. I mentioned that the name was familiar, but that was the extent of it. He proceeded to tell me that Mike Emrick is the voice of the New Jersey Devils but also calls the Stanley Cup Finals.

Actually, I was a bit bummed that I wouldn't be able to work the press box that night, but I understood. I didn't hesitate to do what was being asked of me.

What I didn't expect was the amazing experience of sitting next to New Jersey's broadcaster and hearing his work in real time. Emrick continued being the voice of the New Jersey Devils until 2011, as well as the Stanley Cup and other games.

Toronto Maple Leafs vs. Dallas Stars

January 1, 1996, Noon

My passion and dedication for music would be tested during the season. Several decisions would have to be made.

In 1995, it was a no-brainer that Arlington's Pantera was inching toward the top of the metal world. In March 1994, the band released *Far Beyond Driven*. The album shot to the top of the charts and debuted at number one on the Billboard 100. It was an impressive feat.

Within a year or two, they would be bigger than Metallica. The reason was that Pantera stayed on course metal-wise, whereas the Mighty Met detoured a bit. Any deviation of such was a tad too much for their pre-Black album–era fan base. Plus, Metallica would release some questionable albums, starting with *Load* in June of 1996.

For New Year's Eve 1995, Pantera played a hometown arena show at Tarrant County Convention Center. This was something I really wanted to see. It would be great to close out 1995 seeing a band that had played such an influential role for me.

I had watched them many times in the clubs since February 1985. Eventually, seeing them play was becoming—no pun intended—part of my live music routine. I attended as many of their club gigs as I could. I was immersing myself in the music. Being at their local shows early on was becoming part of my music identity.

It was an extremely difficult decision not to go see them play on

New Year's Eve. I felt as if I needed to be there to complete the 360-degree cycle of a local band playing clubs from Fort Worth to TCCC, the arena that has played a major part in my story. I considered the Pantera show an arena homecoming.

I had to look at two factors, the first being that the show would definitely go to midnight or beyond. Second, game time for the Toronto Maples Leafs and Stars game was set for 12:00 p.m. CST.

That would put me leaving at 9:00 a.m. and getting up at 8:00 a.m. That was the making of a long day. I knew, as with any other game, I needed to be on top of everything.

It was difficult and a mental battle between the two events. I chose not to attend the Pantera show. The decision came down to one consideration—what was more important? Was it the career or bringing in 1996 by watching a band I'd seen many times play TCCC for the first time.

I decided to roll with staying in and getting a good night's rest. I think I was lights out by 10:00 p.m.

I will say on the Pantera *3 Vulgar Videos from Hell* video collection, there is footage from the show. Slo Mo, the Rotting Corpse singer, is in the video walking around the area while wearing one of those large foam cowboy hats.

More than likely, the show was one big throw down in Cowtown.

Los Angeles Kings vs. Dallas Stars

January 8, 1996

The Stars started off December with a six-game road trip beginning on December 2, 1995, in Los Angeles against the Kings. The game ended in a 2–2 OT tie.

The following night, Dallas was in Colorado facing off against who would be the Stanley Cup Champions for the '95–'96 season. Dallas skated away with a 7–6 win over the Avalanche.

Dallas had one day off and traveled east for a series of games starting December 5, 1995, against Boston, Detroit, Toronto, and the New York Rangers. The trek ended on December 11, 1995. The Stars returned back home for a December 13 contest against the Calgary Flames with a day off. Then on December 15, Dallas hosted the Pittsburgh Penguins.

Unfortunately for the Stars, Dallas dropped six games straight starting in Boston. Four on the road, and two upon returning home.

Dallas did break the slide on December 17, 1995, against the San Jose Sharks, followed by an OT tie with the Islanders in Dallas on December 21. That would be it.

Two days later, the Stars hosted the Chicago Blackhawks on December 23 and then traveled to Chicago to face the Blackhawks again on December 26. Then they were off to play the St. Louis Blues on December 28. Dallas returned home to host the Red Wings the following night at Reunion Arena.

Dallas would drop these four games before an OT tie in Detroit on January 3, followed by a much-needed win against the Winnipeg

Jets on January 5. That game was followed by a loss back in Chicago on January 7.

From December 2 through January 7, the Stars played nineteen games, winning three, with four OT ties and twelve losses.

On January 8, the Stars were hosting the Los Angeles Kings, but I sensed an odd vibe. I was informed that Bob Gainey was stepping down from his coaching duties. Ken Hitchcock from the Stars' minor league affiliate, the Kalamazoo Wings of the International Hockey League, would be stepping in. Gainey would be focusing on his general manager duties.

I took care of my normal game-day routine, but word was out that the Stars were having a press conference. While I was setting up the press box, one phone rang and then stopped. A few minutes later, the phone rang again and then stopped. This was the main phone line for the press box.

I was nearby when the phone started ringing a third time. This time, I answered it. A sports editor from a news outlet somewhere in the Northeast identified himself. He started to inquire about the breaking news and was tossing out news scenarios. The individual mainly focused on Mike Modano, one of the key players on the Dallas roster. He was wondering if there was a trade in the works or anything involving Modano.

I replied that I was monitoring the press box. I was not in any position to make a comment or answer any questions, no matter how basic. After a minute or two, he understood that I was in no position to make a comment, though I'd emphasized that all along.

Once I had the press box ready, I reported to a room where the press conference would be held. I stood outside next to the doorway, handing out the press release announcing Hitchcock as the new head coach of the Dallas Stars.

The press release headline read in caps, "Bob Gainey Resigns as Head Coach of Dallas Stars; Ken Hitchcock Named as Successor," and then the subheading read, "Gainey Remains Stars VP of Hockey Operations and General Manager."

Everything was eerily quiet as members of the media filed in and took a seat. The feeling was very strange, as if a somber mood was lingering in the room. At the front of the room, there was an elevated table on a stage riser with the Dallas Stars logo hanging behind it.

I paid close attention to logistics, introductions, paperwork, and other things. There would be a time that I would lead a press conference, and I wanted to make sure I knew how to operate one smoothly from start to finish.

Hitchcock's first game saw the Stars in an OT 4–4 finish with the Los Angeles Kings.

The following day, a second press release about the coaching change was sent out to the media.

The headline for the press release disseminated to the media the next day read, "Ken Hitchcock Head Coach of Dallas Stars," and the subheading read, "Gainey Remains Stars VP of Hockey Operations & General Manager."

The second press release text read exactly the same as the first one that announced the coaching change. Unlike the first press release, the second contained Hitchcock's coaching record with the Kamloops Blazers of the Western Hockey League as well as his time with Kalamazoo.

It took the Stars five more games, four that saw losses with Detroit, New Jersey, Philadelphia, and Edmonton, as well as an OT 6–6 with the Florida Panthers before Hitchcock notched his first win.

The 6–4 win over the Canucks occurred on January 22, 1996, in Vancouver, which was the first date of a three-game road trip with one day off between games.

Dallas took a 5–3 win over Edmonton on January 24 and a 4–2 over Calgary on January 26.

Throughout the rest of the season, Dallas was able to string together two three-game winning streaks, one set of back-to-back wins, four single-game wins, five OT ties, and nineteen losses, which included a four-game skid in March.

The pain was relatively short-lived season-wise, as Hitchcock and the Dallas Stars won the Stanley Cup in the 1998–1999 season.

Florida Panthers vs. Dallas Stars

Friday, January 12, 1996

Some NHL broadcasting teams consist of former players that serve in some capacity, such as color analyst or commentator. This person compliments and adds content for the play-by-play broadcast.

One such afternoon occurred when the Florida Panthers from the Eastern Conference were in town for their one-game regular season game in Dallas.

The Panthers' color commentator at the time was Dennis Potvin.

Potvin's relationship with hockey comes from his time as a defenseman with the New York Islanders from '73–'74 through '87–'88. During that time, the Islanders won the Stanley Cup four years straight from the 1979–'80 through 1983–'84 seasons.

Potvin also served as captain for the Islanders starting with the first Stanley Cup up through 1987, when he relinquished his role of wearing the C on the jersey.

Needless to say, the name Dennis Potvin is legendary in the books of New York Islanders' hockey.

Part of the nightly routine working on game nights was having dinner in the cafeteria with members of the media. That included print, radio, TV personalities, camera operators, and team administration such as the public relations personnel.

On this particular night, Dennis Potvin decided to grab a bite to eat and sit with us. He was very cordial and introduced himself to everyone. After introductions and exchanging pleasantries, it was story time.

Needless to say, he was extremely entertaining and had plenty of stories to share. Every single story he told had the whole table laughing. The experience reminded me of being in high school and having lunch in the cafeteria. At that table, there was one person who told all the hilarious stories. That one person was Dennis Potvin.

That night at the dinner table was the funniest thirty minutes of the season.

Vancouver Canucks vs. Dallas Stars

February 2, 1996

February seems to be the brutal weather month in Dallas Fort Worth. Obviously, the Northern Hemisphere is in full-on winter mode. There are times of mild weather days throughout the month in DFW.

The night Vancouver came to town, serious weather was upon Dallas. With that, another decision was to be made. This time it involved Motorhead playing at the Galaxy Club in Deep Ellum.

I was thinking throughout the day that once I left the arena, I would just drive several miles east of Reunion Arena and catch the Motorhead show. I knew some fun weather was heading in though.

When I was done for the night after locking and securing everything, I made my way to the parking lot. The serious winter weather started to hit during the game. Ice was accumulating.

I was thinking to myself several hours ahead. I concluded it wasn't worth the risk to catch the show and then drive back to Fort Worth.

That would put several additional hours of ice accumulation on the roads.

Even though I was still, at that time, a massive Motorhead fan, I couldn't risk anything. It was very difficult passing up the Motorhead show two miles away. I had to make a commonsense decision. That's what it boiled down to.

This was at a point when Motorhead was playing small venues or rooms. It would be several years before Lemmy/Motorhead would finally receive the respect and admiration they fully deserved.

As for the game, Toronto skated away with a 1-0 win over Dallas on New Year's Day.

THIRTY-FIVE

NHL SEASON PART II

HOCKEY MEMORIES FROM MY Youth

I was a baseball kid growing up in the 1970s. I played a total of six seasons, with five of those in Little League. Players I thought fondly of were obviously Hank Aaron, Brooks Robinson, Johnny Bench, and Carl Yastrzemski. Those were the names of my favorite baseball players.

Hockey wasn't on my radar growing up. Minor league hockey was played in the Dallas-Fort Worth area under the Central Hockey League. The league was in existence from 1963 until 1984 and then came back in 1992 as mentioned earlier in the book.

From 1967–1974, Fort Worth had the Wings. They were a minor league affiliate with the Detroit Red Wings. From 1974–1982, the Fort Worth Wings were the Fort Worth Texans. Their colors, though, were more in line with the New York Islanders, but there was no affiliation.

During those years from 1963–1984, hockey was played at Will Rogers Coliseum.

There was youth hockey as well. A friend of mine who I met in sixth grade played in those youth leagues like my friend Jimmy.

As for NHL hockey in the mid-1970s, I only recognized a few team logos—the Montreal Canadiens, Boston Bruins, and Philadelphia Flyers. When I look back at being a kid in the 1970s, those logos are iconic.

All this information was basically the extent of my hockey knowledge from the 1970s. I was aware of the Miracle on Ice in 1980, but that was several years later.

There wasn't a face or name I was able to place with the Canadiens or Bruins as a kid. There was a face I associated with the Philadelphia Flyers though.

The player had curly, light brownish hair and a hockey smile that consisted of two missing front teeth. His name—Bobby Clarke. He was the captain of the Flyers when the franchise won back-to-back Stanley Cups in 1974 and 1975. The team returned to the Stanley Cup in 1976 but were ironically defeated by the Montreal Canadiens.

Montreal then went on to win the Stanley Cup for the next four years under Scotty Bowman. Oddly, Montreal won the Stanley Cup the year prior (1973) to the Flyers winning the Stanley Cup two years in a row.

These six years of the Stanley Cup, four with Montreal and two with Philadelphia, are probably the reasons why I knew those logos in the 1970s.

---◦---

The Montreal Canadiens and Philadelphia Flyers

Let me fast-forward now back to the 1995–1996 Dallas Stars' season.

There were times I would be in the press box after dinner just making sure everything was tidy and neat. At times personnel or executives from the visiting team would be in the press box an hour or two prior to game time.

Reunion Arena didn't have suites. The closest things to suites would be a vacant booth in the press box. This is why visiting executives would be in the press box.

There are two specific encounters with personnel from two different teams that come to my mind; ironically, the two teams were Montreal and Philadelphia.

When I purchased the Triumph *Allied Forces* album in high school, the band photo on the back cover had guitarist Rik Emmitt wearing a fashionable shirt with the Montreal Canadiens' logo on it. I immediately recognized the logo.

Oddly, though, it was bassist Mike Levine who became known for wearing hockey swag.

Both teams came to Dallas in February; Montreal was on February 7, and Philadelphia was in town on the 28th. It wasn't the last day of the month though, as 1996 was a leap year.

When I entered the press box after dinner, I saw an individual standing in an open area to the side of the stairs. I immediately recognized him as Jacques Demers with the Montreal Canadiens. He'd won the Stanley Cup with Montreal in 1993. That stopped the Pittsburgh Penguins from winning the Cup three years straight. It was also the 100th Anniversary of the Stanley Cup. It was only fitting for Montreal to raise the Stanley Cup in '93.

The following year 1993–1994, Montreal lost in round one, and in the 1994–1995 season, the Canadiens missed the playoffs.

For the 1995–1996 season, the Canadiens started the season off on a five-game skid. At that point, Demers was relieved of his duties.

We chatted for a while. What I remember the most was he was very soft spoken and cordial. I don't recall what we spoke about, but it was a nice little chat with the person who'd guided the Montreal Canadiens to the Stanley Cup at the century mark of the cup.

As with Montreal, I was looking forward to seeing the Philadelphia Flyers against Dallas.

Again as I approached the press box, I saw a sharply dressed man. He had that executive vibe to him. I introduced myself and stated that if he needed anything or assistance to please let me know.

He introduced himself as well, and his name was Bobby Clarke, the name that belonged to the face I remembered from hockey as a kid.

He didn't have curly hair. It was more tamed and ideally styled for an executive. As we spoke, I just couldn't help it, but all I could think about was that 1970's hockey smile with the two missing front teeth.

As with Demers, I don't recall what we spoke about, but he was a super nice and cordial hockey figure. It was a pleasure just to talk with him for a few minutes.

As for the Flyers game, I do have a specific memory. It occurred late in the game. I can't say if it was in the third period or in OT. I will say I was down in the corner where teams would exit, and I would pull the Stars of the Game.

One of the big name players on Philadelphia was #88, Eric Lindros. All I can say is a Stars player came in and executed a perfectly timed hip check on Lindros that sent him into the air. When he hit the ice, he was not a happy person and was chirping to one of the officials.

That check or hit on Lindros was the one hit I remember from the season. It was that memorable.

The Great One, Wayne Gretzky

March 20, 1996

Wayne Gretzky would be on an opposing team a total of four times during the season. One of those visits would be the last preseason game on Monday, October 2, 1995. The other three visits were on November 8, January 8, and March 20.

There would be trade news during the '95–'96 season involving

Gretzky. As the season started, he was with the LA Kings and saw action in the November 8 and January 8 games. He was credited with two assists in each game. It was something else watching him on the ice from up high in the press box. His skating had a smooth, fluid flow. It's hard to explain but amazing to see.

The Kings were only scheduled to visit Dallas twice that season, but a big trade went down.

On February 27, Gretzky was traded to the St. Louis Blues. That would bring Gretzky back to Reunion Arena one more time on Wednesday, March 20, as a St. Louis Blue. That day, as with all the preceding game days, I took care of my duties. By this time, setting up the press box was just a standard routine.

Game day started off like any other day. I stopped by the front office in Valley Ranch and picked up game notes, media guides, and any other material I needed to take to the arena. I arrived at the arena and set up the press box, putting out game notes for all seated media members on press row as well as in the broadcast booths.

I made my way downstairs to the locker rooms, placing a stack of game notes on the table in the center of the Stars' locker room. The tables in each locker room were nothing special, just your typical folding brown banquet table.

I made my way into the St. Louis locker room. I had the stack of game notes ready to place on the table. As I was walking in, I saw Wayne Gretzky sitting back in a chair, relaxing at the table in his blue Bauer hockey garments with his feet up, ankles crossed.

Immediately my mind said to me, "That's Wayne Gretzky." I felt a surge of nervousness rush through me. I didn't want to make any wrong moves, trip, or do something clumsy that would result in pure embarrassment.

As I reached out with the stack of game notes, Gretzky asked for a copy. I replied, "Yes, sir," and handed him a set of game notes.

He then said, "You're a beautiful man," and all I could say was either a thank you or a you're welcome. I don't recall. It was just a weird moment.

It was normal for Gretzky to arrive at the arena early on a game day. This was just another one of those days.

Colorado Avalanche vs. Dallas Stars

Easter Sunday, April 7, 1996

When the season started, one of the games I was looking forward to was the contest between the Montreal Canadiens and Dallas Stars scheduled for Wednesday, February 7, 1996. I wanted to see one person in action—Montreal goalie Patrick Roy. His performance on the ice as a goalie included two Stanley Cups (1986, 1993) and his two Conn Smythe Trophies or MVP in those same two years was reason enough. He's considered one of the 100 Greatest NHL Players in history. He has been referred to as the King of Goaltenders.

I would not see Roy with Montreal, as he was traded to the

Colorado Avalanche on December 6, 1995.

There were only two Colorado vs. Dallas games in the regular season, the first being the eighth home game of the season on Monday, October 30, 1995. The second was on April 7, 1996—Easter Sunday.

After I completed my game-day duties on that Easter Sunday, I was informed that my presence was needed in the Fox Sports production trailer to help track stats. I was looking forward to working in the Fox Sports trailer. It was to be a new and unique behind-the-scenes experience in TV production.

I can't say that I saw one of the greatest goalies in the game, but what I *can* say is that I saw him on monitor screens while I tracked shots on goal in the production truck.

Colorado defeated Dallas 4–1.

When I look back at the whole thing, I just chuckle.

The question is, does it count that I watched Patrick Roy on the live game feed from inside the production truck in the parking lot while the game was underway several hundred feet away?

There was a sad moment associated with the Colorado game. With the end of the Colorado and Dallas game, there was one game left in the regular season, and seeing Dallas in the play-offs was not going to happen.

The Grim Reaper

Sunday, April 14, 1996

This would be the last game of the season, capping off an incredible experience. Something like this wasn't even on my radar when I was watching the Pittsburgh Penguins win Stanley Cups in 1991 and 1992. Here, four years later, I was behind the scenes. It was an amazing opportunity.

The Red Wings and the Stars would face each other six times during the regular season, with three meetings in Detroit and three in Dallas.

This was the third and final time Detroit would visit Dallas. The first visit was Friday, December 29, followed by Wednesday, January 10.

Of the six games, Dallas was able to get a 3–3 OT tie in Detroit on Wednesday, January 3, 1996. All the other meetings resulted in a loss for Dallas.

The Stars closed out their season at home against the Red Wings. It's not unrealistic to say there was friction as Detroit skated away with wins in all six games.

At 1:54 of the first period, Detroit enforcer Stu Grimson and Dallas winger Grant Marshall dropped gloves and went at it. Both players were given five minutes for fighting and spent that time in the penalty box.

Then at 18:22 of the first period, Marshall and Grimson dropped gloves for a second time. Again, both were given five minutes for fighting. I don't know whether or not the two spent time in the penalty box or went to the locker rooms. The remaining time in the second penalty would be served at the beginning of the second period.

I will say Marshall and Grimson behaved for the remainder of the game. There was no more squaring off between the two.

Detroit lit up Dallas with three goals in the third period, handing Dallas a 5–1 loss. This was a bad look for the final game of the regular season.

With this being the last game, it would also be my last time to stand in the corner where players exited and walked to their respective locker rooms.

As Detroit skated off the ice after their sixth win against Dallas, Grimson, the enforcer that spent ten minutes in the penalty box, skated toward me. We made eye contact.

I need to add that Stu "the Grim Reaper" Grimson is a towering and imposing player at 6′ 6″. That's without his skates on. With skates on, add several more inches.

As he skated to the exit and walked onto the padding/runner, he took his right hand still in his hockey glove and rubbed the top of my head. It was something I didn't anticipate from a beast exiting the ice. It just shows you the fun personalities of hockey players.

That was my last interaction with a player for the 1995–1996 season. It was the best, just a quick impromptu moment. A genuine gesture that brought a run of forty-one home games to an end.

This is the End

I learned quite a bit from the PR department and my time running the press box. It was a seven-month learning experience on the major league sports world level. Everything ran so smoothly, even in the press box. I don't recall any hiccups at all. I prided myself on doing the best I could do.

I was more concerned about learning and seeing how a top-notch public relations department ran. In those seven months, October through April, I did just that. I think I utilized the ticket benefit once, maybe twice the entire season. I was more concerned about learning any and everything I could rather than hooking my friends up with tickets to a hockey game.

I do have one regret from the benefit: I didn't treat my parents to a game or two. I don't know why. If my father would've asked, no doubt I would have put a pair of tickets at will call.

It's small things like this that hit you hard when you reflect upon the thought years later. I have so much regret for not making one game possible. I know he would've been proud to see me up there in my element.

My only advice to others is consider the smallest of things no matter how irrelevant you might think it may be in your eyes.

If I was to continue on the path I was carving, I would bring a level of top-notch professionalism with me, and that's what I intended to do.

Probably the biggest gut punch of them all came when I removed the press box key from my keyring and handed it back over. It was as if I didn't want the amazing learning experience to come to an end.

THIRTY-SIX

THE WHIPPLE

THE RESURRECTION OF THE CHL and its success in 1992 showed hockey in Texas was possible. The presence of the Fort Worth Fire and Dallas Freeze was a factor in the relocation of Minnesota North Stars to the DFW area for the '93–'94 season.

The success of the Stars over the first three seasons only fueled the hunger for hockey in Texas.

In the spring, a new league for minor league hockey was announced with five of the six teams based in Texas. The league would be the Western Professional Hockey League, WPHL for short, or Whipple in quick conversation.

This league would bring five teams to Texas. That took the number of hockey teams based in Texas to nine for the '96–'97 season.

These other cities included the Dallas Stars (NHL), Houston Aeros (IHL), Fort Worth and San Antonio (CHL), and the newly added five WPHL teams.

The new Texas teams would be based in Amarillo, Austin, El Paso, Waco, and the Central Texas area, with the team's headquarters in Bell County. The Central Texas team would cater to Belton, Temple, and the Fort Hood/Killeen area. This team would be known as the Central Texas Stampede.

As for the other Texas teams, there would be the Amarillo Rattlers, Austin Ice Bats, El Paso Buzzards, and Waco Wizards.

The sixth team was based in Albuquerque but would be known as the New Mexico Scorpions.

Geographically, the teams were arranged into the Central Texas area and the West Texas/Panhandle/New Mexico area.

Through social media, I learned one team was still in search of a public relations person. I thought to myself, "I need to reach out," and I did.

The phone interview process wasn't long at all. I think it had something to do with being fresh off a public relations internship with the Dallas Stars. Within a day or two, I was hired, but no contract was signed.

The next step for me was to make a road trip, visit and meet the front office, look for housing, and start making preparations to relocate.

The day trip was fairly simple, as I was able to take care of everything needed before packing up and moving. I ended up in the same apartment complex as the players, just on the opposite side, which was fine with me.

Once I relocated, I was welcomed by the front office staff. The team was nice enough to have a luncheon where members of the TV and print media were invited so I could be introduced to them.

On one of my first full days in the front office, I was asking my fellow office workers what team they worked for the previous season or where they relocated from. The answers surprised me.

I was the only person who was coming into a brand-new league and a brand-new franchise with any hockey front office experience. Everyone was local. That was the first red flag, but I wanted to stay positive.

As for the captain who would be piloting the administrative aspect of the team and front office, he was the leading scorer of the AA team where the ownership was located. No front office experience, just on-ice experience of putting the puck in the net.

Locally, there was pushback on the team name, which I found to be odd. That whole event was just weird. Many residents felt the name was not a proper fit for the city. Locals were reading into the name a bit too much. The team name didn't align with the Bible Belt perception and ideology of the residents and region.

I remember sitting at a stoplight in the team van. A blue-collar worker in a work truck pulled up next to me. The man in the vehicle looked at me and said, "We are sure glad you're here, but we wish you would change the name." He was talking about the team and its admin.

I said, "Thank you very much. I am glad we are here, and I can understand where you are coming from."

On my first visit to the coliseum, I noticed there were no press box accommodations. In other words, there was not a press box. The press box would serve several functions. The main purpose in my eyes would be to allow print, radio, and TV home and visitors media an area to report or broadcast the game. The press box area would also serve as a seating area for the off-ice officials to track and report stats during the game. There wasn't enough room to house the entire off-ice official staff. A workstation had to be created for them just outside the press box.

Some people thought that the off-ice officials could just work off of TV trays outside the press box. I found this to be truly insulting, but I wasn't surprised. Coliseum maintenance was nice enough to create a workstation made out of plywood for them. I was impressed with the carpentry of the final product.

The off-ice officials volunteered their time. The least I could do was to feed them before the game. I received pushback on that as well. Eventually, the fine dining of delivered pizzas would serve as dinner.

As for the game program, it wasn't in the standard magazine format as customary with professional sports. It was in a stapled newspaper format. People still remember that when I talk with them about the time I spent in their city.

Opening night was a disaster. The coliseum lacked A/C. All the conditions were present, and fog started accumulating, hovering over the ice. I had never seen or experienced that. The second night, the same thing happened, but industrial-sized fans were brought in, ready to pull the fog out if needed. Yes, the large fans were needed for that second game. People remember that night years later.

The appearance and presence of this fog those first two nights was basically an ill omen for the season.

When the ice was removed for other events in the coliseum, the front office staff was expected to put the ice back in and paint it. Normally, that would be done by coliseum staff.

Part of the duties of a PR person is to travel with the team. This PR person wasn't sent out on the road with the team. It was dumbfounding and a sore spot for me.

Eventually, the team started hosting public skating in the coliseum on non-game days. With that, the team needed to purchase rental skates. By the end of the season, the rental skates needed to be relocated to an empty office space across the parking lot from the team's front office. It was a task that took several hours to do.

Prior to heading over to the coliseum to start loading skates, the general manager told me that the following year, they would send me out with the team. I mentioned that I thought that was a good idea.

Once we got all the skates moved from the coliseum and into the empty office space, I was let go from the team. The statement of telling me they would be sending me out with the team was a bait-and-switch tactic. When I look back on that day, am I surprised that happened? No, not at all.

Actions speak louder than words.

These are just a few examples from the nightmare of the team's inaugural season.

In the end, I thought of an analogy. Ownership wanted the front office to produce cordon bleu but gave us chicken nuggets to work with.

In December, there was a boy, maybe ten years old, who wanted to visit the locker room. I arranged his visit on a game day but several hours prior to when players would arrive. I learned who his favorite player was and made sure that he was able to put on the player's uniform.

I always enjoyed doing stuff like this with the young fans. There really was no effort at all to grant this request. All I needed to do was speak with the player and equipment manager. It does the heart and soul good to make something like this happen. It was all worth it to see joy on the boy's face.

Several days went by, and I received a thank-you card in the mail written by the fan. He thanked me for allowing him to visit the locker room and try on the uniform. He said the best part of his visit was when I gave him a game puck. He added he was looking forward to attending more games in the future. The boy even included a photo of himself in the uniform.

This makes me wonder if the boy who is now an adult still has that game puck and whether it is on display somewhere.

There was a boy named Grant who was a huge fan and supporter of the team. He knew all the players by name and was just a really excited kid experiencing hockey in his hometown, so much so that he wanted to have his ninth birthday party at a game.

His mother went all out. I think the number of his friends totaled nine, so that was ten kids, including the birthday boy, plus his mother. My numbers could be totally off though.

There was a fancy cake, cupcakes, and goodie bags that consisted of fun stuff and a team keychain. The logo keychains were made of rubbery plastic.

Around this time, Grant's mother mentioned to me that she'd inquired about receiving a bulk discount on the keychains. The merchandise person refused and wouldn't budge. This is after tickets for the game—eleven at minimum were purchased, as well as other things.

What Grant really wanted for his birthday was a game-used stick from his favorite player. I made sure that happened. I spoke with the player prior to the game as well as the equipment manager.

Grant was so happy when he was given the stick after the game. His mother took a picture of him with the player and stick. She also wanted me in the photo. I thought that was super-nice.

Several days after the game I received a thank-you card in the mail from Grant's mother, and it read as follows:

"Thank you *so* much for all you have done. You'll never know the joy you have brought to this child! What a difference you've made in his life. It means that someone had a part in bringing joy to another's heart. Thank you for being that someone." His mother signed it and included Grant's name as well.

At some point, maybe when I received the card, I also received an 8×10 of the photo she took.

Grant was such a huge fan that at the end of the season, he presented each player a trophy with their name on it. I thought that was supercool of him to do that. I think there were eighteen players. The cost for this wouldn't be cheap. To top it off, Grant gave me a trophy as well. I was the only front office person to receive one. I truly felt honored, but not surprised.

I reconnected with Grant through social media several years ago. He was shocked that I still had the trophy and that it's on display in my game room.

I had plans to eventually meet up with Grant and have lunch, but it didn't happen and unfortunately it will never happen.

———◆———

While I was with the team, I did two things musically, and there was no way I was going to let these opportunities slip by.

In the spring, it was announced that KISS would be doing a reunion tour with all the original members in full makeup with the 1977 *Love Gun*-era costumes. This announcement was huge to me and every person my age who didn't get to experience the magic of KISS live when we were kids. We would finally get to see our first musical heroes. This tour would be the closest thing to having a time machine.

KISS was scheduled to play July 5, 1996, at Reunion Arena. Tickets were made available to the public on Saturday, May 11, 1996. Obviously, Lee and I grabbed tickets as soon as we could. This was before I reached out to the team and was eventually hired, but I was not going to miss this show.

I traveled to the show in Dallas. Let me say, it was an out-of-body experience. I have never attended a concert where fans on the floor, lower balcony, and upper balcony stood the entire time, singing every word and playing every air guitar riff and solo and drum rhythm and fill.

There were parents who had their kids there. I am curious as to what those young fans thought of the show.

I can't forget to mention fans in makeup. They were all over the place.

And to think KISS wasn't sure if this tour was going to be successful. When forty thousand tickets sold out for the first date at Tiger Stadium in forty-seven minutes, that was a solid indicator.

I also caught the show in Austin on November 5, 1996, but it didn't have the same impact as the Dallas show.

When the '96–'97 NHL preseason or exhibition season kicked in, the Detroit Red Wings and Pittsburgh Penguins were scheduled for a neutral-site game at the Summit in Houston. Coach and I drove to Houston for this game. We didn't have tickets. He had a plan, and it was awesome.

Since Coach played in the World Hockey Association, or WHA, he knew his way around the Houston Summit. Upon our arrival, he directed me to park in the loading dock area. He exited the vehicle, and a security guard approached him. He said he was with the Detroit Red Wings and had just arrived in town. The security guard let him in, and Coach went to the locker room. He was gone for a few minutes and came back out with a Detroit Red Wings staff credential for this game. He gave it to me and said, "You are now Barry Smith."

The security guard let us park the car in the loading dock, and we went in. He introduced me to Scotty Bowman, who was now the interim coach for the Detroit Red Wings. Just several years earlier, Bowman led the Pittsburgh Penguins to their second Stanley Cup Championship, the repeat in 1992. Bowman took over coaching duties when Bob Johnson passed away of cancer during the season.

While in that area, I was able to speak with the Penguins PR person, who I'd met when I was with the Dallas Stars the previous year.

The whole night was amazing. It felt good to be in that NHL element again for a night.

THIRTY-SEVEN

THERE WAS STATIC

OVER THE YEARS, I'VE had people tell me I should work in radio and that my voice is an ideal fit. I really didn't put much thought into the repeated suggestion. I really should have.

After the bait-and-switch about relocating the rental skates from the coliseum, I spoke with a promotions employee from one of several radio stations in the area. She was with the station that did a lot of work with the team. She was sad the team had let me go. Actually, ownership and the front office administration wasn't looked upon favorably by others.

I was told if I needed anything at all to reach out and let her know. That was my ticket to work radio. Unfortunately, I was so hell-bent on working in hockey that I didn't follow up. I should have looked into the invite. I know that if I would have followed up, promotions and on-site promotions would have been "lit," as kids these days say.

My whole life's trajectory would be different if I had gone the radio route. I wonder if I would have ended up back in DFW with a station in a larger market. I am sure that doing promotions, I would have eventually ended up as an on-air personality as well.

The Whipple was turning some heads after completing its first season as a new league.

One person who took notice was an individual in Fort Worth with deep pockets. They wanted to bring a WPHL team to Fort Worth even though there was already another established team in the city.

This ownership group forged ahead like a bull without even receiving permission from the league in the very formative days. The announcement came out of nowhere. It was crazy and unorganized, but I wanted to be part of it. Why? I think it had to do with something along the lines of me coming full circle, returning back to Fort Worth as the PR person with the new Fort Worth hockey team.

I should've stayed away, but that's how badly I wanted to be back in Fort Worth.

Everything came crashing down four months later.

There were power struggles and headbutting between ownership and a general manager. It was chaotic, hectic, and very unorganized. I am surprised the team suited players on the ice for the '97–'98 season. The only thing the team had going for it was the coach, Bill MacDonald. He'd taken the CHL's Fort Worth Fire to the playoffs the year before. The team won the CHL Championship. Now he was going to lead the new Fort Worth team. That meant there were two minor league hockey teams in Fort Worth.

My lease ran out, and I moved back. I was happy to be part of the new team in Fort Worth. I had no idea of the heartache, frustration, and disappointment that was on the horizon several months out.

The new Fort Worth team originally was going to be called the Fort Worth Bulls, but there was an already existing hockey team under the name—the Birmingham Bulls of the ECHL. The new Fort Worth team had to change its name. They settled upon the Fort Worth Brahmas, a name still in existence today relating to hockey in the DFW area.

This was just one example of how unorganized and chaotic it was early on.

After leaving four months in, I was truly devastated. All the hard work and sacrifices I had made to get to that point were quickly flushed away.

By this time, hockey front offices throughout the minor leagues were staffed for the approaching season.

The only good that came out of those four months is that I was introduced to sports marketing. I looked at the game not only from a public relations aspect, but now I was looking at potential sponsorship ideas and promotion angles.

I was able to look at a company and their product and create a concept for a sponsorship that included radio spots, game program ads, in-game mentions, and advertising on the dasher boards.

In those four months, I didn't get to the point of how to create the campaign and pitch the idea to potential sponsors. To this day, I can come up with a concept for a sponsorship and promotion. That brief stint opened up the analytical side of me.

I saw sports marketing coming and anticipated that it would trickle down in the next year or so. What was I seeing? What was it?

It was corporate sponsorships in the sports world at varying levels. Obviously, sponsorships were and still are a common sight at the major league levels. It didn't matter the sport at the time—the sponsorship was there.

I saw sponsorships on the collegiate level, especially in D1, but not to the extent that one would see at a major league level.

I knew at some point sponsorships would trickle down to the high school level in the next year or two at that time. I was paying close attention. I saw it start happening within the year of thinking this way.

Unfortunately, I didn't know where or how to tap in. I am not sure if there were any sports marketing firms or not. Sadly, I just let everything pass me by. Within a year or so, sponsorships made their way to the high school level.

I was actually able to sit down and speak with an athletic director of a large school district. He really didn't know where to point me and didn't have any idea how to go about it.

As I say, I was ahead of the curve. I just didn't know where to turn and capitalize.

High school sports have exploded over the years. Just look at high school football stadiums being built, especially in Texas. It's insane.

The thought of working in radio promotions wasn't on my radar, as I still had tunnel vision to keep things alive; but little by little, reality started to sink in that it was over. I needed to step back and take a look at everything and think beyond the now and more like ten plus years down the road.

I was thinking reality, and that could've happened easier if I had gone the promotions route.

The Best Part of Losing

During the 1997–1998 season, I was watching the box scores of the former team I'd worked for. I never have enjoyed reading game recaps as much as I did during the first part of their season.

The team started 0-4-1, which means they dropped five games straight to start the season. To give them a sprinkling of credit, one of those losses came as a shootout loss, which earned them one point—thus the record of 0-4-1 instead of 0-5-0.

The team pulled off their first win of the season in the sixth game. Then the bottom fell out. The team went on an eighteen-game skid. Only three of those games came from losses in the shootout; all the others were straight up notches in the L column.

It was very comical for me to watch this gong show of a team being handed L after L.

Responsibility starts with the coach, and with a record of 3-21-3, a change was made. A new coach was brought in. The team wrapped up their season at 18-48-3.

Keep in mind, the coach that stepped away was the general manager the previous year and took over as a player/coach in February of the 1996–1997 season. Apparently, the dreams and talk of taking the team to the playoffs under the coaching change fell flat.

To the team's credit, there was an impressive turnaround record-wise in the 1998–1999 season, posting a 40-22-7 record. The team went from the worst to one of the best.

In those formative years of the Whipple, ownership groups that entered the league lacked experience or pockets deep enough to properly operate the team. My former team was a fine example of that.

The original ownership group sold the team prior to their fourth year in existence. I wasn't surprised to learn that in the first part of the 1999–2000 season, the team folded under the new ownership group. The team's last game was December 12, 1999, against the Corpus Christi IceRays.

The franchise was a huge pain for the league. I wouldn't be surprised if there had been a sigh of relief when those doors closed for the last time. With the turn of the key, there was one last echo of the locks.

THIRTY-EIGHT

4, 3, 2

FOR THE NEXT NINE years, I lived in Dallas, as that's where I landed a job. I knew that I needed to work in an industry that was stable—the insurance industry. It wasn't the most glamorous of gigs, but it took care of the bills while seeing a $14K increase in salary.

It didn't take long for me to get pulled back into live music roughly five years after I had my last hurrah with Type O Negative.

A close friend of mine, who just happened to be a hockey equipment manager I worked with, told me that I needed to go check out this band he knew. I took what he was telling me with a grain of salt. He told me this band had a bag of something. I needed to see them. I wasn't sure if I wanted to be part of the scene again, but I relented.

The band was Hellafied Funk Crew out of Dallas. They were packing the club venues just as much as a national act touring on that level. They had something different and had their presentation down. On top of all that, they were good, very good.

The first time I saw them, I was highly impressed, as I had seen numerous bands play on a local level. The first show of theirs I saw was at Trees, a venue in Deep Ellum east of downtown Dallas. Trees is a normal tour stop for national acts. Bands like Nirvana and Soundgarden once graced the stage.

HFC consisted of the standard band setup—drums, bass, and guitar—but there were a total of two vocalists/frontmen who rapped. This was during the rap/rock phase that was sweeping the nation.

Most of all, the band was very marketable. Each member had their own unique stage persona.

The band's logo bore a striking resemblance of KFC's Colonel sporting Ray-Bans, a long goatee, and red devil horns. Eventually, KFC got wind of the Colonel's likeness and asked the band to stop using the image, as the Colonel wasn't being represented in a proper manner.

At that point, their CD that was released locally became a collector's item, as the cover art was changed.

As anticipated, I started hanging out with the band and started photographing them. I was capturing some really nice images because with their personas, each member was very photogenic. As a whole, the band had an image that was pro level. There was even a graphic artist who did artwork.

They had a plywood cutout of the revamped Colonel logo with glowing eyes. This served as the backdrop positioned prominently behind the drummer. The original Colonel would be hung from a second floor window of Trees, basically announcing visually to those outside that HFC was, as people would say, "in the house." It was very impressive, actually.

All the experiences from the past two years were still fresh in my mind. It didn't take long for me to start brainstorming ideas. I wanted to create some possible merchandise ideas for the band. There were so many possibilities. One became a reality.

HFC had a saying, "4, 3, 2, Hellafied Funk Crew."

One evening I glanced at my refrigerator door. I started staring at a Domino's Pizza magnet with the logo attached to the door for a few moments. Then it hit me.

I saw the individual domino sections of light blue and red. The blue section had two white dots, and the red section had one dot. What came to my mind was tweaking the logo that incorporated 4, 3, 2, Hellafied Funk Crew. Instead of two sections of a domino, there would be three. The first would have four dots, the second would have three and then two. The color scheme would remain the same. In the same font, instead of the company name, "Hellafied Funk Crew" would be written.

Then the kicker: on the back of the shirt, it said in large letters, "Free Deviltry."

The shirt was a hit with band members, but their local label wasn't pleased. The only thing I can think of is that they had been outwitted on a piece of merchandise. The label could have capitalized on the idea but didn't, a missed opportunity for funds on their end.

The band's reach wasn't just confined to the Dallas-Fort Worth area. They played out-of-town gigs, including two sets of weekend dates in Maui at the Hard Rock Cafe.

The first set of dates occurred in October 1999 and the second, New Year's Eve. I was invited to go with the band. If there was a place to be for Y2K, Maui was it. All I needed to do was to pay for a plane ticket.

The band had separate units at a condo complex that were walking distance from the Hard Rock Cafe. Food vouchers were provided daily by the Hard Rock. The food portions were so large, it was a meal two people could share with leftovers. That happened daily while there.

During my time there, I spent less than $100, with the majority of my spending happening on the last day of our stay.

Being in Maui, we were one of the last time zones. To put it in perspective, Australia was twenty-one hours ahead of Hawaii. As we were watching the New Year's Eve events in Australia on the

TV, we noticed that nothing was happening in regard to the Y2K scare.

The last sunset of 1999 that Brian shot from the beach in Lahaina. Photo by Brian McLean

I will say it was a nonstop drinking fest while there. It was something I couldn't do and just didn't want to do. I had a shot here and there, but drowning in booze just wasn't my thing. I saw too many hangovers while there.

Unfortunately, there was a lack of business sense within the band. It was all about partying and drinking.

Here's a prime example. We all met an executive from a telecommunications company. He was really impressed with the band. He bought them lots of food on off nights at different bars and even cut the band a $1,000 check to purchase a trailer for out-of-town shows. Members wanted that check cashed since it was "their money." What did some members do? They drank away their portion of the $1,000.

When I look back on these events, this was the beginning of the end.

On the day we were leaving, we were sitting on the outside patio furniture of the Hard Rock Cafe. I was speaking with the bass player, Bob, and I remember twelve distinct words from our conversation.

He said in a soft voice to me, "I just want to get with a band that can make it."

The band was turning heads, and people were taking notice. A major label put a record deal on the table. Unfortunately, a late-night drunken stupor with a threatening phone call killed the deal. That was it.

The chance the band had was gone, flushed away by alcohol. It was really sad.

There's no telling what could've been. I am certain there would've been a platinum record or two, several world tours, and all the other stuff. Members could have reached and lived all of their dreams, but the opportunity never materialized.

Sadly, no other deals were offered. That was it. The golden opportunity had vanished and there were no more.

Thirty-Nine

What Are the Odds?

While living in Dallas, I was meeting a whole new group of friends. Several of us had things in common. The best description would be white-collar, college-educated metalheads.

This new group of friends introduced me to the treasure trove of European metal. Bands I never really knew existed were starting to make waves in the United States. Two of the best examples would be Opeth and Dimmu Borgir. There are others as well, but these two bands had a major impact on me.

Also, along with this new group of friends, Lee had moved back from a reporter job in Temecula, and I was able to speak with him on a more consistent basis. He was also feeding me new music. The band I remember the most that he introduced me to was Primal Fear from Germany. He made me a mix cassette with a lot of bands, but Primal Fear is the one band I remember. I can't even tell you the others.

One of my newfound friends, Scott, was on the same wavelength as me. Like me, Scott was a graduate from a Southwest Conference school. For him, it was SMU with a degree in communications.

Now, prior to meeting Scott, our paths crossed as he managed an underground metal CD store called Bone Daddy's in Dallas. I only went to the store once. I remember what I bought, and I remember him.

Even though he no longer worked at Bone Daddy's when I formally met him and we started hanging out, he still had all of his music distribution contacts. Basically, we, being this small group of friends with a disposable income, had a small, independent record store at our fingertips. Every few weeks, we would place orders for new releases, collector editions, and vinyl releases.

This was at a time that vinyl had yet to make the resurgence we are seeing today.

With this new group of friends that had metal music flowing through their veins, I was able to experience things I had never experienced before.

A group of us would fly out to metal festivals. Between 2002 and 2005, I went to a total of five festivals. Two were in Milwaukee at the Milwaukee Metal Fest, and three were in Atlanta at ProgPower USA. Progpower is a highly respected metal festival that sells out every year. They always have a special band booked.

In 2003, ProgPower USA brought in Gamma Ray, a German power metal outfit. It was noteworthy actually. The show would be the band's first appearance in the United States but second overall in

North America. They'd played in Montreal a night or two prior.

It was amazing to watch their set and how into the band the crowd was. They were singing every word to every song. There was this unified bond of Gamma Ray fans from all over the world. It was an incredible thing to witness.

As I would look around the venue seeing all the people singing and standing up, I was reminded of the time I saw KISS in 1996 on the Reunion Tour.

One night in 2003, Scott and I were heading to the Bronco Bowl in Dallas to see King's X. The band was playing the smaller venue called the Canyon Club and not the main, larger venue known as the Bronco Bowl. As we were driving, I asked him how he was able to go out on tour with bands in the 1980s and early 1990s.

He told me the story from when he was in a fraternity at SMU. He said a friend of his called him from the promoter's office of the Texxas Jam. He was asked if he could help round up and gather some extra people to work security at the Texxas Jam.

He told the promoter assistant no problem. All he did was call in a favor with his fraternity brothers. Basically, Scott provided an additional one hundred or so security personnel with one phone call. He was told he would be repaid for his efforts, and it would be worth it.

Scott was hired up and went out on major arena tours, coordinating local security. He was on the OzzFests, Metallica's Master of Puppets, and Iron Maiden's Fear of the Dark tours and many others. This is a small sampling of the impressive tours he worked on during those years.

From these tours is where and how he obtained his amazing collection of music memorabilia. While we were still driving to the show, I asked him what his favorite piece of memorabilia was. He told me it was an RIAA multi-platinum award for Judas Priest albums. The framed presentation measures several feet across. It's massive and definitely something to be proud of, and it was awarded to him. When seen in person, the piece is just mind-blowing.

I mentioned to Scott that I have several pieces of unique music memorabilia as well, but they consist of bands that I had photographed.

He asked me which of all the pieces I owned was my favorite. I began to explain to him about the black-and-white Bruce Dickinson photo I shot in 1987. The photo was shot on Iron Maiden's *Somewhere in Time* tour at Tarrant County Convention Center in Fort Worth.

I continued that I had hopes of having the photo signed one day. I explained in detail to Scott what the photo looked like and the size of the print, a 16×20.

The opportunity to have Bruce sign the photo presented itself in the summer of 1992 when the sound engineer for my brother's band was on tour with Iron Maiden.

I continued by explaining when we were hanging out in the backstage area before the show, the band members started arriving. Obviously, people flocked toward Bruce Dickinson. My dream of having this photo signed was about to become a reality.

I told Scott that I had the silver paint pen ready to go. When the opportunity presented itself, I laid the photo out on the table in front of Bruce.

Scott then looked at me while he was driving and said, "And Bruce signed the photo on the bottom right."

I was stunned and asked, "How in the **** do you know *that*?"

He replied, "I was standing right next to you. I probably have a photo of you there. I was taking pictures backstage."

Brian with a picture disc in hand standing next to Iron Maiden bassist Steve Harris before their July 8, 1992 show at Starplex Amphitheater in Dallas. Photo by Scott G.

Scott then said that he told Bruce later on that he put a really nice signature on the photo. Bruce replied because it was a nice photo.

In all my life, I have never had my mind blown more than at that moment in his little truck. I was speechless.

About six months later, I received a phone call from one of my friends, and he said, "Guess what? We found a photo of you backstage at Iron Maiden in Scott's photos."

Several days later, I picked up the photograph. It's been tucked into the frame of the Bruce Dickinson photo ever since.

FORTY

REVIEWS AND INTERVIEWS

AROUND 1998 OR 1999, I met an entertainment industry professional named Dave with Head First Entertainment through social media. He was and is still a music publicist, a person who handles PR for bands. His duties include setting up interviews, securing reviews for upcoming releases, setting up media to cover a show, whether as a writer or photographer, and so on. In a nutshell, his job is to secure publicity for his clients, the bands. He's a true professional on the business side of things and a cool dude away from the office. In short, he's an all-around good person. This is why we have remained in contact for years.

Around 2003 or early 2004, he was launching a print publication titled *Hard Attack Magazine*. He approached me to see if I wanted to be a contributing writer. Of course, I jumped at the chance. This would give me a creative outlet to dust off my writer skills and get them back up to par.

I was put on the media mailing list of several record labels where

I would receive advance copies of CDs for review. I also started conducting phone interviews with musicians. Normally, these musicians were in Europe and preparing for a US tour that would begin in a few days. These interviews were last-minute bits of publicity before they would hit the North American shores.

The results would not be just a question-and-answer session, but more of a feature, a human-interest article that touched on the upcoming tour but personal aspects of the musicians as well. In the end, these musicians are just people like you and me. They just have a really cool gig, and they get paid for it.

I remember my very first interview with a musician over the phone. It was Michael Amott from Arch Enemy. We were talking about life, getting ready for the upcoming tour, and other things. During the interview, I could hear the buckles and snaps of stage clothes being tossed around in the dryer. It was just a simple indication of life and getting ready for a tour.

My second interview was with Schmier, bassist and founding member of the German thrash band Destruction. He was very cordial, and I enjoyed talking to him about life in general. I did touch on the fact that at one point he owned a pizzeria named Barracuda. We just talked about things outside of playing on a stage.

Two other individuals I fondly recall speaking with were Peter Tagtgren from Hypocrisy and Devin Townsend of Strapping Young Lad. I had the pleasure of speaking with both of these individuals twice. Each time, I was able to write some really nice, personable stories.

Peter Tagtren may have been my third phone interview. The second time when I was able to interview him, we sat down in the lounge of the tour bus in the parking lot of the Ridglea Theater in Fort Worth. Interviewing a musician on their bus before a show or after was also a special event. Here, I was speaking with individuals who have such an aggressive and menacing presence on stage, but during an interview, they are just soft-spoken and very cordial individuals.

As I was interviewing him, I kept thinking to myself how fortunate I was. Not only is he an incredible musician whose band has produced some great extreme metal, but he's also an amazing and sought-after producer. He owns The Abyss studio in Sweden and has hosted some incredible bands such as Dimmu Borgir, Marduk, Celtic Frost, Children of Bodom, Destruction, and his own bands, Hypocrisy and Pain. This is only a small sampling.

During our sit-down interview in 2005 or so, I inquired about his young son who was maybe ten at the time. He told me that his son liked to paint. All these years later, I often wonder if his son, who would now be approaching thirty, still paints.

I was fortunate enough to sit down with Devin Townsend twice, once after a show at Trees in Dallas. The second time was after a show at the Ridglea Theater in Fort Worth. The first time we spoke was actually my first in-person interview on a bus. I was definitely nervous. I took things one step at a time, listening intently, focusing on what he was saying.

The feature ended up with how difficult things can be on the road and how the sale of merchandise plays an important part for a band while touring.

I vividly recall during their set that night, Devin said, "We are Strapping Young Lad from Canada. Buy T-shirts." That was my lead for the story.

FORTY-ONE

13 MONTHS

FOR SEVERAL YEARS IN the early 2000s, there was a touring Christmas benefit called Rock 4 Xmas. It was a foundation that helped provide toys and the overall Christmas spirit to less fortunate families across the country.

In 2003, the benefit was a thirty-plus date tour that kicked off in Salt Lake City on October 30 with an impressive roster of musicians taking part. It was a generous attempt of those involved to help. If one child was able to have a gift under the tree that resulted from Rock 4 Xmas, then a goal was accomplished.

The benefit featured respected rock musicians who traveled from city to city. These musicians donated their talents and performed. Actually, it was more of an all-star touring line-up with some impressive names attached.

There are dates throughout the tour that some musicians drop off, then new musicians jump aboard to fill the vacated spots.

When the Rock 4 Xmas benefit tour stopped in Arlington in November 2003, it featured Randy Jackson from Zebra, Chris Slade who drummed for AC/DC, Badfinger's Joey Molland, and vocalist Terry Ilous of XYZ as well as others.

Each night on the tour there would be an auction of merchandise. There were regular sales of shirts, CDs, and other items to assist in raising money for the cause. One of the more popular items each night was the signed acoustic guitar up for auction.

The club that played host for the Arlington stop in 2003 was called Division One. The venue was located on Division Street several miles west of Highway 360 on the eastern edge of Arlington and travels north and south.

Division One was a small club that was trying to establish themselves as a live music venue while competing with the more established rooms located in Deep Ellum in Dallas.

There were several separate areas in Division One—the main music room with the stage, the bar area with pool tables and a couch. The upstairs bar served as the VIP room the night the Rock 4 Xmas tour stopped in Arlington. The VIP area gave fans, local music writers and radio personnel the opportunity to mingle with the musicians prior to the show. There was even a massage therapist on hand with a folding table to provide relief from stress or muscle tensions to those who needed it.

Division One was also a place that was frequented by Darrell Abbott and friends, and the night of the Rock 4 Xmas was no different.

Accompanying Abbott on this night were two members of the newly formed band Damage Plan, Bob the bass player from the aforementioned Hellafied Funk Crew and vocalist Patrick Lachman, as well as one or two more individuals.

The night of the Rock 4 Xmas show was the first time I was able to see Bob and speak with him in a while. Most of all, I could congratulate him as a member of Damage Plan. When I saw him, I was greeted with a king-sized bear hug and plenty of pats on the back. Joy filled his eyes.

I was so happy for him. I told him that I remember the day we had left Maui in 2000 and the talk we had on the outside patio of the Hard Rock Café.

His words will forever stick with me. "I just want to get with a band that can make it."

By joining Damage Plan, the dream for Bob was now becoming a reality. I was extremely happy for him. I truly was.

Landing in a band with the level of credibility and status attached with Damage Plan was unmatched. He could not have joined a band with a better list of individuals. Bob deserved it, and I let him know.

We exchanged emails and phone numbers with his contact information written on the last Damage Plan business card he had in his wallet.

Several months down the road, February 10, 2004 to be exact, the Damage Plan debut would be released through Elektra Records. It would be Bob's major label debut as a musician but not the first time a disc would be released with his name attached.

Prior to leaving Division One in a brisk departure, Abbott was in the stage room where the live musicians were performing a jam session. He was standing directly to the left of the black curtains that hung in the doorway watching, taking in the sights. I made eye contact with him but just gave him a smile and head nod. I didn't want to interfere with his personal time.

The Rock 4 Xmas benefit would be the last time I would see Darrell Abbott.

I watched with disappointment as the group of friends walked out the door in a hurry. I was bitter that I didn't get to say bye to Bob but just thought that eventually I would run into them again.

Several weeks later I saw Bob and Pat at the King Diamond show in Fort Worth, but Darrell was not with them. I was happy that I saw Bob, and once again, the brotherly hug was given.

———

Several years later the thought of pulling my VIP pass from the benefit to see what day in November 2003 the show was on never really occurred to me until one day in July 2005. I wanted to use it as a reference point but didn't think much about it. I went through the plastic storage container looking for it, and there it was.

I looked at the pass, and it was dated November 8, 2003. I began to stare in utter disbelief with a sinking feeling. Numbness instantly took over my body like never before. Of all the days in November, why did it have to occur on the eighth day of the month? It was something that I couldn't understand. It was just a coincidence, but it still hit me rather hard.

**DIVISION ONE
NOVEMBER 8, 2003
ARLINGTON, TX**

**MORRISON MUSIC &
PRODUCTION
NEW YORK, NY**

**METALLUM-COR
PROMOTIONS
ARLINGTON, TX**

It would be exactly thirteen months later to that night that I nor anyone else would ever again see Darrell Abbott again in public, whether on stage or out and about.

It's something that I think about often, but I just have to accept it.

What bothers me the most is the feeling that a part of my past is gone now. That past that consisted of watching live music nightly created memories and helped forge friendships that I still have to this day. The memories I have of all those days that began four decades ago still continue. It's something that I cherish.

The exterior of the Division One building. Photo by Brian McLean taken in 2005.

The sign for Division One. Photo taken by Brian McLean taken in 2005.

FORTY-TWO

STREAM OF KEYSTROKES

SOMETIME IN 2004 OR 2005, I stumbled across an independent, online music publication called *Stream of Consciousness*. It was a one-person operation out of Iowa with several writers. I read over some of the content posted and decided to reach out to inquire about becoming a contributor.

I submitted several samples of my work to Rachel, the editor, and was welcomed with open arms.

This outlet gave me more freedom to explore as I wrote. It was with *Stream of Consciousness* that I began attending shows again as an accredited member of the media. Not only was I reviewing shows, but I was photographing the shows as well. This made me more marketable to the publicist when a tour came through town, and I utilized those skills to my advantage.

I wrote for *Stream of Consciousness* for several years, maybe up through 2009, covering a large variety of music. My most meaningful contributions included three pieces, two interviews and one review, that still hold a special place in my heart. They are my in-person interview with Terry Butler, who was at the time touring with Six Feet Under, a phone interview with Rudy Sarzo about his book *Off the Rails*, and a review of Journey's *Live in Houston 1981: The Escape Tour* CD/DVD package.

Butler was on tour with Six Feet Under for the Crossroads to Armageddon tour that stopped at Arlington's Phoenix Music Complex in March of 2006. Butler just isn't another bass player; he's an early death metal pioneer and original dating back to the days of Massacre and Death.

Since then, he spent time in Six Feet Under and then moved onto Obituary, where he's been hammering out bass lines since 2010. More recently, as in 2020, Butler joined forces with two other metal musicians, creating Inhumane Condition.

Needless to say, he stays busy on the death metal front.

What made the interview unique and special is that his middle stepson was on the Six Feet Under tour as a drum tech. It wasn't his first tour with the band, maybe his third or fourth.

Prior to being part of the Six Feet Under road crew, he had never been outside of Florida. He actually saw snow for the first time while on an earlier tour.

For many music fans his age, Pantera was the band. He even made the ultimate sacrifice of his allegiance to the band by having the CFH logo tattooed on his left inner forearm.

363

The interview with Terry was conducted in the afternoon, so there was a bit of downtime after we finished. The venue wasn't far from Moore Memorial Gardens in Arlington. It's where the Abbott family plot is located, and we went there. It was a trek that meant quite a bit to him.

There was a chill to the temperature along with a faint drizzle but nothing drenching when we arrived. Once we parked, he fell silent as we walked on the wet pathway to the plot. I stepped back and watched as he stood at the southern edge, his red cap shielding his eyes from the drizzle.

He eventually and carefully walked around to the opposite side, squatted down like a baseball catcher, reached out, and touched the bronze marker. There, he spent several minutes in his thoughts and solitude, paying his respects.

Upon leaving, there was still a drizzle. I turned on the car radio at a low volume, and Led Zeppelin's "Thank You" was playing. At that moment, the lyrics, "Little drops of rain, whisper of the pain," could be faintly heard.

That was a very emotional and heartfelt moment as we were pulling away.

Not much was said.

On the way back, we stopped at a fast-food restaurant, grabbing a couple of meals before arriving back at the venue.

I wasn't able to stay for the show, as I had commitments to take care of that night, but it was good for me to make this visit happen. It's something I think about every now and then even though it's been roughly eighteen years since that day.

I have taken others out to Moore Memorial Gardens, whether crew members, band members, or both. This one visit in March 2006 hit me the hardest. Actions speak louder than words. There were no words, just actions, and watching was a tug on the heart strings.

By 2005, my musical palette had changed dramatically since my high school days. When I was in high school, 1980–1984, I was a full-blooded hard rocker. Bands like Krokus, Saxon, Motorhead, Riot and many others satisfied my hard rock music cravings.

If I had to list the big bands of my high school years, I would say in alphabetical order, The Cars, Journey, The Police, Styx, and obviously, Van Halen. Those bands dominated the FM airways.

A year or two after high school, I started adding the Styx albums *Equinox* and *Paradise Theater* to my collection. Styx could do no wrong music-wise until that abomination of an album titled *Kilroy Was Here* was released in 1983. That album literally killed the band's career and all momentum they had been riding. Everything fell apart with the release of that one album. The damage was done.

It took seven years for a new album, but the greatness and superstardom that Styx achieved in the 1970s and '80s never came back.

In 1990 or so, I noticed that my diversity in rock bands was starting to expand. I specifically remember purchasing *Candy-O* by The Cars in the mall. Thus, that started my journey, no pun intended, into the more mainstream rock bands of my high school days.

The Cars music collection I now have consists of all original pressed albums, the debut through *Door to Door*, CDs, cassettes, and even the 8-tracks that were produced.

Various compilations and live recordings have been released and I have those in early pressings as well.

Along with The Cars, I started diving into the Steve Perry–era Journey around this time. That consisted of the albums *Infinity* through *Frontiers*. Even though I saw all three Dallas dates of the *Frontiers* tour, Journey albums, cassettes, or CDs didn't occupy any slots in my music collection.

At the peak of Journey's *Escape* album, their November 6, 1981, show at Houston's Summit was filmed and aired on MTV's Saturday night concert series. The band was firing on all cylinders and seemed unstoppable. It was an amazing time in Journey's history. As for when this showed aired on MTV, I do not know.

In 2005, it was announced that this legendary performance at the height of *Escape* would be released in CD and DVD formats on November 11, 2005. I was all over this and actually went on a hunt to find the DVD/CD edition. I ventured to several stores before I was finally able to purchase a copy.

Me, being the collector I am, purchased the DVD/CD edition as well as the CD. I don't think the DVD was released on its own.

I remember this run of shows though. Journey played two nights,

November 5 and 6, 1981, at the Summit in Houston and then two nights at Reunion Arena on November 7 and 8, 1981. Loverboy was the supporting act.

Even though at the time, I wasn't a huge fan, I understood what a great pairing it was to have Loverboy on the *Get Lucky* album opening for Journey on this tour.

The Houston shows were Thursday and Friday, putting the Dallas shows on Saturday and Sunday. That Monday at school, Journey concert shirts were everywhere. It reminded me of the times Van Halen came through on *Women and Children First* and *Fair Warning*. Everywhere I looked, there were Journey shirts.

For some odd reason, I have a specific memory of a girl in my homeroom, Vanessa, wearing the *Escape* three-quarter-sleeve baseball jersey with red sleeves that Monday. I think maybe we briefly talked about the show, but I recall she still seemed to be on a cloud nine high of happiness from attending the show.

For those wondering how close the Houston and Dallas dates were to the release date of the *Live in Houston 1981* DVD/CD package, it was November 11, 2005. Journey played Amarillo twenty-four years earlier on November 11, 1981, for one show.

Steve Perry was the producer of the DVD and CD for this release, and I will use the words I used to bring my review to a close: "Thank you, Mr. Perry."

This release is a must-have for any fan of music. The best thing—it has been released in vinyl format in the last several years in standard black vinyl as well as a white-and-red release. One piece is red, and the other is white. Yes, I do have the vinyl releases as well.

———◇———

In chapter 13, I wrote how missing the *Diary of a Madman* tour was something that I still feel the sting of to this day. I just never thought I would reflect back on that day some forty-two years later, but what teenager thinks that far into the future?

If someone had told me one day in 2007, "You will be conducting a phone interview with Rudy Sarzo," I would have been totally confused. Journalism wasn't on my radar back in 1982. I was just a hard rock–loving teenager discovering music.

To explain to those who may not know who Rudy Sarzo is, he was the bass player on the *Diary of a Madman* tour and close friends with Rhoads, which dates back to before their days with Ozzy. Sarzo and Rhoads were in Quiet Riot. This would be six years prior to the release of *Metal Health* in 1983, with the release of *Quiet Riot I* and *Quiet Riot II* in 1978.

Prior to going out on the tour, Sarzo was advised to maintain records of his travels and expenses for tax purposes. These diligently kept records and journals, vivid memories of his first two tours, his degree in mass communications, and press clippings allowed him to write *Off the Rails*. It's an accurate and factual account of his time on tour with Rhoads, but also that fateful day.

There is so much detail in the book, and it's an amazing and wonderful read. It's a shame that it took so long for *Off the Rails* to be published, as there were people who didn't want this book to be released.

It's a very informative, must-read for every fan of music and Randy Rhoads.

Forty-Three

Corpse, Corpse, Rotting Corpse

Around early 2005, the name Rotting Corpse started to surface and generate a buzz. I reached out to the contact person who was disseminating the information being put out. His name was Steve. He was in the later incarnations of Rotting Corpse as the bassist. He was not #75.

I emailed and explained that I had the photos from the first shoot behind Rascals in Arlington. After speaking with Steve, I learned the band was scheduled to rehearse for the first time in years. The practice would take place at a rehearsal studio not far from me. I had to be there to witness this moment.

I was looking forward to seeing Walt, as it had been years since I last saw him, along with Mo, who I also hadn't seen in years. It would be my first time meeting Luke (guitarist) and Gribbs (drummer), who were both in the later version of Rotting Corpse.

It was a wild feeling hearing those songs played in person at the rehearsal facility.

Attending the rehearsal was a major milestone in my life. This was the first time I allowed anyone besides my parents to watch E. Steve's wife was more than happy to do it for me, but putting trust into her to do so was a major feat.

At the time, Steve was a new father, as in within a couple of weeks. I remember my daughter peering over the bassinet to look at Steve's daughter, who was only a few weeks old.

My daughter really wasn't fazed with me leaving for an hour or two that day. I think it may have had something to do with Steve's dog, Bubba. He was huge, and to a two-year-old, the dog was massive. I won't ever forget the big hug my daughter gave Bubba when we were about to leave.

To celebrate the band's twentieth anniversary, the band booked a run of dates through the larger Texas markets. In other words, it booked a small Texas tour. The Rotting Corpse Memorial Day Massacre Tour 2005 consisted of four consecutive dates in Corpus Christi, Houston, Arlington, and Austin that ran May 26–29.

A week prior, Corpse had played a one-off show in Austin on Saturday, May 21. The show was more of a trial run and warm-up show before heading out for the four consecutive dates five days later.

During the week of the Memorial Day Massacre Tour, Corpse released *The Demos* in CD format. The disc featured all the old-school thrash songs that were laid down on tape early in the band's career. The release was significant in that it marked the first time *ever* Rotting Corpse's music had been officially released in any other format besides the four cassette demo tapes.

During the Arlington date, SPLarsen, who was directing and producing the Rotting Corpse documentary *Circus of Fools*, was in town to obtain interviews for the DVD. He interviewed present and former band members as well as yours truly.

At one point CM Distro wanted to purchase ten thousand copies of the documentary. Why SPLarsen didn't follow, I am not certain. It was capitalism at its finest.

I will say it was nice and thoughtful to be included in the documentary.

Later in 2005, there would be a handful of shows with Rigor Mortis and/or Gammacide on select dates, the big one being October 29 with both Rigor Mortis and Gammacide. It was the first time the three Texas metal bands ever played a show together. For the connoisseurs of Texas metal, it was a historic event.

Sometime in 2024, Rotting Corpse music will be put out on vinyl. The first run will consist of red vinyl and red-and-yellow splatter. The second pressing will be the old-school black vinyl.

———◇———

The handful of Rotting Corpse dates in 2005 opened an unexpected door for me.

A locally printed and distributed Dallas-Fort Worth music

publication asked me to write a review of a Rotting Corpse show. I was more than happy to do so, as it now put my name in print for covering music. One of the more important reviews I wrote came from the October 29 show with Rigor Mortis, Gammacide, and Rotting Corpse.

Eventually, I took over a column titled "Extremities" that consisted of local, national, and international news that leaned more toward extreme metal bands. Information could include tour dates, releases, bands in the studio, new band signings, partnerships, and other things.

The only negative in regard to the music reviews, especially local band reviews, was that everything had to be positive no matter how awful the release was.

I would have people approach me at shows and ask why everything was always sugar coated. The reason why I never said it was that it boiled down to advertising revenue.

I did enjoy writing legit feature stories on bands or people. When I think of these features, the one that immediately comes to mind is the one I wrote on KNON, titled "Thrashin' and Beggin' with KNON's Thrashin' Alan and Dave Chaos."

I recall how appreciative Alan was of the article. He told me people would come up to him in public and talk about the article. I sincerely believe the article brought a nice bit of awareness to the station as a whole.

Hard Time Radio hosted by Alan has been delivering the metal goods to listeners since 1996 and continues to do so. It's an impressive run for a metal-formatted show on public radio. I will say that it's always good to run into Thrashin' Alan out in the wild. He's a good man and a true ambassador for the Dallas-Fort Worth metal scene.

———— ◆ ————

With my column, I had an outlet for creativity. I was fully immersed into the scene, not only locally but nationally as well. The shows I attended always ended up with reviews in print, and label publicists sincerely appreciated every piece.

During this time, which lasted about four years, my daughter and I would head to Fort Worth. I would catch a show as an escape from Single Dad Duty.

The Ridglea Theater in west Fort Worth was a mid-size venue that saw lots of concert action, not only for metal but other genres as well. It seemed at least twice a month I was traveling to Fort Worth for a show at the Ridglea. After the show, I would stay at my parents' house, and the next morning, we would drive back to Dallas. These concert outings to Fort Worth were a much-needed escape from the working world, especially in April 2007.

July 2009 was the last run of the publication, and it hasn't been resurrected since. It's a shame, as there is some talent in DFW that deserves publicity, but the market has become saturated with mediocrity and "headache metal."

FORTY-FOUR

THE PLANETS ALIGNED

THERE ARE EVENTS IN people's lives that literally change the trajectory of their lives. I know this for a fact because this happened to me in April 2007. Add to this, the location of this event is the same location where I would have my film developed in 1985 at 60 Minute Photo. It could be considered real-time foreshadowing. The only difference is, instead of a few pages of text, twenty-two years have passed by. Some would call it the circle of life, and it has happened more than once to me.

To begin with, I drove to Fort Worth for just another weekend music event on a Saturday at the Ridglea Theater. This time, though, I went earlier than normal because I had a standard haircut appointment. Nothing fancy, just something that occurred every six weeks or so.

While I was sitting in the chair with clippers buzzing and scissors snipping, I could see a lady in the mirror looking at me from the mirror in front of her. Her back was toward me and off to my right.

I didn't have my glasses on, so I really couldn't be certain if she was looking, staring, or what.

When my appointment was finished, I was walking to the front counter to pay when the lady asked, "What is your name?"

At first I was thinking that this person was someone I'd pissed off by denying a claim, or they recognized me from my "Extremities" column. I stopped dead in my tracks and cautiously said my first name.

She said, "Brian McLean."

I replied, "I don't mean to be rude, but I don't recognize you."

She stated we had gone to school together.

I thought for a moment and mentioned that it had to be elementary school because I would recognize her if we went to middle school or high school.

She said, "You're right. We went to elementary school together." Then she told me her name.

I was floored and couldn't believe it. She was my good friend in fourth grade who I'd hung out with a lot.

My mind was blown. I wished her a nice day and left.

When I arrived home, I started thinking that I should've grabbed her phone number to catch up. With the availability of the internet, I went online and started to search for her. I didn't find anything at all, not even a brief mention in a public record.

It didn't occur to me though to just reach out to her parents. They still lived in the same house that I would ride my bicycle to, and the phone number was the same.

After twenty minutes or so of a failed internet search, I walked away and really didn't think much about it.

———◦———

By this time, things were not good at the insurance company. The head of the claims service center was calculating how to terminate senior employees who made a decent salary. The plan was to bring in recent college graduates and pay them a much lower salary. Heads were on the chopping block, including mine. This was a low, bottom-feeder move, if you ask me.

I was beyond stressed. I was a single father with a daughter who was four years old. I was her provider of stability and security and her safety net.

Several weeks after the salon encounter, my mother called me during the middle of the week and said, "Your father was at the salon today. Janice left her phone number for you to call her."

At this point, my father was retired from Delta, and to keep himself busy, he was one of the drivers at a retirement home for seniors. Once every few weeks, he would take the nice little old ladies to the salon for their monthly hair appointments. In other words, he was driving Miss Daisy, as he would say, but there was more than one Miss Daisy in the little bus.

Janice's number had been sitting at the salon for several weeks when my father went in that day. I immediately called her after speaking with my mother. It was nice to speak with an old friend after going our separate ways after elementary school.

One of the first things Janice asked me was what I was doing. I proceeded to tell her that I worked for the insurance company, but things were not looking great. Management was documenting any and everything to build a file to get rid of the senior employees. I told her I was worried.

I then asked her what she was doing. She said that she worked for a school district and had two master's and a Ph.D. That was something I was not expecting.

She asked if I ever thought about becoming a teacher. I explained I did take a class at TCU once. With the way the professor taught and presented the material for the Philosophy of Education class, I lost any interest.

Janice then mentioned to me that even though she hadn't seen me in years, she knew my personality and that I would make a great teacher. She wanted to meet for dinner the next time I was in Fort Worth and talk.

I said I would be in Fort Worth on Saturday.

———◇———

We met for dinner. She started asking me if I knew about alternative certification. I had no idea what she was referring to. She had to explain.

Alternative certification, or alternative cert, is when an individual with a college degree that wasn't an education major becomes a teacher. She stated that I should look at ELA. I had no idea what that meant. It stands for *English language arts* (reading and writing). She explained that would be the ideal route for me to go since I had a background in communications.

Since she was fairly well connected in the education realm throughout DFW, she made some phone calls and was able to have me accepted into an alternative certification program even though the deadlines had passed several months prior.

The next step for me was to sign up for an English language arts content test. The closest location for an ELA test three weeks out was in Abilene, two hours and 149 miles west of Fort Worth. The three-week gap gave me time to study. I needed to become familiar with the ELA learning standards as well as the numerous acronyms, best practices, and other things.

The day finally came in mid-May. I drove to Abilene on a Friday, stayed at a hotel, took the test at a high school on Saturday and then drove back to Fort Worth.

The waiting for results stressed me out beyond comprehension. Even though the test answer document was a Scantron sheet, it took six weeks for the results to arrive.

I knew that passing the content test was my ticket out of the insurance company and that my life would be changing.

Finally, one afternoon, I went and checked the mail, and the results were in. I opened the document with the perforated edges and looked at all the information. I was so nervous that my hands were shaking. It seemed like information overload due to the individual scores of the various domains. After a few moments of looking at all the numbers, I saw the word "PASSED."

I felt a huge weight lifted off my shoulders.

That meant I'd passed the content test. I was cleared to start the process of interviewing to land a teaching job.

That night, I spoke with my mother on the phone and told her that I'd passed the test. She recommended I speak with the longtime neighbor across the street who'd spent forty years as an elementary teacher.

Our neighbor shared with me a few very important things when I was speaking with her.

First, she said, "You don't need that insurance company. You go in tomorrow morning and resign."

Second, "You are a male, and you will find a teaching job. There is a need for male role models."

The only recommendation she made was for me to look at elementary and not middle school. There was more of a demand for male teachers on the elementary level than there was on the middle school level. This is still true today.

I had a lot to think about and reflect upon as I turned out the lights that Wednesday night.

The next morning, I woke up earlier than normal and got E ready for daycare. I mentally readied myself for a life-changing event.

I wanted to get my desk and everything cleared out before employees started to arrive at their normal times. By 6:45 a.m., I had already spoken with one manager, the only manager I wanted to speak with. I didn't want to see my unit manager, service manager, or anyone else—just that one manager, Thomas.

It was a bit of a shock for an employee approaching the seven-year mark to up and leave without giving a two-week notice. I didn't care at that point. With the way top brass of the service center were treating the senior employees, they didn't deserve a two-week notice. Plus, I don't know if I had the luxury of working my final two weeks.

Thomas asked me if I had a plan, and I told him that I did.

At that moment, he wasn't aware that I didn't have anything lined up. He thanked me for my time with the company and authorized two weeks' additional pay as well as two weeks' additional vacation pay.

That was something I wasn't expecting, but that just shows his character and fabric as a manager. He's a good person.

By 7:20, I had everything boxed up, and I was out the door, headed back home. By 8:00 a.m., I called Janice and let her know that I had resigned. She was definitely caught off guard and hadn't anticipated that news from me.

She said that she knew several principals who were hiring and would reach out to them. Within ten minutes, she called me back and said I had an interview at 10:00 a.m. the next morning. The school was listed as a Title I school, and the student population was predominantly Hispanic. She then stated that I really needed to think about it.

By 8:30, my cell phone would not stop ringing from my coworkers who'd sat near me. Around 9:00 a.m., probably the most genuine call came in with a voicemail.

Big John had sat behind me, and we'd spoken many times with our hearts on our sleeves about how we needed to get out and move on to the next chapter of life. His call came in, but I didn't answer.

The voicemail he left went something like this: "Hey Brian, it's Big John. It's almost 9:00. I am sitting in the parking lot. I don't see your car. I am wondering if you pulled the trigger." The best part of the message—he laughed.

Since I was anticipating interviews with principals, I'd had my suit dry-cleaned a week or two in advance, and it was ready to go. I called my parents' house and let them know we were coming over and that we needed to stay the night. I was so happy to tell them I had an interview scheduled for the next morning.

Friday morning, I arrived for my interview roughly ten minutes early and walked into the school. The principal was the person who greeted me when I entered the school. He was expecting my arrival.

We went to his office. I was extremely nervous and never thought I would be sitting in a principal's office as an adult. It was a weird feeling.

I was in a new environment, but I did the best I could answer-wise, and then things took a turn for the positive and felt less pressured. We started talking about photography.

For a decent amount of time, we talked shop. I will admit that in the past, my photography resume had had some impressive and cool entries. He was curious about that. Our conversation was on a more personal level.

By the end of our interview, I had a job offer. Not wanting to look too eager or desperate, I told him I would give it the weekend and reach out to him Monday morning.

Obviously, I knew I was going to take the job. It was a new start, but most importantly, I was moving back home, as in moving back to Fort Worth after being in Dallas for nearly a decade.

After the interview, I called a dear friend at the claim center who was a big Elvis fan. I told her that I'd landed a teaching job. She was so happy, and I wanted her to be one of the first to know.

I was only unemployed for twenty-six hours.

Now, since it was summertime, I had three weeks to get packed, find a place in Fort Worth, move, unpack, and get ready for new teacher training in early August.

I was pressed for time.

FORTY-FIVE

15-YEAR-LONG CHAPTER

BECOMING AN EDUCATOR WAS probably the best move career-wise as a single father I could make. Not only did it allow me to move back home, as in Fort Worth, the city I grew up in, but it also gave me great peace of mind.

In my first year of teaching, E was in kindergarten. Since my daughter was attending school in the same district I was teaching, that meant our schedules aligned. For Thanksgiving break, winter break, spring break, summer break, and holidays, we were both off from school. This schedule stayed consistent all the way through her senior year in high school.

I spent fifteen years as an educator on three different campuses, starting out as an English language arts teacher and transitioning solely into science.

The first three years I taught ELA, and in the fourth year, I began to teach science and ELA. My fourth year also saw a new principal come in. The administrator who hired me in 2007 went to another campus.

I will say that I learned a lot operations-wise from the new principal. We were actually close in age, maybe just a year or two difference. He was a great principal and just had a way of taking care of things.

I recall during one staff meeting, all teachers were instructed to bring a relic that would best describe yourself. I brought in my copy of Queen's *Live Killers* album. When he saw that, he went and grabbed an administrator from the district that was at the meeting and said, "You have to see this."

I remember sitting down with him one time, and he told me the story about when he was listening to Pink Floyd's *The Wall* as a teenager in his room upstairs. "Another Brick in the Wall" was playing, and he said his mother rushed upstairs and scolded him about the song. Here he was, thirty years later, leading an elementary school as an amazing principal. He had a reputation in the district as one of the best. It's a shame I was only under him for one year. I truly did miss working under him.

By this time in the 2010–2011 school year, the dual language program finally made its way up and would be implemented in fifth grade the following year. That meant the four fifth-grade teachers were shuttled out for the following school year. It was something the principal didn't want to do but had to due to the language program.

For the 2011–2012 school year, I was picked up by a middle school to teach 6th Pre-AP Science. It was actually what I was looking for, to be honest, once I left elementary. I spent nine years at the middle school, and in that time, I accomplished a lot.

I earned my M.Ed. in secondary science education, traveled abroad teaching four days of middle school science in Ecuador while working on the master's, and spent five days in the Galapagos on the same trip. Most importantly to me, I wrote a research paper on how vital parental involvement truly is for student success.

Brian with the original photo in front of his junior year high school locker. Photo taken by Jason B.

For an independent study class, I wrote a two papers. The first on the flora and fauna of the Galapagos Islands and the other on the geology, meteorology and oceanography of the Galapagos archipelago.

I created an interactive graphic organizer, or core model, out of a paper plate that I presented at the Conference for Advancement for Science Teaching. My paper plate creation came out of boredom while sitting in professional development after winter break one year, maybe 2013.

The first year I presented, I was conservative with the number of people and the size of the room. I requested a small room that held no more than thirty-five people. I utilized that room for two separate presentations. The room was full for both presentations.

The following year, I went to San Antonio and presented. This time, I put in a request for a room that held seventy people and presented twice, back-to-back.

When I arrived with my co-presenter, my main graduate professor, there was a line of people waiting to get in. She pointed to the line of people and said they were waiting in line for my presentation. I didn't believe her, but she was correct. It was a very weird feeling.

The following year, I went to Houston. This time I requested an even larger room to present in. The room set for my presentation consisted of three banquet rooms as one. Ten minutes before my presentation, I was at capacity, 210 people. People were being turned away at the door. It was mind-blowing to me.

During my nine years at the school, the advanced program declined year after year, little by little. There were no standards for admissions or anything like that. If a student applied, they were placed in the program.

By my ninth year, I had three advanced classes and two regular classes. In this area of the city, students didn't care about receiving an education, nor did they possess an ounce of respect. That not only wore me out, but my fellow colleagues as well.

I will say there were a few students each year who were superstars. I often wonder where they are now.

If there was no better time for the pandemic to hit, it was during this school year. I had no idea that once I left for spring break in March 2020, I would never deal with that group of disrespectful kids again.

I reluctantly signed a contract for the next year, but I wasn't happy about it.

During the pandemic, I started upgrading my photography equipment to pro-level gear. I had plenty of time to photograph, as school wasn't in session except for a few hours a day. It took six weeks to get to that point.

———◦———

Several days after the school year was finished, I was recruited by another district that was closer to the house. It was for a position I was seeking.

I was so excited that there was an opportunity for me to leave my previous district. I just had to show that I was the one for the position I was being interviewed for. The timing of the interview was quick. I received an email at 10:00 a.m. for an interview at 2:00 p.m. Keep in mind, this interview was remote, and four people total were interviewing me.

I made sure the area I would sit in my office was clean and clutter-free. I had one of my science journals to my right with a lesson bookmarked. I also had index cards with campus data on the cards so I could reference those during the interview. All of these things that I did to prepare for the interview occurred within a four-hour window, including getting a haircut.

I will admit that I was very nervous, but everything ran smoothly in the interview. There was one point toward the end of the interview that I was asked what my favorite lesson that I taught was. I reached over to my right for the science journal that had a lesson marked. I showed the principal and other three educators my paper plate core model of the Earth's layers. The model is actually impressive when looking at it. All four educators complimented me on how unique the model made out of just a paper plate was.

Before signing off, the director of Elementary Science for the district had a question that was in a way related to the interview but not really at the same time; she was just curious.

She asked me if I had presented the paper plate model at the Conference for Advancement for Science Teaching in San Antonio several years back. I replied, "Yes, I did."

She proceeded to tell me that she was in one of the presentations. She actually brought the idea back to the district and implemented the model into the curriculum.

I was blown away. I didn't know what to say. That curious brief moment is what sealed the deal for the district to hire me. After the interview, they called me twenty minutes later and made the offer.

I was ecstatic. I was leaving the middle school and moving to another school. There would be more respect for the teachers and a bit more parental support.

I spent two years in the district. Eventually, I was at a point where I could walk away, and I did.

Unfortunately, the burning passion and thinking-outside-the-box lesson creativity I had going for me was destroyed in two years. I grew tired of working six, sometimes seven days a week from paperwork and data overload. All that extra useless busy work and data didn't make a difference.

In my second year, I would get home from school around 4:30. I would be so tired that I would take a two-hour nap. Several hours later, I would turn out the light for the night only to repeat the process when I would wake up at 5:45 to be in my classroom by 6:50 a.m.

I was not alone in wanting to escape the classroom; I just had an out. Others are not so fortunate.

The issue I see with education is that districts are looking for that magic formula for student success. What I was seeing was a lack of accountability from the students as well as very little parent involvement.

Students are falling further and further behind. Teachers are being worn out. Many with an out like me are walking away, but low numbers of hopeful educators are signing up. I truly feel for the education majors graduating from college and stepping into the classroom. Many won't even last five years. Many have no idea what they will be walking into.

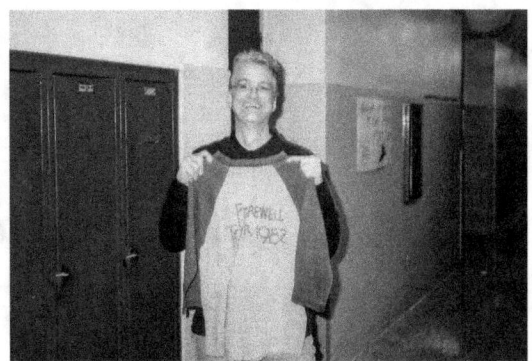

Brian showing off the back of his Doobie Brothers shirt next to his junior year high school locker. Photo taken by Jason B.

FORTY-SIX

NICE TO SEE YOU, MR. PHOTO PIT

IN 2018, I STARTED to get the urge to write about music again. It had been just a little over nine years since I'd written or photographed anything related to music. Dave, my publicist friend, put the word out that a new online music publication was looking for contributors and would be launching in January 2019. I found this too ironic.

I reached out to Eric, the editor of *Brutal Planet Magazine*, about being part of his new venture. I explained that not only could I write, but I could photograph as well. At this time, I just had a basic Canon kit camera I'd purchased several years prior to photograph E playing volleyball. By this point, she was no longer playing, and my camera was sitting idle.

BPM launched in January 2019. I was banging out reviews and thinking about features that I could write, and I covered my first show in March: Hypocrisy.

This was Hypocrisy's first appearance in the Dallas-Fort Worth area in a long time. It was January 2006 when I last interviewed Peter Tatgren, the founder of the band, on the tour bus in the parking lot of the Ridglea Theater. If there was a band for me to cover first for *BPM*, it was Hypocrisy.

From that point, I was covering show after show after show. I even traveled to Houston to cover Hell's Heroes II. While down there, I did an interview with Dan Beehler, drummer and vocalist for Exciter. It was surreal sitting down with him. I had so many questions that I needed answers for once we concluded our interview.

We talked about the Motorhead, Mercyful Fate, and Exciter tour in 1984 and how Daniel Dekay, their new guitarist, was bringing new blood and energy to the metal trio. The show at Hell's Heroes II was actually Dekay's first show with the band, so it was a historic moment for the band. Since then, the band hasn't slowed down, playing all over the world.

The day of the interview was the day Paul Raymond from UFO passed away. I learned about his passing minutes before I sat down with Beehler.

I was able to catch up again with Exciter when they played Hell's Heroes in 2023. It was great to see Dan again and then to formally meet bassist Alan Johnson and Dekay.

For the remainder of 2019, I was covering so many shows and was extremely happy that I felt as if I was back in my element.

Toward the end of 2019, I was talking gear with Eric, and he made some recommendations to me gear-wise. I just didn't think I could afford to make the upgrades he was recommending. He told me that if I did, it would be a game changer for image quality.

I had someone close to me say that I had made countless sacrifices for my daughter over the years. It was now time to think about myself.

In late December, I did just that. I made my first gear upgrade, picking up a Canon 5D Mark III as well as a 70-200mm 2.8.

The first show I shot with this one camera setup was Queensrÿche with support from John 5 in January 2020. He was right; this setup was a game changer for my photos. There was just no comparison between the kit and what I shot the show with.

The next piece I added was a 24-70mm 2.8, but then I needed a second body, and that's what I purchased, an additional camera body.

For the next few shows, I shot with the two bodies and two lenses. It allowed me to get a larger variety, and I even started capturing overalls of the venue when a second level was available.

I was content with this setup but then became interested in photographing aviation at DFW International Airport. This was new territory for me, but I was really enjoying it. Even though I had only those two bodies and lenses, I utilized my editorial background to capture images others wouldn't see.

Then the lockdown hit, but I continued to photograph at DFW during the day when time allowed. It was at this point that I picked my first major piece of glass, or in simpler terms, lens. I purchased a 400mm 2.8. This allowed me more reach photographically and started to separate me from others.

Over time, I added a third 5D Mark III and an 8-15 4.0 Fisheye, 300mm 2.8, 600mm 4.0, 85mm 1.2, and 50mm 1.2.

———◇———

I had the gear to photograph high school sports but no outlet to photograph for. By this time, I was in a new district, but I didn't want to be too eager about photographing high school football. I was patient time-wise and waited for my second year in the district.

Before the end of my first year, I reached out and introduced myself to the athletic director and told him about my background. He provided me with a season credential for the 2021–2022 school year, as well as a UIL pass that would grant me access to any school in the district.

I found a small suburban newspaper to submit photos to and went from there. During the course of the 2021 high school football season, I discovered a new editorial-based high school sports publication that covered high schools nationwide. I reached out and was put in touch with the VP of content and started covering games for them. I recall covering a game seventy miles away on a Thursday night, editing and processing images, and submitting for the deadline. I finally was able to turn out the lights around 12:00 a.m. only to have the alarm go off at 5:45 a.m. to get ready for school.

I continued to photograph for the remainder of the athletic school year. Things slowed down a bit, as a director of photography came aboard and was using his network photographers. I covered four games that spring.

When the school year came to an end, I walked away from the classroom. I was spent, mentally and energy-wise. I can say I was very fortunate that I could devote my time to shooting.

Football kicked back in, and I was all over North Texas, from Stephenville to Allen. I didn't have to worry about grading papers, getting up early, and heading to the classroom or working six and seven days a week on school-related items. I was out, and I was done.

FORTY-SEVEN

BACK TO WHERE I BELONG

BEFORE I KNEW IT, football season was done, and now I was back photographing basketball, softball, and some baseball. My friend Sammy suggested I reach out to her younger brother. He just happened to be a softball coach for a NCCAA school—National Christian College Athletic Association, not the NCAA.

I photographed their season when I could and their post-season play that saw the team earn a return trip back to the NCCAA Softball World Series 2023. I thoroughly enjoyed it, as I was photographing a step above high school. I witnessed some great softball and come-from-behind wins and captured some really nice images with the access I had. I was craving more though.

In early April, I took a leap of faith and submitted a contributor's inquiry form to the photography liaison at a press agency and wire service. He eventually got back to me and apologized for the delay.

I had several questions to answer in regard to what I was hoping to accomplish photographing for them. I gave serious thought to my responses and approached each reply as if I was answering a short essay question.

Eventually, I signed my contract and was given the green light. The only thing was that I needed approval to apply for credentials. The reason is simple: to keep photographers from overlapping on events.

Joining their global network of photographers, I was now and still am associated with a reputable media outlet. I already understood the credential game, and I was all in, whether for sports or entertainment.

My lenses have remained the same, but I made a switch with my bodies. I now shoot with a 1DX Mark II. I have three that I shoot with, and there's been a noticeable change in what I capture.

My first big photographic outing for the wire service was the Gold Cup matches at AT&T Stadium in July 2023. I shot Panama versus Qatar and Mexico versus Costa Rica. I was covering big-time soccer and was just blown away by the atmosphere in the stadium. I was floored, and this was only the beginning.

In mid-July, I reached out to the TCU Killer Frogs contact. I explained who I was and that I'd graduated from TCU. I wanted to look into becoming a contributor with the TCU Horned Frogs on SI site.

We met for about an hour at the university bookstore and talked about how I could contribute. A fellow writer I had worked with in the past did some work for them as well. He was my reference, and along with my website galleries, I was welcomed aboard.

In the fall, Mexico and Australia would play a Concacaf Friendly Match at AT&T Stadium. Along with that, I would cover Baylor football, several D1 basketball tournaments, bowl games, baseball tournaments, and large concerts in a stadium, arenas, and smaller venues, all of this through the wire service.

There's a feature called Best Pictures of the Day. Editors select photos that are being submitted throughout the day to feature on this daily website. I wasn't even aware of this feature early on until I stumbled upon it in late 2023. I went back to my first event and started inputting the dates I submitted.

I learned that my photos were being selected on a regular basis, and by this time, my photos have been featured numerous times. It's really nice and a great sense of accomplishment seeing my work recognized on a global scale. It only motivates me further.

For the TCU Horned Frogs on SI, football wasn't the only sport I would cover at TCU. There was women's soccer, volleyball, basketball, and equestrian as well as men's basketball and baseball.

I was surprised how fast things were happening, but I think it came down to how much I wanted it. In early 2023 I was thinking how I could get my foot in the door and start photographing NCAA D1 sports. To me, it didn't matter who or where I photographed; I just wanted to shoot NCAA D1.

As of this writing, it's the first week of April 2024, and I have a D1 baseball championship on the books as well as FC Dallas, North Texas Soccer Club, the FC Dallas farm team, minor league baseball, and the NCAA Women's Gymnastics National Championship to name a few. There will be more concerts, including several stadium shows and major arena shows as well.

There's more to come on the horizon. No telling what new adventures await my cameras.

I am very happy to be back at this juncture, photographing again. At one point, I actually thought I would not be shooting anymore at this level. So much has changed, but I am grateful for my editorial photography experience that has allowed me to get back to this level of shooting.

I don't like the phrase "living the dream," but this is something I wanted to make happen, and it has. To me, it's just a different office environment that changes with every event I cover.

I brought to life my desire to shoot at this level again. I am very grateful for everything that has occurred in the last year, and I am looking forward to the fall.

FORTY-EIGHT

LIFE

I FEEL THAT THE following two passages should be in a chapter together and on their own. I find it fitting to start bringing my book to a close with these two events. These really did impact me as an older teen.

Originally, I just wished I could recall exactly when in the school year what I am about to write occurred. I am thinking sometime in the spring, 1982. With a little research, I was able to determine when: March 1, 1982.

One morning I was getting ready. I was blow-drying my hair, and my mother asked me if I knew a student named Larry *****.

I replied, "Yes, he's in my World History class."

She then proceeded to tell me he was hit by a car at Hulen/Altamesa and was killed.

My heart sank. I just couldn't believe it. His desk was directly to my left. We always talked.

His family had moved from Seattle. I remember him telling me about the Mount St. Helens eruption.

I always arrived to class on time. I never could understand people who were late. I think it was because I had the first half of the day's books with me, and after lunch I changed them out for the second half of the day.

Before class outside in the hallway, a mutual friend asked if I had seen Larry.

I looked at her and said, "You haven't heard?"

"Heard what?" she asked.

I then looked at her, took a big swallow, and said, "Larry was hit by a car last night at Hulen and Altamesa and was killed."

She looked at me and said, "That's a sick joke. Why would you say something like that?"

I tried to reason with her, but she would hear nothing of it.

I just looked at her and walked to my desk. I sat down in complete silence next to Larry's desk.

The teacher closed the door and said that he had something to tell the class. Obviously, I knew what he was going to say.

As he started to speak, I listened intently, but I wasn't looking at him. Instead, I was looking at our mutual friend to watch her expression when our teacher told us we'd lost a classmate the previous night.

She never apologized to me, but I know deep down, she was really hurting.

I learned several years ago the reason she asked me if I'd seen Larry. She and Larry had had an argument the day before. She wanted to apologize to Larry, but she never had the opportunity.

Life lesson: don't hold back. If something needs to be said, then say it and clear the air.

As for me, the moment I sat down at my desk and looked over at Larry's desk, it produced a feeling I never want to experience again. The previous day he was sitting next to me; the next day he was gone.

No student should ever have to experience that. Unfortunately, it's inevitable, and there is no way around it. Larry was a good person. I am thankful for the classroom friendship we had.

By 1982, it was no secret I was a huge Lynyrd Skynyrd fan. I had all of their albums and overall just enjoyed their music. The first speech I ever gave in Coach Freeman's class was a speech of interest. My topic, Lynyrd Skynyrd.

I had a baseball jersey with red sleeves, and on the front was a Lynyrd Skynyrd iron-on. The image was a skull with dark glasses and a cowboy hat, with a cigar hanging from its mouth. There was a Confederate flag wrapped around the shoulders of the skull. It was vintage Skynyrd, plain and simple.

The saxophone section in the marching band had a new person join in with us at the beginning of 1982. His name was Jay, and he was a silly, funny, and solid tenor saxophone player. In other words, he fit right in. He was one year ahead of me, so that put him graduating in 1983.

At one point early in the year, he said he could tell how much I liked the band Lynyrd Skynyrd. He told me that he had the Confederate flag Skynyrd logo belt buckle. He wanted to give it to me because I was such a fan of the band.

I was blown away by his generosity.

The next day, he brought it. I was speechless because I was holding an authentic piece of official Lynyrd Skynyrd merchandise. I wore that belt buckle religiously, basically every day with my belt that had my name on the back.

I never forgot Jay doing that for me, and I never will.

I am not sure what route he took directly after graduating high school, but I know that in the months following my graduation in 1984, he was a manager of a pizza delivery shop.

On January 14, 1985, he was shot and killed in an armed robbery that was committed by an employee who was on an armed robbery spree.

With the research capabilities of the last several years, I was finally able to get some answers as to what happened to my friend. I have always wanted to know the details about what had occurred. I needed some type of closure.

During my research, I also learned his father passed away in August 2019. If only I was able to get that information, I would have been more than happy to visit him where he was residing. I would've taken the belt buckle with me. I would've explained how much the buckle meant to me, as it was a gift. Now it's much more than a gift.

There was a documentary on Oxygen with a teaser on YouTube titled "Robbery Rampage in Fort Worth Stuns Police." This allowed me to get the information I sought.

Over the years, I tried to recall where Jay's service was held, but I couldn't remember. All I could remember was that I attended his service on a very cold winter day in January 1985. Even though we were out of high school, several band students were present, including the one who was dismissed from marching band boot camp. I am not sure how he knew Jay.

I learned that when I visit my father at Greenwood Memorial Park, I drive by Jay's plot every time. I have visited Jay a few times, but I wonder if anybody else has or does. He shouldn't be forgotten.

FORTY-NINE

CLOSING TIME

I FIND IT APPROPRIATE to pull up the Legs Diamond debut album as I write this final chapter taking me back to where it all started.

I wrote in the last sentence of the Introduction that my story consisted of hopes, teenage daydreams, detours, and disappointments. What I didn't mention was the tragedies I would endure. There's no way around a tragedy or the passing of those close to you. No matter how close or how far it is from your soul, it just hits differently. You can get through it, just not over it.

As I close in on the Big 60, I can say with certainty I have lived a very cool life. I have experienced things that were not even on my radar as I navigated life in my formative rock music years.

Things I have done are now mind-blowing to me when I reflect on them from the perspective of a teenager with a burning, soul-scorching passion for music. It was that dedication to music, though, that set me on the paths I followed. One thing just led to another.

Were there disappointments as I made my way? Of course, but that's life, and I always tried not to let it get me down. I really never tried to look back, as I always tended to look forward to what was possible.

I have "no regerts" as those who had an unfortunate tattoo experience with poor spelling.

With that said, it's been a crazy ride and I am always looking for the next boarding call. Along with the photographing of live music, especially metal, sports provide the same rush. I never thought by this age I would be favoring the flavors of extreme metal. I guess it's true, I grew up, I just never grew old.

Acknowledgements

To my kiddo, who would've thought our little adventure in July 2012 would result in what you're holding in your hands? This book is for you.

To my father, what I would give to have you here and able to hold this book in your hand. I wanted to make you proud one more time.

To my mother, it's strange how my passion and love for music have taken me on the paths I have traveled. It's safe to say music is a never-ending journey for me.

To my cousin Jimmy, I wish you were still here to read my book. I know you would have gotten more than a few laughs out of it. We created some great memories in Ohio and Texas.

To Penny Fool, Joylita Mama, and others I confided in, thank you for listening to the stories of all my crazy adventures and the whacky plans for this book. Your feedback was greatly appreciated.

To everybody mentioned directly or indirectly in this book, thank you for being part of my story whether I like you or not.

To Ace, Gene, Paul, and Peter, just the mention of these four names says it all.

To Joe D. and Joe G., thank you for your profound words of wisdom as I entered the world of photojournalism.

To all the athletic directors, assistant athletic directors, media relation professionals, public relations professionals, label publicists, promoters, tour managers, and anyone else, past, present and future, thank you for the credential approvals.

To Peter Walker, thank you for being the final piece of inspiration for this book. You have no idea how much you inspired me. I just kept it to myself. I would not be surprised if our paths crossed at Richfield Coliseum on May 11, 1987, if you were not out on the road with Maleki.

To my editors Jenna B. and Stacey K., thank you so very much for your hard work. I sincerely appreciate it.

To Randi R., thank you for your assistance, wisdom, guidance, and everything in between.

To Gwendolyn S., thank you for your legal guidance.

CREDITS

Thank you to Photos on the Vine for the cover photo and Cody Grubbs for the back cover photo.

Thank you to Andra Bennett from the Fort Worth Convention Center, formerly known as Tarrant County Convention Center, for access on a down day to a clean and silent arena for the cover photo.

Thank you to Tom Dodson for your outstanding graphics work, as usual, for the cover and back cover. Mc A Doodle is very grateful.

Thank you to Dave Tedder for your publicity magic and extra eyes.

Some names have been changed to respect the privacy of individuals.

ABOUT THE AUTHOR

With 13 years of editorial experience and three collegiate journalism awards under his belt, TCU graduate, single father and native Texan, Brian McLean's work has been published globally in print and digital formats. His work though is not just limited to just music where he has several albums and promotional materials to his credit.

McLean also has hockey trading cards for Topps Finest, Fleer Power Play, Premier Hockey Magazine, Pro Hockey Magazine, The Hockey News, various game programs and a poster in Swedish Hockey Magazine to his name.

Prior to returning to his cameras in a digital photography world, Brian McLean spent 15 years as an educator. While working in education, McLean earned a M.Ed in Science Education from Texas Wesleyan University and studied abroad in Ecuador where he taught four days in a middle school science classroom. He also presented at the Conference for the Advancement of Science Teaching (CAST) in Fort Worth, San Antonio and Houston.

McLean's life may have veered in a different direction but he has picked up where he left off and is looking to capture new images from news, sports and entertainment.

McLean's other love is for animals. Specifically his cats Elvis and Priscilla as well as all the opossums, raccoons, skunks and foxes that visit his backyard.